The Simple Mediterranean Diet
Cookbook for Beginners

2000+
Days Quick, Tasty and Nutritious Recipes Book for a Balanced Diet | 28-Day Meal Plan for Better Eating Habits

Tressa H. Smith

Table of Contents

Chapter 5 Beef, Pork, and Lamb   34

Chapter 6 Poultry   42

Chapter 7 Fish and Seafood   51

Chapter 8 Snacks and Appetizers 61

Chapter 9 Vegetables and Sides 71

Chapter 10 Vegetarian Mains 84

Chapter 11 Desserts 95

Chapter 12 Salads 105

Chapter 13 Pizzas, Wraps, and Sandwiches — 113

Chapter 14 Pasta — 119

Chapter 15 Staples, Sauces, Dips, and Dressings — 125

Appendix 1: Measurement Conversion Chart — 129

Appendix 2: The Dirty Dozen and Clean Fifteen — 130

INTRODUCTION

Welcome, dear reader, to a gastronomic odyssey that will transport your taste buds to the sun-soaked shores of the Mediterranean. Prepare to embark on a culinary adventure like no other—a journey that promises not only tantalizing flavors but also a remarkable transformation in your approach to food and well-being. Within the pages of the Mediterranean Diet Cookbook, a delightful world of deliciousness and laughter awaits, where healthy eating meets whimsy and flavor dances on your tongue like a joyful celebration.

Now, let's flip open the pages of our Mediterranean Diet Cookbook and discover the culinary treasures that await you. This cookbook is like a treasure map leading you to a bounty of mouthwatering recipes inspired by the Mediterranean's rich culinary heritage. It's a astonishing blend of fresh produce, lean proteins, heart-healthy fats, and an abundance of aromatic herbs and spices.

First up, say hello to our Freekeh, Chickpea, and Herb Salad! These salad wizards know how to transform simple greens into culinary masterpieces. From the refreshing Greek Salad, bursting with juicy tomatoes, baby spinach leaves, and crumbled feta cheese, to the exotic Moroccan Tomato and Roasted Chile Salad, with its medley of vibrant colors and exotic spices, these salads will take your taste buds on a wild adventure.

But wait, there's more! Our Mediterranean Cookbook is a treasure trove of delicious and nutritious recipes for every meal. Imagine waking up to a leisurely breakfast of creamy Greek Yogurt Parfait topped with a drizzle of cream and a sprinkle of crunchy nuts. Or perhaps you'd prefer a slice of Whole-Wheat Toast with Apricots, Blue Cheese, and Honey slathered with luscious apricot, cheese and honey—the perfect start to your day.

As we venture further into the cookbook, you'll encounter our seafood aficionados. These culinary maestros know how to work their magic with fresh catches from the sea. Indulge in succulent Mediterranean Grilled Shrimp marinated in fragrant garlic and zesty lemon, or savor a perfectly Lemon Pesto Salmon with a tangy herb-infused sauce. These dishes not only tantalize your taste buds but also provide a dose of heart-healthy omega-3 fatty acids.

Oh, and let's not forget the Mediterranean's love affair with colorful veggies! Our cookbook is brimming with vibrant recipes that showcase the natural goodness of vegetables. From Roasted Veggie Bowl drizzled with coconut oil and sprinkled with aromatic herbs, to tender Savory Zucchini Muffins stuffed with a savory medley of parsley, Parmesan cheese, and onion, your plate will become a canvas of flavor and beauty.

And for all you sweet teeth out there, fear not! Our Mediterranean Diet Cookbook has a selection of delightful desserts that will satisfy your cravings without derailing your healthy lifestyle. Treat yourself to a slice of light and airy Blueberry-Lemon Tea Cakes infused with extraordinary flavors, or indulge in a luscious bowl of Dried Fruit Compote drizzled with a touch of juice and a sprinkle of raisins.

So, my friend, if you're ready to embrace a deliciously wholesome lifestyle and let the Mediterranean breeze sweep you away, our cookbook is your passport to culinary bliss. Say goodbye to complicated diets and restrictive rules, and say hello to a joyful and easy-going approach to eating. Let the Mediterranean flavors dance on your tongue and nourish your body and soul. Bon appétit!

Chapter 1 Dive into the Mediterranean Diet

A Dash of History, a Pinch of Tradition

Before we delve into the realm of recipes and culinary marvels, let's take a moment to appreciate the rich tapestry of history that forms the foundation of the Mediterranean diet. Picture yourself wandering through ancient Greek marketplaces, inhaling the aromas of freshly baked bread, sampling ripe olives, and savoring the simplicity of a juicy tomato. From the olive groves of Greece to the vineyards of Italy, this diet embodies the timeless traditions and cultural heritage of the Mediterranean region—a symphony of flavors passed down through generations.

The Mediterranean diet is a dietary pattern that originated in the countries surrounding the Mediterranean Sea, such as Greece, Italy, Spain, and parts of North Africa. It is characterized by the consumption of plant-based foods, such as fruits, vegetables, whole grains, legumes, and nuts, as well as olive oil as the primary source of fat. Moderate amounts of dairy products, fish, and poultry are also included, while red meat and sweets are consumed in small quantities.

The origins of the Mediterranean diet can be traced back thousands of years to ancient civilizations that thrived in the Mediterranean region. These civilizations, including the Ancient Greeks and Romans, relied heavily on agriculture and had access to a wide variety of fruits, vegetables, legumes, and grains. Their diets were based on what was locally available, and they consumed foods such as olives, grapes, figs, wheat, and barley.

The term "Mediterranean diet" was coined in the 1950s by the American nutritionist Ancel Keys, who observed that people in the Mediterranean region had lower rates of heart disease compared to other populations. Keys conducted a study called the Seven Countries Study, which found that the Mediterranean diet, rich in fruits, vegetables, whole grains, and olive oil, was associated with better health outcomes, particularly in terms of cardiovascular health.

Since then, numerous studies have been conducted to investigate the health benefits of the Mediterranean diet. Research has shown that this dietary pattern is associated with a reduced risk of heart disease, stroke, type 2 diabetes, certain types of cancer, and overall mortality. It is also known to have a positive impact on weight management and cognitive function.

The Mediterranean diet gained international recognition and popularity in the 1990s when it was promoted by organizations such as the World Health Organization (WHO) and the Food and Agriculture Organization of the United Nations (FAO). It was included in the dietary guidelines of several countries and has since been adopted by many people around the world as a healthy and balanced way of eating.

Today, the Mediterranean diet is not only a dietary pattern but also represents a cultural and social lifestyle. It emphasizes the enjoyment of food, the importance of meals shared with family and friends, and physical activity. The traditional Mediterranean diet continues to inspire new recipes, cookbooks, and restaurant menus, promoting a healthful and flavorful approach to eating.

The Joyful Secrets of Health

While we certainly can't promise six-pack abs overnight or a magic potion for eternal youth, the Mediterranean diet does hold a few secrets that can help you feel your best. Imagine indulging in delectable dishes while nourishing your body with the essential nutrients it craves. Research has shown that this diet can lower the risk of heart disease, boost brain health, and even contribute to a longer, more vibrant life. So, why not embark on a journey of wellness that doesn't involve rabbit food and calorie counting? Let's uncover the joyful secrets that the Mediterranean diet holds for your well-being.

1. Rich in Nutrient-Dense Foods: The Mediterranean diet emphasizes the consumption of nutrient-dense foods such as fruits, vegetables, whole grains, legumes, and nuts. These foods are abundant in vitamins, minerals, fiber, antioxidants, and phytochemicals, which contribute to overall health and well-being.

2. Heart-Healthy Fats: Olive oil is a staple in the Mediterranean diet and serves as the primary source of fat. It is rich in monounsaturated fats, particularly oleic acid, which has been associated with numerous health benefits, including a reduced risk of heart disease. The diet also includes other sources of healthy fats, such as nuts, seeds, and fatty fish, which provide omega-3 fatty acids that support heart health.

3. Reduced Risk of Cardiovascular Disease: Studies have consistently shown that the Mediterranean diet is associated with a lower risk of cardiovascular diseases, including heart disease and stroke. This is attributed to its emphasis on plant-based foods, which are naturally low in saturated fats and high in fiber, as well as its inclusion of healthy fats and moderate consumption of fish and poultry.

4. Anti-Inflammatory Properties: The Mediterranean diet is known to have anti-inflammatory effects in the body. The abundance of fruits, vegetables, whole grains, and olive oil, along with the consumption of

fatty fish rich in omega-3 fatty acids, helps reduce chronic inflammation, which is linked to various diseases, including cardiovascular disease, diabetes, and certain types of cancer.

5. Improved Blood Sugar Control: Following the Mediterranean diet has been shown to improve blood sugar control and reduce the risk of developing type 2 diabetes. The diet's emphasis on whole grains, legumes, fruits, and vegetables provides a steady release of carbohydrates, preventing rapid spikes in blood sugar levels.

6. Protection Against Chronic Diseases: The Mediterranean diet has been associated with a reduced risk of various chronic diseases, including certain types of cancer (such as breast and colorectal cancer), Parkinson's disease, Alzheimer's disease, and age-related macular degeneration. The abundance of antioxidants and anti-inflammatory compounds in the diet's plant-based foods may contribute to these protective effects.

7. Weight Management: The Mediterranean diet is not only health-promoting but also supports weight management. Its emphasis on whole, unprocessed foods, along with portion control and mindful eating practices, can help individuals achieve and maintain a healthy weight.

It's important to note that the Mediterranean diet is not just about the foods consumed but also encompasses a lifestyle that includes regular physical activity, social interactions, and enjoyment of meals. These factors contribute to overall well-being and make the Mediterranean diet a sustainable and enjoyable way of eating for long-term health benefits.

Flavors that Tickle the Senses

Ah, the flavors! Brace yourself for a symphony of tastes that will ignite your senses and leave you craving more. Picture yourself biting into a succulent Greek moussaka, each layer of eggplant and creamy béchamel sauce creating a melodic harmony on your palate. Or imagine the burst of sunshine in your mouth as you taste a perfectly roasted tomato drizzled with fragrant olive oil. From the aromatic spices of Morocco to the delicate balance of herbs in Italian pasta sauces, the Mediterranean diet presents a vibrant and diverse palette of flavors that will transport you to a world of culinary ecstasy.

The Mediterranean diet is characterized by a specific dietary structure that prioritizes certain food groups while moderating the consumption of others. Here's a detailed breakdown of the dietary structure of the Mediterranean diet:

◊ Abundant Plant-Based Foods: The Mediterranean diet emphasizes the consumption of plant-based foods. These include:

- Fruits: Fresh fruits such as apples, oranges, berries, pears, and grapes are commonly consumed.

- Vegetables: A wide variety of vegetables, including leafy greens, tomatoes, peppers, onions, broccoli, zucchini, eggplant, and artichokes, are staples.

- Whole Grains: Whole grains like wheat, barley, oats, rice, and corn are consumed in the form of bread, pasta, rice dishes, and cereals.

- Legumes: Beans, lentils, chickpeas, and other legumes are frequently included in soups, stews, salads, and side dishes.

◊ Healthy Fats and Oils: Healthy fats, particularly olive oil, are a fundamental component of the Mediterranean diet. It is used as the primary cooking oil and salad dressing. Other sources of healthy fats include:

- Nuts and Seeds: Almonds, walnuts, cashews, pistachios, flaxseeds, chia seeds, and sesame seeds are commonly consumed for their healthy fats, protein, and fiber.

- Avocado: Rich in monounsaturated fats, avocados are a popular ingredient in Mediterranean cuisine.

◊ Moderate Consumption of Dairy Products: Dairy products are consumed in moderate amounts in the Mediterranean diet. Common options include:

- Cheese: Feta, mozzarella, halloumi, and ricotta are popular choices.

- Yogurt: Greek yogurt, often unsweetened and plain, is favored for its probiotic content.

◊ Moderate Intake of Fish, Poultry, and Eggs: The Mediterranean diet encourages moderate consumption of fish and poultry as sources of lean protein. Eggs are also consumed in moderation.

- Fish: Fatty fish like salmon, mackerel, sardines, and trout are rich in omega-3 fatty acids and are recommended at least twice a week.

- Poultry: Chicken and turkey are consumed in smaller quantities compared to fish.

- Eggs: Whole eggs are enjoyed but typically limited to a few times per week.

◊ Limited Red Meat and Sweets: Red meat and sweets are consumed sparingly in the Mediterranean diet.

- Red Meat: Consumption of red meat, such as beef, lamb, and pork, is limited to occasional portions and usually reserved for special occasions.

- Sweets and Desserts: Sugary treats and desserts like cakes, cookies, and pastries are enjoyed infrequently.

◊ Flavorful Herbs and Spices: Herbs and spices play a crucial role in Mediterranean cuisine, adding flavor without relying on excessive salt or unhealthy condiments. Common choices include garlic, basil, oregano, thyme, parsley, rosemary, and cinnamon.

◊ Red Wine in Moderation: While not mandatory, moderate consumption of red wine is often associated with the Mediterranean diet. It is typically consumed in small quantities during meals, primarily for its potential health benefits. However, it's important to note that excessive alcohol consumption is not encouraged.

The Art of Gathering and Celebration

In the Mediterranean, food is not just sustenance; it is a celebration of life itself. Picture a lively family gathering, where laughter fills the air, glasses clink, and plates overflow with mouthwatering delicacies. The Mediterranean Diet Cookbook encourages you to embrace the art of gathering, bringing loved ones together around a shared table to create lasting memories. Discover the joy of preparing a Mediterranean feast, where the process of cooking becomes an act of love and the act of eating becomes a communal celebration of life's simple pleasures.

The Pyramid of Mediterranean Diet

The pyramid is actually the Mediterranean diet structure. The bottom of the pyramid is carbohydrates, including staples, vegetables and fruit; up are various soy and dairy products; then olive oil; then fish, shrimp, and poultry; the tip of the pyramid is dessert, pork, beef and lam, which should be consumed sparingly.

Tips for You

◊ Don't consume too much:The Mediterranean diet includes a wide variety of foods and beverages. So it is important to make wise choices and balance the nutrition in each meal you have. Just a small piece of cake at a birthday party, a few thin slices of roast meat at a field dinner, a glass or two of red wine at a family reunion, you still can enjoy the delicacy, and your body will not be overwhelmed by unhealthy food. A few bites or sips keep you healthy and bring you happiness. Also, you should not forget to eat less fried food. Nuts protect the heart blood vessels, but should be consumed moderately because there are so many calories. People with high blood triacylglycerols or abnormal liver function should avoid drinking alcohol.

◊ Eat with Your Loved Ones

Mediterranean people place great importance on family and friendships. The dinner table is an important arena for bringing everyone closer. Sharing a good meal with friends and family is a great way to enjoy the physical and mental benefits.

◊ Exercise

Daily exercise is very important for health. Based on your own situation, you can choose to exercise for no matter how long you like.

◊ Weight control

This is the essential part of keeping your body fit. Consult your doctor or use the Internet to find out what weight range is good for you. If you are overweight, it is urgent to eat less, drink less and take exercise regularly. But when controlling your weight, don't always keep an eye on the amount of energy (calories) you take in because if you do so you might never be happy anymore and even give up weight control.

Remember that the Mediterranean style of eating is suitable for most adults. However, children and pregnant women have different diets and need additional supplements for certain nutrients. For these special cases, recipes need to be adjusted, or you can consult a nutrition specialist or doctor.

Chapter 2 Beyond the Kitchen

What does the Mediterranean Lifestyle Bring Us

The Food and Agriculture Organization of the United Nations has described Mediterranean diet culture as a "way of life", which many believe that it is the philosophy of food, socialization and time.

The Mediterranean diet culture is not only an important historical and cultural product of the countries and regions involved, but also a great contribution to world civilization. 2010 UNESCO declared the Mediterranean diet on the World Heritage List, and included range of skills, knowledge, recipes and traditions into Mediterranean lifestyle, such as crop cultivation, fishing, processing, and food consumption, among other industries. The Mediterranean way of life has contributed to the birth of abundant knowledge, odes, aphorisms, stories and legends, preserves geographical and biological diversity, and the greatly develops traditions and crafts of fishing and agriculture. It's noted by UNESCO that the important role of women in spreading Mediterranean diet culture, the main force who preserve the cooking technique of the Mediterranean diet, and pass on diverse values to the next generation.

The Mediterranean diet culture also has a positive effect on the regional economy. The Mediterranean diet stands for health and sustainability, and is closely related to current tensions, such as food security, climate change, youth unemployment, etc. Local studies in Spain have shown that the Mediterranean diet can contribute to global food security by reducing greenhouse gas emissions, saving agricultural land, reducing energy consumption and water use, and promotes global sustainability.

Before You Get Started

Hey, before you really go to the kitchen and try our recipes, know some about the key ingredients and seasonings often used in Mediterranean cuisine:

1.Herbs: Common herbs used in Mediterranean cooking include basil, bay leaf, oregano, parsley, thyme, rosemary, sage, mint, dill, marjoram, lavender, and savory.

2.Spices: Some of the spices frequently used in Mediterranean dishes are black pepper, cloves, coriander, cumin, paprika, saffron, sumac, tarragon, turmeric, cinnamon, red pepper flakes, allspice, and nutmeg.

3.Olive oil: Extra virgin olive oil is a staple ingredient in the Mediterranean diet and is used for cooking, dressings, and dipping.

4.Fresh vegetables and fruits: The Mediterranean diet emphasizes the consumption of fresh vegetables and fruits, such as tomatoes, potatoes, spinach, kale, apples, bananas, oranges, and pears.

5.Whole grains: Whole grains like barley, bulgur, couscous, farro, and quinoa are commonly used in Mediterranean dishes.

6.Legumes: Legumes such as chickpeas, cannellini beans, fava beans, kidney beans, and lentils are an essential part of the Mediterranean diet.

7.Nuts and seeds: Almonds, walnuts, sunflower seeds, and other nuts and seeds are often used in Mediterranean cooking4.

8.Fish: Fish, especially oily fish like salmon, mackerel, and sardines, are an important source of protein in the Mediterranean diet.

Practicality meets Playfulness

Now, we understand that life can sometimes get a bit hectic, and spending hours in the kitchen might not be everyone's cup of tea (or glass of wine, in this case!). That's why the Mediterranean Diet Cookbook embraces the principles of practicality and playfulness. We'll guide you through easy-to-follow recipes that fit seamlessly into your busy lifestyle. Whether you're a kitchen novice or a seasoned chef, our instructions and tips will make cooking a breeze. So put on your apron, let your culinary creativity run wild, and prepare to amaze yourself and your loved ones with flavorful dishes that will make your taste buds dance with joy.

28-Day Mediterranean Diet Meal Plan

DAYS	BREAKFAST	LUNCH	DINNER	SNACK/DESSERT
1	Blueberry-Banana Bowl with Quinoa	Chickpea Fritters	Greek Frittata with Tomato-Olive Salad	Lemon Berry Cream Pops
2	Spinach Pie	Pilaf with Eggplant and Raisins	Roasted Portobello Mushrooms with Kale and Red Onion	Strawberry Panna Cotta
3	Mashed Chickpea, Feta, and Avocado Toast	White Bean Cassoulet	Stuffed Portobellos	Grilled Stone Fruit with Whipped Ricotta
4	Baklava Hot Porridge	Greek-Style Black-Eyed Pea Soup	Provençal Ratatouille with Herbed Breadcrumbs and Goat Cheese	Koulourakia (Olive Oil Cinnamon Cookies)
5	Smoked Salmon Egg Scramble with Dill and Chives	Barley Risotto	Fava Bean Purée with Chicory	Red-Wine Poached Pears
6	Sunny-Side Up Baked Eggs with Swiss Chard, Feta, and Basil	Mediterranean Lentils and Rice	Pesto Vegetable Skewers	Cranberry-Orange Cheesecake Pears
7	Green Spinach & Salmon Crepes	Garbanzo and Pita No-Bake Casserole	Root Vegetable Soup with Garlic Aioli	Mascarpone and Fig Crostini
8	Crostini with Smoked Trout	Asparagus Salad	Lentil Chili	Tortilla Fried Pies
9	Egg in a "Pepper Hole" with Avocado	Mediterranean Salad with Bulgur	Black-Eyed Peas with Olive Oil and Herbs	Crunchy Sesame Cookies
10	Blueberry-Lemon Tea Cakes	Panzanella (Tuscan Bread and Tomatoes Salad)	Domatorizo (Greek Tomato Rice)	Honey-Vanilla Apple Pie with Olive Oil Crust
11	Whole Wheat Blueberry Muffinsl	Roasted Cauliflower and Arugula Salad with Pomegranate and Pine Nuts	Vegetable Barley Soup	Crispy Apple Phyllo Tart
12	Savory Zucchini Muffins	Yellow and White Hearts of Palm Salad	Rice Pilaf	Peaches Poached in Rose Water
13	Whole-Wheat Toast with Apricots, Blue Cheese, and Honey	Melon Caprese Salad	Couscous with Apricots	Karithopita (Greek Juicy Walnut Cake)
14	Peach Sunrise Smoothie	Greek Black-Eyed Pea Salad	Pan-Fried Pork Chops with Peppers and Onions	Grilled Fruit Kebabs with Honey Labneh
15	Spiced Scrambled Eggs	Root Vegetable Soup with Garlic Aioli	Salmon with Cauliflower	Mediterranean Orange Yogurt Cake
16	Spinach, Sun-Dried Tomato, and Feta Egg Wraps	Roasted Ratatouille Pasta	Italian Fish	Crispy Chili Chickpeas

DAYS	BREAKFAST	LUNCH	DINNER	SNACK/DESSERT
17	Crunchy Vanilla Protein Bars	Eggplants Stuffed with Walnuts and Feta	South Indian Split Yellow Pigeon Peas with Mixed Vegetables	Taco-Spiced Chickpeas
18	Gluten-Free Granola Cereal	Tortellini in Red Pepper Sauce	Rice with Blackened Fish	Feta and Quinoa Stuffed Mushrooms
19	Marinara Eggs with Parsley	Moroccan Vegetable Tagine	Farro and Mushroom Risotto	Baked Eggplant Baba Ganoush
20	Veggie Hash with Eggs	Crustless Spinach Cheese Pie	Mediterranean Creamed Green Peas	Pesto Cucumber Boats
21	Ricotta and Fruit Bruschetta	Freekeh, Chickpea, and Herb Salad	Garlic-Asparagus Israeli Couscous	Roasted Za'atar Chickpeas
22	Enjoy-Your-Veggies Breakfast	White Bean Soup with Kale and Lemon	Taverna-Style Greek Salad	Fried Baby Artichokes with Lemon-Garlic Aioli
23	Avocado Toast with Smoked Trout	Greek Chickpeas with Coriander and Sage	Italian Summer Vegetable Barley Salad	Greek Yogurt Deviled Eggs
24	Breakfast Polenta	Gigantes (Greek Roasted Butter Beans)	Watermelon Burrata Salad	Kale Chips
25	Mushroom-and-Tomato Stuffed Hash Browns	Fava and Garbanzo Bean Fūl	Roasted Golden Beet, Avocado, and Watercress Salad	Stuffed Cucumber Cups
26	Greek Yogurt Parfait	Cilantro Lime Rice	Spinach Salad with Pomegranate, Lentils, and Pistachios	Roasted Chickpeas with Herbs and Spices
27	Spanish Tuna Tortilla with Roasted Peppers	Lentils with Spinach	Marinated Greek Salad with Oregano and Goat Cheese	Red Pepper Tapenade
28	Heart-Healthy Hazelnut-Collagen Shake	Vegetable Risotto with Beet Greens	Four-Bean Salad	Bravas-Style Potatoes

Chapter 3 Breakfasts

Blueberry-Banana Bowl with Quinoa

Prep time: 5 minutes | Cook time: 20 minutes | Serves 4

1½ cups water
¾ cup uncooked quinoa, rinsed
2 tablespoons honey, divided
1 cup blueberries (preferably frozen)
2 bananas (preferably frozen), sliced

½ cup sliced almonds or crushed walnuts
½ cup dried cranberries
1 cup granola
1 cup milk or nondairy milk of your choice

1. Combine the water and quinoa in a medium saucepan. Bring to a boil over medium-high heat, cover, reduce the heat to low, and simmer for 15 to 20 minutes, until the water has been absorbed. Remove from the heat and fluff the quinoa with a fork. 2. Evenly divide the quinoa among four bowls, about ½ cup for each bowl. Evenly divide the honey among the bowls and mix it in well. Top evenly with the blueberries, bananas, almonds, cranberries, granola, and milk. Serve.

Per Serving:
calories: 469 | fat: 15g | protein: 12g | carbs: 77g | fiber: 9g | sodium: 31mg

Breakfast Pita

Prep time: 5 minutes | Cook time: 6 minutes | Serves 2

1 whole wheat pita
2 teaspoons olive oil
½ shallot, diced
¼ teaspoon garlic, minced
1 large egg

¼ teaspoon dried oregano
¼ teaspoon dried thyme
⅛ teaspoon salt
2 tablespoons shredded Parmesan cheese

1. Preheat the air fryer to 380°F(193ºC). 2. Brush the top of the pita with olive oil, then spread the diced shallot and minced garlic over the pita. 3. Crack the egg into a small bowl or ramekin, and season it with oregano, thyme, and salt. 4. Place the pita into the air fryer basket, and gently pour the egg onto the top of the pita. Sprinkle with cheese over the top. 5. Bake for 6 minutes. 6. Allow to cool for 5 minutes before cutting into pieces for serving.

Per Serving:
calories: 191 | fat: 10g | protein: 8g | carbs: 19g | fiber: 3g | sodium: 312mg

Smoked Salmon Egg Scramble with Dill and Chives

Prep time: 5 minutes | Cook time: 5 minutes | Serves 2

4 large eggs
1 tablespoon milk
1 tablespoon fresh chives, minced
1 tablespoon fresh dill, minced
¼ teaspoon kosher salt

⅛ teaspoon freshly ground black pepper
2 teaspoons extra-virgin olive oil
2 ounces (57 g) smoked salmon, thinly sliced

1. In a large bowl, whisk together the eggs, milk, chives, dill, salt, and pepper. 2. Heat the olive oil in a medium skillet or sauté pan over medium heat. Add the egg mixture and cook for about 3 minutes, stirring occasionally. 3. Add the salmon and cook until the eggs are set but moist, about 1 minute.

Per Serving:
calories: 325 | fat: 26g | protein: 23g | carbs: 1g | fiber: 0g | sodium: 455mg

Grilled Halloumi with Whole-Wheat Pita Bread

Prep time: 5 minutes | Cook time: 10 minutes | Serves 4

2 teaspoons olive oil
8 (½-inch-thick) slices of halloumi cheese
4 whole-wheat pita rounds

1 Persian cucumber, thinly sliced
1 large tomato, sliced
½ cup pitted Kalamata olives

1. Brush a bit of olive oil on a grill pan and heat it over medium-high heat. 2. Brush the cheese slices all over with olive oil. Add the cheese slices in a single layer and cook until grill marks appear on the bottom, about 3 minutes. Flip the slices over and grill until grill marks appear on the second side, about 2 to 3 minutes more. 3. While the cheese is cooking, heat the pita bread, either in a skillet or in a toaster. 4. Serve the cheese inside of the pita pockets with the sliced cucumber, tomato, and olives.

Per Serving:
calories: 358 | fat: 24g | protein: 17g | carbs: 21g | fiber: 4g | sodium: 612mg

Green Spinach & Salmon Crepes

Prep time: 10 minutes | Cook time: 5 minutes |

Serves 1

Green Spinach Crepe:
1 cup fresh spinach or thawed and drained frozen spinach
1 small bunch fresh parsley
½ teaspoon fresh thyme leaves or ¼ teaspoon dried thyme
1 tablespoon nutritional yeast
1 tablespoon flax meal
Salt and black pepper, to taste
2 large eggs
2 teaspoons extra-virgin

avocado oil or ghee for cooking
Salmon Filling:
3 ounces (85 g) wild smoked salmon
½ large avocado, sliced
2 tablespoons crumbled goat's cheese or feta
1 teaspoon fresh lemon or lime juice
Optional: fresh herbs or microgreens, to taste

Make the green spinach crepe: 1. Place the spinach, herbs, nutritional yeast, flax meal, salt, and pepper in a food processor or blender. Process well until the spinach is finely chopped. Add the eggs and process on low speed until the mixture is just combined. 2. Heat half of the oil in a large skillet and add half of the mixture. Swirl the pan so the mixture completely covers the bottom. Cook for about 3 minutes or until just set, then add the salmon and avocado. Sprinkle the crepe with the goat's cheese and drizzle with the lemon juice. Slide onto a plate and optionally garnish with fresh herbs or microgreens. Serve warm.

Per Serving:

calories: 673 | fat: 48g | protein: 44g | carbs: 23g | fiber: 15g | sodium: 762mg

Mashed Chickpea, Feta, and Avocado Toast

Prep time: 10 minutes |Cook time: 0 minutes|

Serves: 4

1 (15-ounce / 425-g) can chickpeas, drained and rinsed
1 avocado, pitted
½ cup diced feta cheese (about 2 ounces / 57 g)
2 teaspoons freshly squeezed

lemon juice or 1 tablespoon orange juice
½ teaspoon freshly ground black pepper
4 pieces multigrain toast
2 teaspoons honey

1. Put the chickpeas in a large bowl. Scoop the avocado flesh into the bowl. 2. With a potato masher or large fork, mash the ingredients together until the mix has a spreadable consistency. It doesn't need to be totally smooth. 3. Add the feta, lemon juice, and pepper, and mix well. 4. Evenly divide the mash onto the four pieces of toast and spread with a knife. Drizzle with honey and serve.

Per Serving:

calories: 301 | fat: 14g | protein: 12g | carbs: 35g | fiber: 11g | sodium: 450mg

Egg in a "Pepper Hole" with Avocado

Prep time: 15 minutes | Cook time: 5 minutes |

Serves 4

4 bell peppers, any color
1 tablespoon extra-virgin olive oil
8 large eggs
¾ teaspoon kosher salt, divided
¼ teaspoon freshly ground

black pepper, divided
1 avocado, peeled, pitted, and diced
¼ cup red onion, diced
¼ cup fresh basil, chopped
Juice of ½ lime

1. Stem and seed the bell peppers. Cut 2 (2-inch-thick) rings from each pepper. Chop the remaining bell pepper into small dice, and set aside. 2. Heat the olive oil in a large skillet over medium heat. Add 4 bell pepper rings, then crack 1 egg in the middle of each ring. Season with ¼ teaspoon of the salt and ⅛ teaspoon of the black pepper. Cook until the egg whites are mostly set but the yolks are still runny, 2 to 3 minutes. Gently flip and cook 1 additional minute for over easy. Move the egg-bell pepper rings to a platter or onto plates, and repeat with the remaining 4 bell pepper rings. 3. In a medium bowl, combine the avocado, onion, basil, lime juice, reserved diced bell pepper, the remaining ¼ teaspoon kosher salt, and the remaining ⅛ teaspoon black pepper. Divide among the 4 plates.

Per Serving:

2 egg-pepper rings: calories: 270 | fat: 19g | protein: 15g | carbs: 12g | fiber: 5g | sodium: 360mg

Blueberry-Lemon Tea Cakes

Prep time: 10 minutes | Cook time: 25 minutes |

Serves 12

4 eggs
½ cup granulated sugar
Grated peel of 1 lemon
1½ cups all-purpose flour
¾ cup fine cornmeal

2 teaspoons baking powder
1 teaspoon kosher salt
1 cup extra-virgin olive oil
1½ cups fresh or frozen blueberries

1. Preheat the oven to 350°F(180°C). Grease a 12-cup muffin pan or line with paper liners. 2. With an electric mixer set to medium speed, beat the eggs and sugar together until they are pale and fluffy. Stir in the lemon peel. 3. In a medium bowl, stir together the flour, cornmeal, baking powder, and salt. With the mixer on low speed, alternate adding the flour mixture and oil to the egg mixture. Fold in the blueberries. 4. Dollop the batter into the muffin pan. Bake until the tops are golden and a toothpick inserted in the middle comes out clean, 20 to 25 minutes.

Per Serving:

calories: 317 | fat: 20g | protein: 4g | carbs: 31g | fiber: 2g | sodium: 217mg

Crostini with Smoked Trout

Prep time: 10 minutes | Cook time: 5 minutes | Serves 4

½ French baguette, cut into
1-inch-thick slices
1 tablespoon olive oil
¼ teaspoon onion powder
1 (4-ounce / 113-g) can smoked

trout
¼ cup crème fraîche
¼ teaspoon chopped fresh dill,
for garnish

1. Drizzle the bread on both sides with the olive oil and sprinkle with the onion powder. 2. Place the bread in a single layer in a large skillet and toast over medium heat until lightly browned on both sides, 3 to 4 minutes total. 3. Transfer the toasted bread to a serving platter and place 1 or 2 pieces of the trout on each slice. Top with the crème fraîche, garnish with the dill, and serve immediately.

Per Serving:

calories: 206 | fat: 10g | protein: 13g | carbs: 15g | fiber: 1g | sodium: 350mg

Spinach Pie

Prep time: 10 minutes | Cook time: 25 minutes | Serves 8

Nonstick cooking spray
2 tablespoons extra-virgin olive
oil
1 onion, chopped
1 pound (454 g) frozen spinach,
thawed
¼ teaspoon garlic salt
¼ teaspoon freshly ground
black pepper

¼ teaspoon ground nutmeg
4 large eggs, divided
1 cup grated Parmesan cheese,
divided
2 puff pastry doughs,
(organic, if available), at room
temperature
4 hard-boiled eggs, halved

1. Preheat the oven to 350°F(180ºC). Spray a baking sheet with nonstick cooking spray and set aside. 2. Heat a large sauté pan or skillet over medium-high heat. Put in the oil and onion and cook for about 5 minutes, until translucent. 3. Squeeze the excess water from the spinach, then add to the pan and cook, uncovered, so that any excess water from the spinach can evaporate. Add the garlic salt, pepper, and nutmeg. Remove from heat and set aside to cool. 4. In a small bowl, crack 3 eggs and mix well. Add the eggs and ½ cup Parmesan cheese to the cooled spinach mix. 5. On the prepared baking sheet, roll out the pastry dough. Layer the spinach mix on top of dough, leaving 2 inches around each edge. 6. Once the spinach is spread onto the pastry dough, place hard-boiled egg halves evenly throughout the pie, then cover with the second pastry dough. Pinch the edges closed. 7. Crack the remaining egg in a small bowl and mix well. Brush the egg wash over the pastry dough. 8. Bake for 15 to 20 minutes, until golden brown and warmed through.

Per Serving:

calories: 417 | fat: 28g | protein: 17g | carbs: 25g | fiber: 3g | sodium: 490mg

Baklava Hot Porridge

Prep time: 5 minutes | Cook time: 5 minutes | Serves 2

2 cups riced cauliflower
¾ cup unsweetened almond,
flax, or hemp milk
4 tablespoons extra-virgin olive
oil, divided
2 teaspoons grated fresh orange
peel (from ½ orange)
½ teaspoon ground cinnamon

½ teaspoon almond extract or
vanilla extract
⅛ teaspoon salt
4 tablespoons chopped walnuts,
divided
1 to 2 teaspoons liquid stevia,
monk fruit, or other sweetener
of choice (optional)

1. In medium saucepan, combine the riced cauliflower, almond milk, 2 tablespoons olive oil, grated orange peel, cinnamon, almond extract, and salt. Stir to combine and bring just to a boil over medium-high heat, stirring constantly. 2. Remove from heat and stir in 2 tablespoons chopped walnuts and sweetener (if using). Stir to combine. 3. Divide into bowls, topping each with 1 tablespoon of chopped walnuts and 1 tablespoon of the remaining olive oil.

Per Serving:

calories: 414 | fat: 38g | protein: 6g | carbs: 16g | fiber: 4g | sodium: 252mg

Sunny-Side Up Baked Eggs with Swiss Chard, Feta, and Basil

Prep time: 15 minutes | Cook time: 10 to 15 minutes | Serves 4

1 tablespoon extra-virgin olive
oil, divided
½ red onion, diced
½ teaspoon kosher salt
¼ teaspoon nutmeg
⅛ teaspoon freshly ground

black pepper
4 cups Swiss chard, chopped
¼ cup crumbled feta cheese
4 large eggs
¼ cup fresh basil, chopped or
cut into ribbons

1. Preheat the oven to 375ºF (190ºC). Place 4 ramekins on a half sheet pan or in a baking dish and grease lightly with olive oil. 2. Heat the remaining olive oil in a large skillet or sauté pan over medium heat. Add the onion, salt, nutmeg, and pepper and sauté until translucent, about 3 minutes. Add the chard and cook, stirring, until wilted, about 2 minutes. 3. Split the mixture among the 4 ramekins. Add 1 tablespoon feta cheese to each ramekin. Crack 1 egg on top of the mixture in each ramekin. Bake for 10 to 12 minutes, or until the egg white is set. 4. Allow to cool for 1 to 2 minutes, then carefully transfer the eggs from the ramekins to a plate with a fork or spatula. Garnish with the basil.

Per Serving:

calories: 140 | fat: 10g | protein: 9g | carbs: 4g | fiber: 4g | sodium: 370mg

Breakfast Polenta

Prep time: 5 minutes |Cook time: 10 minutes|

Serves: 6

2 (18-ounce / 510-g) tubes plain polenta
2¼ to 2½ cups 2% milk, divided

2 oranges, peeled and chopped
½ cup chopped pecans
¼ cup 2% plain Greek yogurt
8 teaspoons honey

1. Slice the polenta into rounds and place in a microwave-safe bowl. Heat in the microwave on high for 45 seconds. 2. Transfer the polenta to a large pot, and mash it with a potato masher or fork until coarsely mashed. Place the pot on the stove over medium heat. 3. In a medium, microwave-safe bowl, heat the milk in the microwave on high for 1 minute. Pour 2 cups of the warmed milk into the pot with the polenta, and stir with a whisk. Continue to stir and mash with the whisk, adding the remaining milk a few tablespoons at a time, until the polenta is fairly smooth and heated through, about 5 minutes. Remove from the stove. 4. Divide the polenta among four serving bowls. Top each bowl with one-quarter of the oranges, 2 tablespoons of pecans, 1 tablespoon of yogurt, and 2 teaspoons of honey before serving.

Per Serving:

calories: 319 | fat: 9g | protein: 8g | carbs: 54g | fiber: 4g | sodium: 428mg

Mushroom-and-Tomato Stuffed Hash Browns

Prep time: 10 minutes | Cook time: 20 minutes |

Serves 4

Olive oil cooking spray
1 tablespoon plus 2 teaspoons olive oil, divided
4 ounces (113 g) baby bella mushrooms, diced
1 scallion, white parts and green parts, diced

1 garlic clove, minced
2 cups shredded potatoes
½ teaspoon salt
¼ teaspoon black pepper
1 Roma tomato, diced
½ cup shredded mozzarella

1. Preheat the air fryer to 380°F(193ºC). Lightly coat the inside of a 6-inch cake pan with olive oil cooking spray. 2. In a small skillet, heat 2 teaspoons olive oil over medium heat. Add the mushrooms, scallion, and garlic, and cook for 4 to 5 minutes, or until they have softened and are beginning to show some color. Remove from heat. 3. Meanwhile, in a large bowl, combine the potatoes, salt, pepper, and the remaining tablespoon olive oil. Toss until all potatoes are well coated. 4. Pour half of the potatoes into the bottom of the cake pan. Top with the mushroom mixture, tomato, and mozzarella. Spread the remaining potatoes over the top. 5. Bake in the air fryer for 12 to 15 minutes, or until the top is golden brown. 6. Remove from the air fryer and allow to cool for 5 minutes before slicing and serving.

Per Serving:

calories: 165 | fat: 9g | protein: 6g | carbs: 16g | fiber: 3g | sodium: 403mg

Spinach, Sun-Dried Tomato, and Feta Egg Wraps

Prep time: 10 minutes | Cook time: 7 minutes |

Serves 2

1 tablespoon olive oil
¼ cup minced onion
3 to 4 tablespoons minced sun-dried tomatoes in olive oil and herbs
3 large eggs, beaten

1½ cups packed baby spinach
1 ounce (28 g) crumbled feta cheese
Salt
2 (8-inch) whole-wheat tortillas

1. In a large skillet, heat the olive oil over medium-high heat. Add the onion and tomatoes and sauté for about 3 minutes. 2. Turn the heat down to medium. Add the beaten eggs and stir to scramble them. 3. Add the spinach and stir to combine. Sprinkle the feta cheese over the eggs. Add salt to taste. 4. Warm the tortillas in the microwave for about 20 seconds each. 5. Fill each tortilla with half of the egg mixture. Fold in half or roll them up and serve.

Per Serving:

calories: 435 | fat: 28g | protein: 17g | carbs: 31g | fiber: 6g | sodium: 552mg

Crunchy Vanilla Protein Bars

Prep time: 10 minutes | Cook time: 5 minutes |

Serves 8

Topping:
½ cup flaked coconut
2 tablespoons raw cacao nibs
Bars:
1½ cups almond flour
1 cup collagen powder
2 tablespoons ground or whole chia seeds
1 teaspoon vanilla powder or 1

tablespoon unsweetened vanilla extract
¼ cup virgin coconut oil
½ cup coconut milk
1½ teaspoons fresh lemon zest
⅓ cup macadamia nuts, halved
Optional: low-carb sweetener, to taste

1. Preheat the oven to 350°F (180°C) fan assisted or 380°F (193ºC) conventional. 2. To make the topping: Place the coconut flakes on a baking tray and bake for 2 to 3 minutes, until lightly golden. Set aside to cool. 3. To make the bars: In a bowl, combine all of the ingredients for the bars. Line a small baking tray with parchment paper or use a silicone baking tray. A square 8 × 8–inch (20 × 20 cm) or a rectangular tray of similar size will work best. 4. Press the dough into the pan and sprinkle with the cacao nibs, pressing them into the bars with your fingers. Add the toasted coconut and lightly press the flakes into the dough. Refrigerate until set, for about 1 hour. Slice to serve. Store in the refrigerator for up to 1 week.

Per Serving:

calories: 285 | fat: 27g | protein: 5g | carbs: 10g | fiber: 4g | sodium: 19mg

Gluten-Free Granola Cereal

Prep time: 7 minutes | Cook time: 30 minutes |
Makes 3½ cups

Oil, for spraying
1½ cups gluten-free rolled oats
½ cup chopped walnuts
½ cup chopped almonds
½ cup pumpkin seeds
¼ cup maple syrup or honey

1 tablespoon toasted sesame oil
or vegetable oil
1 teaspoon ground cinnamon
½ teaspoon salt
½ cup dried cranberries

1. Preheat the air fryer to 250ºF (121ºC). Line the air fryer basket with parchment and spray lightly with oil. (Do not skip the step of lining the basket; the parchment will keep the granola from falling through the holes.) 2. In a large bowl, mix together the oats, walnuts, almonds, pumpkin seeds, maple syrup, sesame oil, cinnamon, and salt. 3. Spread the mixture in an even layer in the prepared basket. 4. Cook for 30 minutes, stirring every 10 minutes. 5. Transfer the granola to a bowl, add the dried cranberries, and toss to combine. 6. Let cool to room temperature before storing in an airtight container.

Per Serving:

calories: 322 | fat: 17g | protein: 11g | carbs: 35g | fiber: 6g | sodium: 170mg

Veggie Hash with Eggs

Prep time: 20 minutes | Cook time: 6¼ hours |
Serves 2

Nonstick cooking spray
1 onion, chopped
2 garlic cloves, minced
1 red bell pepper, chopped
1 yellow summer squash, chopped
2 carrots, chopped
2 Yukon Gold potatoes, peeled and chopped
2 large tomatoes, seeded and

chopped
¼ cup vegetable broth
½ teaspoon salt
⅛ teaspoon freshly ground black pepper
½ teaspoon dried thyme leaves
3 or 4 eggs
½ teaspoon ground sweet paprika

1. Spray the slow cooker with the nonstick cooking spray. 2. In the slow cooker, combine all the ingredients except the eggs and paprika, and stir. 3. Cover and cook on low for 6 hours. 4. Uncover and make 1 indentation in the vegetable mixture for each egg. Break 1 egg into a small cup and slip the egg into an indentation. Repeat with the remaining eggs. Sprinkle with the paprika. 5. Cover and cook on low for 10 to 15 minutes, or until the eggs are just set, and serve.

Per Serving:

calories: 381 | fat: 8g | protein: 17g | carbs: 64g | fiber: 12g | sodium: 747mg

Ricotta and Fruit Bruschetta

Prep time: 5 minutes | Cook time: 0 minutes | Serves 2

¼ cup full-fat ricotta cheese
1½ teaspoons honey, divided
3 drops almond extract
2 slices whole-grain bread, toasted
½ medium banana, peeled and

cut into ¼-inch slices
½ medium pear (any variety), thinly sliced
2 teaspoons chopped walnuts
2 pinches of ground cinnamon

1. In a small bowl, combine the ricotta, ¼ teaspoon honey, and the almond extract. Stir well. 2. Spread 1½ tablespoons of the ricotta mixture over each slice of toast. 3. Divide the pear slices and banana slices equally on top of each slice of toast. 4. Drizzle equal amounts of the remaining honey over each slice, and sprinkle 1 teaspoon of the walnuts over each slice. Top each serving with a pinch of cinnamon.

Per Serving:

calories: 207 | fat: 7g | protein: 8g | carbs: 30g | fiber: 4g | sodium: 162mg

Marinara Eggs with Parsley

Prep time: 5 minutes |Cook time: 15 minutes|
Serves: 6

1 tablespoon extra-virgin olive oil
1 cup chopped onion (about ½ medium onion)
2 garlic cloves, minced (about 1 teaspoon)
2 (14½-ounce / 411-g) cans Italian diced tomatoes, undrained, no salt added
6 large eggs
½ cup chopped fresh flat-leaf (Italian) parsley
Crusty Italian bread and grated Parmesan or Romano cheese, for serving (optional)

1. In a large skillet over medium-high heat, heat the oil. Add the onion and cook for 5 minutes, stirring occasionally. Add the garlic and cook for 1 minute. 2. Pour the tomatoes with their juices over the onion mixture and cook until bubbling, 2 to 3 minutes. While waiting for the tomato mixture to bubble, crack one egg into a small custard cup or coffee mug. 3. When the tomato mixture bubbles, lower the heat to medium. Then use a large spoon to make six indentations in the tomato mixture. Gently pour the first cracked egg into one indentation and repeat, cracking the remaining eggs, one at a time, into the custard cup and pouring one into each indentation. Cover the skillet and cook for 6 to 7 minutes, or until the eggs are done to your liking (about 6 minutes for soft-cooked, 7 minutes for harder cooked). 4. Top with the parsley, and serve with the bread and grated cheese, if desired.

Per Serving:

calories: 127 | fat: 7g | protein: 8g | carbs: 8g | fiber: 2g | sodium: 82mg

Spiced Scrambled Eggs

Prep time: 15 minutes | Cook time: 28 minutes | Serves 4

2 tablespoons olive oil
1 small red onion, chopped
1 medium green pepper, cored, seeded, and finely chopped
1 red Fresno or jalapeño chili pepper, seeded and cut into thin strips
3 medium tomatoes, chopped
Sea salt and freshly ground pepper, to taste
1 tablespoon ground cumin
1 teaspoon ground coriander
4 large eggs, lightly beaten

1. Heat the olive oil in a large, heavy skillet over medium heat. 2. Add the onion and cook until soft and translucent, 6–7 minutes. 3. Add the peppers and continue to cook until soft, another 4–5 minutes. Add in the tomatoes and season to taste. 4. Stir in the cumin and coriander. 5. Simmer for 10 minutes over medium-low heat. 6. Add the eggs, stirring them into the mixture to distribute. 7. Cover the skillet and cook until the eggs are set but still fluffy and tender, about 5–6 minutes more. 8. Divide between 4 plates and serve immediately.

Per Serving:
calories: 169 | fat: 12g | protein: 8g | carbs: 8g | fiber: 2g | sodium: 81mg

Enjoy-Your-Veggies Breakfast

Prep time: 20 minutes | Cook time: 10 minutes | Serves 4

1 tablespoon olive oil
1 small sweet onion, peeled and diced
2 large carrots, peeled and diced
2 medium potatoes, peeled and diced
1 stalk celery, diced
1 large red bell pepper, seeded and diced
1 tablespoon low-sodium soy
sauce
¼ cup water
1 cup diced peeled zucchini or summer squash
2 medium tomatoes, peeled and diced
2 cups cooked brown rice
½ teaspoon ground black pepper

1. Press the Sauté button on the Instant Pot® and heat oil. Add onion and cook until just tender, about 2 minutes. 2. Stir in carrots, potatoes, celery, and bell pepper and cook until just tender, about 2 minutes. Add soy sauce and water. Press the Cancel button. 3. Close lid, set steam release to Sealing, press the Manual button, and set time to 2 minutes. When the timer beeps, quick-release the pressure until the float valve drops. Press the Cancel button. 4. Open lid and add squash and tomatoes, and stir. Close lid, set steam release to Sealing, press the Manual button, and set time to 1 minute. When the timer beeps, quick-release the pressure until the float valve drops. Press the Cancel button and open lid. 5. Serve over rice and sprinkle with black pepper.

Per Serving:
calories: 224 | fat: 5g | protein: 6g | carbs: 41g | fiber: 5g | sodium: 159mg

Greek Yogurt Parfait

Prep time: 5 minutes | Cook time: 0 minutes | Serves 1

½ cup plain whole-milk Greek yogurt
2 tablespoons heavy whipping cream
¼ cup frozen berries, thawed with juices
½ teaspoon vanilla or almond
extract (optional)
¼ teaspoon ground cinnamon (optional)
1 tablespoon ground flaxseed
2 tablespoons chopped nuts (walnuts or pecans)

1. In a small bowl or glass, combine the yogurt, heavy whipping cream, thawed berries in their juice, vanilla or almond extract (if using), cinnamon (if using), and flaxseed and stir well until smooth. Top with chopped nuts and enjoy.

Per Serving:
calories: 333 | fat: 27g | protein: 10g | carbs: 15g | fiber: 4g | sodium: 71mg

Peach Sunrise Smoothie

Prep time: 10 minutes | Cook time: 0 minutes | Serves 1

1 large unpeeled peach, pitted and sliced (about ½ cup)
6 ounces (170 g) vanilla or
peach low-fat Greek yogurt
2 tablespoons low-fat milk
6 to 8 ice cubes

1. Combine all ingredients in a blender and blend until thick and creamy. Serve immediately.

Per Serving:
calories: 228 | fat: 3g | protein: 11g | carbs: 42g | fiber: 3g | sodium: 127mg

Avocado Toast with Smoked Trout

Prep time: 10 minutes | Cook time: 0 minutes | Serves 2

1 avocado, peeled and pitted
2 teaspoons lemon juice, plus more for serving
¾ teaspoon ground cumin
¼ teaspoon kosher salt
¼ teaspoon red pepper flakes,
plus more for sprinkling
¼ teaspoon lemon zest
2 pieces whole-wheat bread, toasted
1 (3.75-ounce / 106-g) can smoked trout

1. In a medium bowl, mash together the avocado, lemon juice, cumin, salt, red pepper flakes, and lemon zest. 2. Spread half the avocado mixture on each piece of toast. Top each piece of toast with half the smoked trout. Garnish with a pinch of red pepper flakes (if desired), and/or a sprinkle of lemon juice (if desired).

Per Serving:
calories: 300 | fat: 20g | protein: 11g | carbs: 21g | fiber: 6g | sodium: 390mg

Peachy Green Smoothie

Prep time: 10 minutes | Cook time: 0 minutes |
Serves 2

1 cup almond milk
3 cups kale or spinach
1 banana, peeled
1 orange, peeled

1 small green apple
1 cup frozen peaches
¼ cup vanilla Greek yogurt

1. Put the ingredients in a blender in the order listed and blend on high until smooth. 2. Serve and enjoy.

Per Serving:

calories: 257 | fat: 5g | protein: 9g | carbs: 50g | fiber: 7g | sodium: 87mg

Mediterranean Fruit Bulgur Breakfast Bowl

Prep time: 5 minutes |Cook time: 15 minutes|
Serves: 6

1½ cups uncooked bulgur
2 cups 2% milk
1 cup water
½ teaspoon ground cinnamon
2 cups frozen (or fresh, pitted) dark sweet cherries

8 dried (or fresh) figs, chopped
½ cup chopped almonds
¼ cup loosely packed fresh mint, chopped
Warm 2% milk, for serving (optional)

1. In a medium saucepan, combine the bulgur, milk, water, and cinnamon. Stir once, then bring just to a boil. Cover, reduce the heat to medium-low, and simmer for 10 minutes or until the liquid is absorbed. 2. Turn off the heat, but keep the pan on the stove, and stir in the frozen cherries (no need to thaw), figs, and almonds. Stir well, cover for 1 minute, and let the hot bulgur thaw the cherries and partially hydrate the figs. Stir in the mint. 3. Scoop into serving bowls. Serve with warm milk, if desired. You can also serve it chilled.

Per Serving:

calories: 273 | fat: 7g | protein: 10g | carbs: 48g | fiber: 8g | sodium: 46mg

Poached Eggs on Whole Grain Avocado Toast

Prep time: 5 minutes | Cook time: 7 minutes | Serves 4

Olive oil cooking spray
4 large eggs
Salt
Black pepper

4 pieces whole grain bread
1 avocado
Red pepper flakes (optional)

1. Preheat the air fryer to 320°F(160°C). Lightly coat the inside of four small oven-safe ramekins with olive oil cooking spray. 2. Crack one egg into each ramekin, and season with salt and black pepper. 3. Place the ramekins into the air fryer basket. Close and set the timer to 7 minutes. 4. While the eggs are cooking, toast the bread in a toaster. 5. Slice the avocado in half lengthwise, remove the pit, and scoop the flesh into a small bowl. Season with salt, black pepper, and red pepper flakes, if desired. Using a fork, smash the avocado lightly. 6. Spread a quarter of the smashed avocado evenly over each slice of toast. 7. Remove the eggs from the air fryer, and gently spoon one onto each slice of avocado toast before serving.

Per Serving:

calories: 232 | fat: 14g | protein: 11g | carbs: 18g | fiber: 6g | sodium: 205mg

Heart-Healthy Hazelnut-Collagen Shake

Prep time: 5 minutes | Cook time: 0 minutes | Serves 1

1½ cups unsweetened almond milk
2 tablespoons hazelnut butter
2 tablespoons grass-fed collagen powder
½–1 teaspoon cinnamon

⅛ teaspoon LoSalt or pink Himalayan salt
⅛ teaspoon sugar-free almond extract
1 tablespoon macadamia oil or hazelnut oil

1. Place all of the ingredients in a blender and pulse until smooth and frothy. Serve immediately.

Per Serving:

calories: 507 | fat: 41g | protein: 3g | carbs: 35g | fiber: 12g | sodium: 569mg

Quinoa Porridge with Apricots

Prep time: 10 minutes | Cook time: 12 minutes |
Serves 4

1½ cups quinoa, rinsed and drained
1 cup chopped dried apricots
2½ cups water

1 cup almond milk
1 tablespoon rose water
½ teaspoon cardamom
¼ teaspoon salt

1. Place all ingredients in the Instant Pot®. Stir to combine. Close lid, set steam release to Sealing, press the Rice button, and set time to 12 minutes. When the timer beeps, let pressure release naturally, about 20 minutes. 2. Press the Cancel button, open lid, and fluff quinoa with a fork. Serve warm.

Per Serving:

calories: 197 | fat: 2g | protein: 3g | carbs: 44g | fiber: 4g | sodium: 293mg

Spanish Tuna Tortilla with Roasted Peppers

Prep time: 15 minutes | Cook time: 15 minutes |

Serves 4

6 large eggs
¼ cup olive oil
2 small russet potatoes, diced
1 small onion, chopped
1 roasted red bell pepper, sliced
1 (7-ounce / 198-g) can tuna

packed in water, drained well and flaked
2 plum tomatoes, seeded and diced
1 teaspoon dried tarragon

1. Preheat the broiler on high. 2. Crack the eggs in a large bowl and whisk them together until just combined. Heat the olive oil in a large, oven-safe, nonstick or cast-iron skillet over medium-low heat. 3. Add the potatoes and cook until slightly soft, about 7 minutes. Add the onion and the peppers and cook until soft, 3–5 minutes. 4. Add the tuna, tomatoes, and tarragon to the skillet and stir to combine, then add the eggs. 5. Cook for 7–10 minutes until the eggs are bubbling from the bottom and the bottom is slightly brown. 6. Place the skillet into the oven on 1 of the first 2 racks, and cook until the middle is set and the top is slightly brown. 7. Slice into wedges and serve warm or at room temperature.

Per Serving:

calories: 247 | fat: 14g | protein: 12g | carbs: 19g | fiber: 2g | sodium: 130mg

Portobello Eggs Benedict

Prep time: 10 minutes | Cook time: 10 to 14 minutes | Serves 2

1 tablespoon olive oil
2 cloves garlic, minced
¼ teaspoon dried thyme
2 portobello mushrooms, stems removed and gills scraped out
2 Roma tomatoes, halved lengthwise
Salt and freshly ground black

pepper, to taste
2 large eggs
2 tablespoons grated Pecorino Romano cheese
1 tablespoon chopped fresh parsley, for garnish
1 teaspoon truffle oil (optional)

1. Preheat the air fryer to 400°F (204°C). 2. In a small bowl, combine the olive oil, garlic, and thyme. Brush the mixture over the mushrooms and tomatoes until thoroughly coated. Season to taste with salt and freshly ground black pepper. 3. Arrange the vegetables, cut side up, in the air fryer basket. Crack an egg into the center of each mushroom and sprinkle with cheese. Air fry for 10 to 14 minutes until the vegetables are tender and the whites are firm. When cool enough to handle, coarsely chop the tomatoes and place on top of the eggs. Scatter parsley on top and drizzle with truffle oil, if desired, just before serving.

Per Serving:

calories: 189 | fat: 13g | protein: 11g | carbs: 7g | fiber: 2g | sodium: 87mg

Italian Egg Cups

Prep time: 5 minutes | Cook time: 10 minutes |

Serves 4

Olive oil
1 cup marinara sauce
4 eggs
4 tablespoons shredded Mozzarella cheese

4 teaspoons grated Parmesan cheese
Salt and freshly ground black pepper, to taste
Chopped fresh basil, for garnish

1. Lightly spray 4 individual ramekins with olive oil. 2. Pour ¼ cup of marinara sauce into each ramekin. 3. Crack one egg into each ramekin on top of the marinara sauce. 4. Sprinkle 1 tablespoon of Mozzarella and 1 tablespoon of Parmesan on top of each egg. Season with salt and pepper. 5. Cover each ramekin with aluminum foil. Place two of the ramekins in the air fryer basket. 6. Air fry at 350°F (177°C) for 5 minutes and remove the aluminum foil. Air fry until the top is lightly browned and the egg white is cooked, another 2 to 4 minutes. If you prefer the yolk to be firmer, cook for 3 to 5 more minutes. 7. Repeat with the remaining two ramekins. Garnish with basil and serve.

Per Serving:

calories: 123 | fat: 7g | protein: 9g | carbs: 6g | fiber: 1g | sodium: 84mg

Whole Wheat Blueberry Muffins

Prep time: 10 minutes | Cook time: 15 minutes |

Serves 6

Olive oil cooking spray
½ cup unsweetened applesauce
¼ cup raw honey
½ cup nonfat plain Greek yogurt
1 teaspoon vanilla extract
1 large egg

1½ cups plus 1 tablespoon whole wheat flour, divided
½ teaspoon baking soda
½ teaspoon baking powder
½ teaspoon salt
½ cup blueberries, fresh or frozen

1. Preheat the air fryer to 360°F (182°C). Lightly coat the inside of six silicone muffin cups or a six-cup muffin tin with olive oil cooking spray. 2. In a large bowl, combine the applesauce, honey, yogurt, vanilla, and egg and mix until smooth. 3. Sift in 1½ cups of the flour, the baking soda, baking powder, and salt into the wet mixture, then stir until just combined. 4. In a small bowl, toss the blueberries with the remaining 1 tablespoon flour, then fold the mixture into the muffin batter. 5. Divide the mixture evenly among the prepared muffin cups and place into the basket of the air fryer. Bake for 12 to 15 minutes, or until golden brown on top and a toothpick inserted into the middle of one of the muffins comes out clean. 6. Allow to cool for 5 minutes before serving.

Per Serving:

calories: 186 | fat: 2g | protein: 7g | carbs: 38g | fiber: 4g | sodium: 318mg

Greek Breakfast Power Bowl

3 tablespoons extra-virgin avocado oil or ghee, divided
1 clove garlic, minced
2 teaspoons chopped fresh rosemary
1 small eggplant, roughly chopped
1 medium zucchini, roughly chopped
1 tablespoon fresh lemon juice
2 tablespoons chopped mint

1 tablespoon chopped fresh oregano
Salt and black pepper, to taste
6 ounces (170 g) Halloumi cheese, cubed or sliced
¼ cup pitted Kalamata olives
4 large eggs, soft-boiled (or hard-boiled or poached)
1 tablespoon extra-virgin olive oil, to drizzle

1. Heat a skillet (with a lid) greased with 2 tablespoons (30 ml) of the avocado oil over medium heat. Add the garlic and rosemary and cook for 1 minute. Add the eggplant, zucchini, and lemon juice. Stir and cover with a lid, then reduce the heat to medium-low. Cook for 10 to 15 minutes, stirring once or twice, until tender. 2. Stir in the mint and oregano. Optionally, reserve some herbs for topping. Season with salt and pepper to taste. Remove from the heat and transfer to a plate. Cover with the skillet lid to keep the veggies warm. 3. Grease the same pan with the remaining 1 tablespoon (15 ml) avocado oil and cook the Halloumi over medium-high heat for 2 to 3 minutes per side until lightly browned. Place the slices of cooked Halloumi on top of the cooked veggies. Top with the olives and cooked eggs and drizzle with the olive oil. 4. Always serve warm, as Halloumi hardens once it cools. Reheat before serving if necessary.

Per Serving:

calories: 748 | fat: 56g | protein: 40g | carbs: 25g | fiber: 10g | sodium: 275mg

Savory Zucchini Muffins

1 tablespoon extra virgin olive oil plus extra for brushing
2 medium zucchini, grated
⅛ teaspoon fine sea salt
1 large egg, lightly beaten
1½ ounces (43 g) crumbled feta
¼ medium onion (any variety), finely chopped
1 tablespoon chopped fresh parsley

1 tablespoon chopped fresh dill
1 tablespoon chopped fresh mint
¼ teaspoon freshly ground black pepper
3 tablespoons unseasoned breadcrumbs
1 tablespoon grated Parmesan cheese

1. Preheat the oven to 400°F (205°C), and line a medium muffin pan with 6 muffin liners. Lightly brush the bottoms of the liners with olive oil. 2. Place the grated zucchini in a colander and sprinkle with the sea salt. Set aside for 10 minutes to allow the salt to penetrate. 3. Remove the zucchini from the colander, and place it on a tea towel. Pull the edges of the towel in and then twist and squeeze the towel to remove as much of the water from the zucchini as possible. (This will prevent the muffins from becoming soggy.) 4. In a large bowl, combine the egg, feta, onions, parsley, dill, mint, pepper, and the remaining tablespoon of olive oil. Mix well, and add the zucchini to the bowl. Mix again, and add the breadcrumbs. Use a fork to mash the ingredients until well combined. 5. Divide the mixture among the prepared muffins liners and then sprinkle ½ teaspoon grated Parmesan over each muffin. Transfer to the oven, and bake for 35 minutes or until the muffins turn golden brown. 6. When the baking time is complete, remove the muffins from the oven and set aside to cool for 5 minutes before removing from the pan. Store in an airtight container in the refrigerator for 3 days, or tightly wrap individual muffins in plastic wrap and freeze for up to 3 months.

Per Serving:

calories: 39 | fat: 2g | protein: 2g | carbs: 3g | fiber: 1g | sodium: 80mg

Polenta with Sautéed Chard and Fried Eggs

For the Polenta:
2½ cups water
½ teaspoon kosher salt
¾ cups whole-grain cornmeal
¼ teaspoon freshly ground black pepper
2 tablespoons grated Parmesan cheese
For the Chard:
1 tablespoon extra-virgin olive oil
1 bunch (about 6 ounces / 170

g) Swiss chard, leaves and stems chopped and separated
2 garlic cloves, sliced
¼ teaspoon kosher salt
⅛ teaspoon freshly ground black pepper
Lemon juice (optional)
For the Eggs:
1 tablespoon extra-virgin olive oil
4 large eggs

Make the Polenta: 1. Bring the water and salt to a boil in a medium saucepan over high heat. Slowly add the cornmeal, whisking constantly. 2. Decrease the heat to low, cover, and cook for 10 to 15 minutes, stirring often to avoid lumps. Stir in the pepper and Parmesan, and divide among 4 bowls. Make the Chard: 3. Heat the oil in a large skillet over medium heat. Add the chard stems, garlic, salt, and pepper; sauté for 2 minutes. Add the chard leaves and cook until wilted, about 3 to 5 minutes. 4. Add a spritz of lemon juice (if desired), toss together, and divide evenly on top of the polenta. Make the Eggs: 5. Heat the oil in the same large skillet over medium-high heat. Crack each egg into the skillet, taking care not to crowd the skillet and leaving space between the eggs. Cook until the whites are set and golden around the edges, about 2 to 3 minutes. 6. Serve sunny-side up or flip the eggs over carefully and cook 1 minute longer for over easy. Place one egg on top of the polenta and chard in each bowl.

Per Serving:

calories: 310 | fat: 18g | protein: 17g | carbs: 21g | fiber: 1g | sodium: 500mg

Breakfast Quinoa with Figs and Walnuts

Prep time: 10 minutes | Cook time: 12 minutes | Serves 4

1½ cups quinoa, rinsed and drained
2½ cups water
1 cup almond milk
2 tablespoons honey
1 teaspoon vanilla extract

½ teaspoon ground cinnamon
¼ teaspoon salt
½ cup low-fat plain Greek yogurt
8 fresh figs, quartered
1 cup chopped toasted walnuts

1. Place quinoa, water, almond milk, honey, vanilla, cinnamon, and salt in the Instant Pot®. Stir to combine. Close lid, set steam release to Sealing, press the Rice button, and set time to 12 minutes. When the timer beeps, let pressure release naturally, about 20 minutes. 2. Press the Cancel button, open lid, and fluff quinoa with a fork. Serve warm with yogurt, figs, and walnuts.

Per Serving:

calories: 413 | fat: 25g | protein: 10g | carbs: 52g | fiber: 7g | sodium: 275mg

Whole-Wheat Toast with Apricots, Blue Cheese, and Honey

Prep time: 5 minutes | Cook time: 5 minutes | Serves 2

2 thick slices crusty whole-wheat bread
1 tablespoon olive oil
2 apricots, halved and cut into ¼-inch-thick slices

2 ounces (57 g) blue cheese
2 tablespoons honey
2 tablespoons toasted slivered almonds

1. Preheat the broiler to high. 2. Brush the bread on both sides with the olive oil. Arrange the slices on a baking sheet and broil until lightly browned, about 2 minutes per side. 3. Arrange the apricot slices on the toasted bread, dividing equally. Sprinkle the cheese over the top, dividing equally. Return the baking sheet to the broiler and broil for 1 to 2 minutes until the cheese melts and just begins to brown. Remove from the oven and serve drizzled with honey and garnished with the toasted almonds.

Per Serving:

calories: 379 | fat: 20g | protein: 13g | carbs: 40g | fiber: 4g | sodium: 595mg

Spiced Antioxidant Granola Clusters

Prep time: 10 minutes | Cook time: 1 hour 10 minutes | Serves 10

1 cup unsweetened fine coconut flakes
1 cup unsweetened large coconut flakes
¼ cup packed flax meal
¼ cup chia seeds
½ cup pecans, chopped
1 cup blanched almonds, roughly chopped, or flaked almonds
2 teaspoons cinnamon
1 teaspoon ground anise seed
½ teaspoon ground nutmeg

½ teaspoon ground cloves
1 tablespoon fresh lemon zest
¼ teaspoon black pepper
¼ teaspoon salt
⅓ cup light tahini
¼ cup virgin coconut oil
2 large egg whites
Optional: unsweetened almond milk, coconut cream, coconut yogurt, or full-fat goat's yogurt, to serve

1. Preheat the oven to 265°F (130°C) conventional or 230°F (110°C) fan assisted convection. Line a baking tray with parchment paper. 2. Place all of the dry ingredients, including the lemon zest, in a large bowl. Stir to combine. In a small bowl, mix the tahini with the coconut oil, then add to the dry ingredients. Add the egg whites and mix to combine. 3. Spoon onto the lined baking tray and crumble all over. Bake for 1 hour and 10 minutes to 1 hour and 20 minutes, until golden. Remove from the oven and let cool completely; it will crisp up as it cools. Serve on its own or with almond milk, coconut cream or coconut yogurt, or full-fat goat's yogurt. Store in a jar at room temperature for up to 2 weeks or freeze for up to 3 months.

Per Serving:

calories: 291 | fat: 25g | protein: 6g | carbs: 15g | fiber: 6g | sodium: 128mg

Chapter 4 Beans and Grains

Chickpea Fritters

Prep time: 15 minutes | Cook time: 15 minutes |
Serves 4

3 tablespoons olive oil, plus
extra for frying
1 onion, chopped
2 garlic cloves, minced
1 (15-ounce/ 425-g) can
chickpeas, drained and rinsed
1 teaspoon dried thyme

1 teaspoon dried oregano
1 teaspoon dried parsley
Sea salt
Freshly ground black pepper
¾ cup all-purpose flour, plus
more as needed

1. In a large skillet, heat 1 tablespoon of the olive oil over medium-high heat. Add the onion and garlic and sauté for 5 to 7 minutes, until the onion is soft. Transfer the onion-garlic mixture to a food processor and add the remaining 2 tablespoons olive oil, the chickpeas, thyme, oregano, and parsley. Season with salt and pepper and purée until a paste forms. (If the mixture is too wet, add 1 to 2 tablespoons of flour and pulse to incorporate.) 2. Place the flour in a bowl. Scoop about 2 tablespoons of the chickpea mixture and roll it into a ball. Dredge the ball in the flour to coat, then flatten the ball slightly and place it on a plate. Repeat with the remaining chickpea mixture. 3. Wipe out the skillet and pour in 2 inches of olive oil. Heat the oil over medium-high heat. Working in batches, fry the fritters in a single layer until golden, about 3 minutes per side. Transfer them to a paper towel–lined plate. Repeat to fry the remaining fritters. Serve immediately.

Per Serving:

calories: 290 | fat: 12g | protein: 8g | carbs: 38g | fiber: 6g | sodium: 45mg

Greek-Style Black-Eyed Pea Soup

Prep time: 10 minutes | Cook time: 26 minutes |
Serves 8

2 tablespoons light olive oil
2 stalks celery, chopped
1 medium white onion, peeled
and chopped
2 cloves garlic, peeled and
minced
2 tablespoons chopped fresh
oregano
1 teaspoon fresh thyme leaves

1 pound (454 g) dried black-eyed peas, soaked overnight
and drained
¼ teaspoon salt
1 teaspoon ground black pepper
4 cups water
1 (15-ounce / 425-g) can diced
tomatoes

1. Press the Sauté button on the Instant Pot® and heat oil. Add celery and onion, and cook until just tender, about 5 minutes.

Add garlic, oregano, and thyme, and cook until fragrant, about 30 seconds. Press the Cancel button. 2. Add black-eyed peas, salt, pepper, water, and tomatoes to the Instant Pot® and stir well. Close lid, set steam release to Sealing, press the Manual button, and set time to 20 minutes. When the timer beeps, let pressure release naturally, about 20 minutes. 3. Open lid and stir well. Serve hot.

Per Serving:

calories: 153 | fat: 3g | protein: 8g | carbs: 25g | fiber: 5g | sodium: 189mg

Pilaf with Eggplant and Raisins

Prep time: 10 minutes | Cook time: 30 minutes |
Serves 4

4 eggplant (preferably thinner,
about 6 ounces/170g each) cut
into ¼-inch (.5cm) thick slices
(if the slices are too large, cut
them in half)
1½ teaspoons fine sea salt,
divided
½ cup extra virgin olive oil
1 medium onion (any variety),
diced
4 garlic cloves, thinly sliced
¼ cup white wine

1 cup uncooked medium-grain
rice
1 (15-ounce / 425-g) can
crushed tomatoes
3 cups hot water
4 tablespoons black raisins
4 teaspoons finely chopped
fresh parsley
4 teaspoons finely chopped
fresh mint
¼ teaspoon freshly ground
black pepper to serve

1. Place the eggplant in a colander and sprinkle with ½ teaspoon of the sea salt. Set aside to rest for 10 minutes, then rinse well and squeeze to remove any remaining water. 2. Add the olive oil to a medium pot placed over medium heat. When the oil begins to shimmer, add the eggplant and sauté for 7 minutes or until soft, moving the eggplant continuously, then add the onions and continue sautéing and stirring for 2 more minutes. 3. Add the garlic and sauté for 1 additional minute, then add the white wine and deglaze the pan. After about 1 minute, add the rice and stir until the rice is coated with the oil. 4. Add the crushed tomatoes, hot water, and remaining sea salt. Stir and bring to a boil, then reduce the heat to low and simmer for 20 minutes.Add more hot water, ¼ cup at a time, if the water level gets too low. 5. Add the raisins, stir, then cover the pot and remove from the heat. Set aside to cool for 15 minutes. 6. To serve, sprinkle 1 teaspoon of the mint and 1 teaspoon of the parsley over each serving, then season each serving with black pepper. Store covered in the refrigerator for up to 3 days.

Per Serving:

calories: 612 | fat: 29g | protein: 11g | carbs: 84g | fiber: 21g | sodium: 859mg

Garbanzo and Pita No-Bake Casserole

Prep time: 10 minutes | Cook time: 10 minutes |

Serves 4

4 cups Greek yogurt
3 cloves garlic, minced
1 teaspoon salt
2 (16-ounce/ 454-g) cans garbanzo beans, rinsed and

drained
2 cups water
4 cups pita chips
5 tablespoons unsalted butter

1. In a large bowl, whisk together the yogurt, garlic, and salt. Set aside. 2. Put the garbanzo beans and water in a medium pot. Bring to a boil; let beans boil for about 5 minutes. 3. Pour the garbanzo beans and the liquid into a large casserole dish. 4. Top the beans with pita chips. Pour the yogurt sauce over the pita chip layer. 5. In a small saucepan, melt and brown the butter, about 3 minutes. Pour the brown butter over the yogurt sauce.

Per Serving:

calories: 772 | fat: 36g | protein: 39g | carbs: 73g | fiber: 13g | sodium: 1,003mg

Mediterranean Lentils and Rice

Prep time: 5 minutes |Cook time: 25 minutes|

Serves: 4

2¼ cups low-sodium or no-salt-added vegetable broth
½ cup uncooked brown or green lentils
½ cup uncooked instant brown rice
½ cup diced carrots (about 1 carrot)
½ cup diced celery (about 1 stalk)
1 (2¼-ounce / 64-g) can sliced olives, drained (about ½ cup)
¼ cup diced red onion (about ⅛

onion)
¼ cup chopped fresh curly-leaf parsley
1½ tablespoons extra-virgin olive oil
1 tablespoon freshly squeezed lemon juice (from about ½ small lemon)
1 garlic clove, minced (about ½ teaspoon)
¼ teaspoon kosher or sea salt
¼ teaspoon freshly ground black pepper

1. In a medium saucepan over high heat, bring the broth and lentils to a boil, cover, and lower the heat to medium-low. Cook for 8 minutes. 2. Raise the heat to medium, and stir in the rice. Cover the pot and cook the mixture for 15 minutes, or until the liquid is absorbed. Remove the pot from the heat and let it sit, covered, for 1 minute, then stir. 3. While the lentils and rice are cooking, mix together the carrots, celery, olives, onion, and parsley in a large serving bowl. 4. In a small bowl, whisk together the oil, lemon juice, garlic, salt, and pepper. Set aside. 5. When the lentils and rice are cooked, add them to the serving bowl. Pour the dressing on top, and mix everything together. Serve warm or cold, or store in a sealed container in the refrigerator for up to 7 days.

Per Serving:

calories: 183 | fat: 6g | protein: 4.9g | carbs: 29.5g | fiber: 3.3g | sodium: 552mg

Black-Eyed Peas with Olive Oil and Herbs

Prep time: 15 minutes | Cook time: 20 minutes |

Serves 8

¼ cup extra-virgin olive oil
4 sprigs oregano, leaves minced and stems reserved
2 sprigs thyme, leaves stripped and stems reserved
4 sprigs dill, fronds chopped and stems reserved

1 pound (454 g) dried black-eyed peas, soaked overnight and drained
¼ teaspoon salt
1 teaspoon ground black pepper
4 cups water

1. In a small bowl, combine oil, oregano leaves, thyme leaves, and dill fronds, and mix to combine. Cover and set aside. 2. Tie herb stems together with butcher's twine. Add to the Instant Pot® along with black-eyed peas, salt, pepper, and water. Close lid, set steam release to Sealing, press the Manual button, and set time to 20 minutes. When the timer beeps, let pressure release naturally, about 20 minutes. 3. Open lid, remove and discard herb stem bundle, and drain off any excess liquid. Stir in olive oil mixture. Serve hot.

Per Serving:

calories: 119 | fat: 7g | protein: 6g | carbs: 9g | fiber: 3g | sodium: 76mg

Lentil Chili

Prep time: 15 minutes | Cook time: 30 minutes |

Serves 6

2 tablespoons olive oil
1 medium yellow onion, peeled and chopped
1 large poblano pepper, seeded and chopped
¼ cup chopped fresh cilantro
2 cloves garlic, peeled and minced
1 tablespoon chili powder
½ teaspoon ground cumin
½ teaspoon ground black

pepper
¼ teaspoon salt
2 cups dried red lentils, rinsed and drained
6 cups vegetable broth
1 (10-ounce / 283-g) can tomatoes with green chilies, drained
1 (15-ounce / 425-g) can kidney beans, drained and rinsed
1 tablespoon lime juice

1. Press the Sauté button on the Instant Pot® and heat oil. Add onion and poblano pepper, and cook until just tender, about 3 minutes. Add cilantro, garlic, chili powder, cumin, black pepper, and salt, and cook until fragrant, about 30 seconds. Press the Cancel button. 2. Add lentils and broth, close lid, set steam release to Sealing, press the Manual button, and set time to 25 minutes. When the timer beeps, let pressure release naturally, about 15 minutes. 3. Open lid and stir in tomatoes, beans, and lime juice. Let stand uncovered on the Keep Warm setting for 10 minutes. Serve warm.

Per Serving:

calories: 261 | fat: 6g | protein: 15g | carbs: 42g | fiber: 9g | sodium: 781mg

Barley Risotto

Prep time: 10 minutes | Cook time: 30 minutes | Serves 6

2 tablespoons olive oil
1 large onion, peeled and diced
1 clove garlic, peeled and minced
1 stalk celery, finely minced
1½ cups pearl barley, rinsed and drained
⅓ cup dried mushrooms

4 cups low-sodium chicken broth
2¼ cups water
1 cup grated Parmesan cheese
2 tablespoons minced fresh parsley
¼ teaspoon salt

1. Press the Sauté button on the Instant Pot® and heat oil. Add onion and sauté 5 minutes. Add garlic and cook 30 seconds. Stir in celery, barley, mushrooms, broth, and water. Press the Cancel button. 2. Close lid, set steam release to Sealing, press the Manual button, and set time to 18 minutes. When the timer beeps, quick-release the pressure until the float valve drops and open the lid. 3. Drain off excess liquid, leaving enough to leave the risotto slightly soupy. Press the Cancel button, then press the Sauté button and cook until thickened, about 5 minutes. Stir in cheese, parsley, and salt. Serve immediately.

Per Serving:

calories: 175 | fat: 9g | protein: 10g | carbs: 13g | fiber: 2g | sodium: 447mg

Domatorizo (Greek Tomato Rice)

Prep time: 10 minutes | Cook time: 12 minutes | Serves 6

2 tablespoons extra-virgin olive oil
1 large onion, peeled and diced
1 cup Arborio rice
1 cup tomato juice
3 tablespoons dry white wine
2 cups water
1 tablespoon tomato paste

½ teaspoon salt
½ teaspoon ground black pepper
½ cup crumbled or cubed feta cheese
⅛ teaspoon dried Greek oregano
1 scallion, thinly sliced

1. Press the Sauté button on the Instant Pot® and heat oil. Add onion and cook until just tender, about 3 minutes. Stir in rice and cook for 2 minutes. 2. Add tomato juice and wine to rice. Cook, stirring often, until the liquid is absorbed, about 1 minute. 3. In a small bowl, whisk together water and tomato paste. Add to pot along with salt and pepper and stir well. Press the Cancel button. 4. Close lid, set steam release to Sealing, press the Manual button, and set time to 5 minutes. When the timer beeps, let pressure release naturally for 10 minutes, then quick-release any remaining pressure until the float valve drops. 5. Open lid and stir well. Spoon rice into bowls and top with feta, oregano, and scallion. Serve immediately.

Per Serving:

calories: 184 | fat: 9g | protein: 6g | carbs: 20g | fiber: 1g | sodium: 537mg

Vegetable Barley Soup

Prep time: 30 minutes | Cook time: 26 minutes | Serves 8

2 tablespoons olive oil
½ medium yellow onion, peeled and chopped
1 medium carrot, peeled and chopped
1 stalk celery, chopped
2 cups sliced button mushrooms
2 cloves garlic, peeled and minced
½ teaspoon dried thyme
½ teaspoon ground black pepper
1 large russet potato, peeled and cut into ½" pieces
1 (14½-ounce / 411-g) can

fire-roasted diced tomatoes, undrained
½ cup medium pearl barley, rinsed and drained
4 cups vegetable broth
2 cups water
1 (15-ounce / 425-g) can corn, drained
1 (15-ounce / 425-g) can cut green beans, drained
1 (15-ounce / 425-g) can Great Northern beans, drained and rinsed
½ teaspoon salt

1. Press the Sauté button on the Instant Pot® and heat oil. Add onion, carrot, celery, and mushrooms. Cook until just tender, about 5 minutes. Add garlic, thyme, and pepper. Cook 30 seconds. Press the Cancel button. 2. Add potato, tomatoes, barley, broth, and water to pot. Close lid, set steam release to Sealing, press the Soup button, and cook for the default time of 20 minutes. 3. When the timer beeps, let pressure release naturally, about 15 minutes. Open lid and stir soup, then add corn, green beans, and Great Northern beans. Close lid and let stand on the Keep Warm setting for 10 minutes. Stir in salt. Serve hot.

Per Serving:

calories: 190 | fat: 4g | protein: 7g | carbs: 34g | fiber: 8g | sodium: 548mg

Rice Pilaf

Prep time: 5 minutes | Cook time: 30 minutes | Serves 6

2 tablespoons olive oil
1 medium onion, diced
¼ cup pine nuts
1½ cups long-grain brown rice
2 ½ cups hot chicken stock

1 cinnamon stick
¼ cup raisins
Sea salt and freshly ground pepper, to taste

1. Heat the olive oil in a large saucepan over medium heat. 2. Sauté the onions and pine nuts for 6–8 minutes, or until the pine nuts are golden and the onion is translucent. 3. Add the rice and sauté for 2 minutes until lightly browned. Pour the chicken stock into the pan and bring to a boil. 4. Add the cinnamon and raisins. 5. Lower the heat, cover the pan, and simmer for 15–20 minutes, or until the rice is tender and the liquid is absorbed. 6. Remove from the heat and fluff with a fork. Season and serve.

Per Serving:

calories: 293 | fat: 10g | protein: 7g | carbs: 45g | fiber: 2g | sodium: 35mg

Greek Chickpeas with Coriander and Sage

Prep time: 20 minutes | Cook time: 22 minutes | Serves 6 to 8

1½ tablespoons table salt, for brining
1 pound (454 g) dried chickpeas, picked over and rinsed
2 tablespoons extra-virgin olive oil, plus extra for drizzling
2 onions, halved and sliced thin
¼ teaspoon table salt
1 tablespoon coriander seeds, cracked
¼–½ teaspoon red pepper flakes
2½ cups chicken broth
¼ cup fresh sage leaves
2 bay leaves
1½ teaspoons grated lemon zest plus 2 teaspoons juice
2 tablespoons minced fresh parsley

1. Dissolve 1½ tablespoons salt in 2 quarts cold water in large container. Add chickpeas and soak at room temperature for at least 8 hours or up to 24 hours. Drain and rinse well. 2. Using highest sauté function, heat oil in Instant Pot until shimmering. Add onions and ¼ teaspoon salt and cook until onions are softened and well browned, 10 to 12 minutes. Stir in coriander and pepper flakes and cook until fragrant, about 30 seconds. Stir in broth, scraping up any browned bits, then stir in chickpeas, sage, and bay leaves. 3. Lock lid in place and close pressure release valve. Select low pressure cook function and cook for 10 minutes. Turn off Instant Pot and let pressure release naturally for 15 minutes. Quick-release any remaining pressure, then carefully remove lid, allowing steam to escape away from you. 4. Discard bay leaves. Stir lemon zest and juice into chickpeas and season with salt and pepper to taste. Sprinkle with parsley. Serve, drizzling individual portions with extra oil.

Per Serving:

calories: 190 | fat: 6g | protein: 11g | carbs: 40g | fiber: 1g | sodium: 360mg

Gigantes (Greek Roasted Butter Beans)

Prep time: 10 minutes | Cook time: 1 hour 45 minutes | Serves 4

1 pound (454 g) uncooked gigantes or butter beans
2 bay leaves
¾ cup extra virgin olive oil, divided
2 medium red onions, chopped
4 garlic cloves, thinly sliced
1½ cups canned crushed tomatoes
2 tablespoons tomato paste mixed with 2 tablespoonsp
water
1 teaspoon paprika
1 teaspoon dried oregano
3 tablespoons chopped fresh parsley
2 tablespoons chopped fresh dill
1 teaspoon fine sea salt, divided
¼ teaspoon freshly ground black pepper
Pinch of kosher salt

1. Place the beans in a large bowl and cover with cold water. Soak for 10 hours or overnight, then drain and rinse. 2. When ready to cook, add the beans to a large pot and fill the pot with enough fresh water to cover the beans. Add the bay leaves and place the pot over high heat. Bring the beans to a boil, cover, and reduce the heat to low. Simmer for about 40 minutes to 1 hour or until the beans are soft but not mushy. 3. While the beans are cooking, begin preparing the sauce by adding ¼ cup olive oil to a medium pan placed over medium heat. When the oil begins to shimmer, add the onions and sauté for 5 minutes or until the onions are soft. Add the garlic and sauté for 1 more minute. 4. Add the crushed tomatoes, tomato paste mixture, paprika, oregano, parsley, dill, ½ teaspoon of the sea salt, black pepper, and another ¼ cup of the olive oil, then stir to combine. Let the sauce simmer for about 10 minutes or until it thickens. 5. Preheat the oven to 350° (180°C). When the beans are done cooking, remove them from the heat. Reserve 2 cups of the cooking water, drain the remaining water from the pot, and remove the bay leaves. 6. Add the sauce to the beans, then add the remaining ½ teaspoon of sea salt, and mix gently. Pour the mixture into a baking dish and spread it evenly. Add the reserved cooking water to one corner of the dish and tilt the dish to spread the water across the beans. Drizzle the remaining ¼ cup of olive oil over the beans. Transfer the beans to the oven and bake for 45 minutes or until the sauce is thick and the beans are tender. 7. Remove the beans from the oven and set aside to cool for 15 minutes. Sprinkle a pinch of kosher salt over the top before serving warm or at room temperature. Store covered in the refrigerator for up to 3 days.

Per Serving:

calories: 564 | fat: 42g | protein: 2g | carbs: 13g | fiber: 3g | sodium: 596mg

Farro and Mushroom Risotto

Prep time: 10 minutes | Cook time: 20 minutes | Serves 6

2 tablespoons olive oil
1 medium yellow onion, peeled and diced
16 ounces (454 g) sliced button mushrooms
½ teaspoon salt
½ teaspoon ground black pepper
½ teaspoon dried thyme
½ teaspoon dried oregano
1 clove garlic, peeled and minced
1 cup farro, rinsed and drained
1½ cups vegetable broth
¼ cup grated Parmesan cheese
2 tablespoons minced fresh flat-leaf parsley

1. Press the Sauté button on the Instant Pot® and heat oil. Add onion and mushrooms and sauté 8 minutes. Add salt, pepper, thyme, and oregano and cook 30 seconds. Add garlic and cook for 30 seconds. Press the Cancel button. 2. Stir in farro and broth. Close lid, set steam release to Sealing, press the Manual button, and set time to 10 minutes. When timer beeps, let pressure release naturally for 10 minutes, then quick-release the remaining pressure until the float valve drops. 3. Top with cheese and parsley before serving.

Per Serving:

calories: 215 | fat: 8g | protein: 11g | carbs: 24g | fiber: 3g | sodium: 419mg

Rice with Blackened Fish

Prep time: 10 minutes | Cook time: 2 to 4 hours |
Serves 4

1 teaspoon ground cumin
1 teaspoon ground coriander
1 teaspoon garlic powder
1 teaspoon paprika
½ teaspoon sea salt
½ teaspoon freshly ground
black pepper
½ teaspoon onion powder

1 pound (454 g) fresh salmon
fillets
1 cup raw long-grain brown
rice, rinsed
2½ cups low-sodium chicken
broth
¼ cup diced tomato

1. In a small bowl, stir together the cumin, coriander, garlic powder, paprika, salt, pepper, and onion powder. Generously season the salmon fillets with the blackening seasoning. 2. In a slow cooker, combine the rice, chicken broth, and tomato. Stir to mix well. 3. Place the seasoned salmon on top of the rice mixture. 4. Cover the cooker and cook for 2 to 4 hours on Low heat.

Per Serving:

calories: 318 | fat: 6g | protein: 29g | carbs: 38g | fiber: 3g | sodium: 337mg

White Bean Cassoulet

Prep time: 30 minutes | Cook time: 45 minutes |
Serves 8

1 tablespoon olive oil
1 medium onion, peeled and
diced
2 cups dried cannellini beans,
soaked overnight and drained
1 medium parsnip, peeled and
diced
2 medium carrots, peeled and
diced
2 stalks celery, diced
1 medium zucchini, trimmed

and chopped
½ teaspoon fennel seed
¼ teaspoon ground nutmeg
½ teaspoon garlic powder
1 teaspoon sea salt
½ teaspoon ground black
pepper
2 cups vegetable broth
1 (14½-ounce / 411-g) can
diced tomatoes, including juice
2 sprigs rosemary

1. Press the Sauté button on the Instant Pot® and heat oil. Add onion and cook until translucent, about 5 minutes. Add beans and toss. 2. Add a layer of parsnip, then a layer of carrots, and next a layer of celery. Finally, add a layer of zucchini. Sprinkle in fennel seed, nutmeg, garlic powder, salt, and pepper. Press the Cancel button. 3. Gently pour in broth and canned tomatoes. Top with rosemary. 4. Close lid, set steam release to Sealing, press the Bean button, and cook for the default time of 30 minutes. When the timer beeps, let pressure release naturally for 10 minutes. Quick-release any remaining pressure until the float valve drops and open lid. Press the Cancel button. 5. Press the Sauté button, then press the Adjust button to change the temperature to Less, and simmer bean mixture uncovered for 10 minutes to thicken. Transfer to a serving bowl and carefully toss. Remove and discard rosemary and serve.

Per Serving:

calories: 128 | fat: 2g | protein: 6g | carbs: 21g | fiber: 5g | sodium: 387mg

Mediterranean Creamed Green Peas

Prep time: 5 minutes | Cook time: 25 minutes |
Serves 4

1 cup cauliflower florets, fresh
or frozen
½ white onion, roughly
chopped
2 tablespoons olive oil
½ cup unsweetened almond
milk
3 cups green peas, fresh or
frozen
3 garlic cloves, minced

2 tablespoons fresh thyme
leaves, chopped
1 teaspoon fresh rosemary
leaves, chopped
½ teaspoon salt
½ teaspoon black pepper
Shredded Parmesan cheese, for
garnish
Fresh parsley, for garnish

1. Preheat the air fryer to 380°F(193°C). 2. In a large bowl, combine the cauliflower florets and onion with the olive oil and toss well to coat. 3. Put the cauliflower-and-onion mixture into the air fryer basket in an even layer and bake for 15 minutes. 4. Transfer the cauliflower and onion to a food processor. Add the almond milk and pulse until smooth. 5. In a medium saucepan, combine the cauliflower purée, peas, garlic, thyme, rosemary, salt, and pepper and mix well. Cook over medium heat for an additional 10 minutes, stirring regularly. 6. Serve with a sprinkle of Parmesan cheese and chopped fresh parsley.

Per Serving:

calories: 313 | fat: 16.4g | protein: 14.7g | carbs: 28.8g | fiber: 8.3g | sodium: 898mg

White Bean Soup with Kale and Lemon

Prep time: 15 minutes | Cook time: 27 minutes |
Serves 8

1 tablespoon light olive oil
2 stalks celery, chopped
1 medium yellow onion, peeled
and chopped
2 cloves garlic, peeled and
minced
1 tablespoon chopped fresh
oregano
4 cups chopped kale

1 pound (454 g) dried Great
Northern beans, soaked
overnight and drained
8 cups vegetable broth
¼ cup lemon juice
1 tablespoon extra-virgin olive
oil
1 teaspoon ground black pepper

1. Press the Sauté button on the Instant Pot® and heat light olive oil. Add celery and onion and cook 5 minutes. Add garlic and oregano and sauté 30 seconds. Add kale and turn to coat, then cook until just starting to wilt, about 1 minute. Press the Cancel button. 2. Add beans, broth, lemon juice, extra-virgin olive oil, and pepper to the Instant Pot® and stir well. Close lid, set steam release to Sealing, press the Manual button, and set time to 20 minutes. When the timer beeps, let pressure release naturally, about 20 minutes. Open lid and stir well. Serve hot.

Per Serving:

calories: 129 | fat: 3g | protein: 7g | carbs: 22g | fiber: 6g | sodium: 501mg

Cilantro Lime Rice

Prep time: 10 minutes | Cook time: 32 minutes |

Serves 8

2 tablespoons extra-virgin olive oil
½ medium yellow onion, peeled and chopped
2 cloves garlic, peeled and minced
½ cup chopped fresh cilantro, divided

2 cups brown rice
2¼ cups water
2 tablespoons lime juice
1 tablespoon grated lime zest
¼ teaspoon salt
½ teaspoon ground black pepper

1. Press the Sauté button on the Instant Pot® and heat oil. Add onion and cook until soft, about 6 minutes. Add garlic and ¼ cup cilantro and cook until fragrant, about 30 seconds. Add rice and cook, stirring constantly, until well coated and starting to toast, about 3 minutes. Press the Cancel button. 2. Stir in water. Close lid, set steam release to Sealing, press the Manual button, and set time to 22 minutes. When the timer beeps, let pressure release naturally for 10 minutes, then quick-release the remaining pressure. Open lid and fluff rice with a fork. Fold in remaining ¼ cup cilantro, lime juice, lime zest, salt, and pepper. Serve warm.

Per Serving:

calories: 95 | fat: 4g | protein: 1g | carbs: 14g | fiber: 1g | sodium: 94mg

Lentils with Spinach

Prep time: 10 minutes | Cook time: 20 minutes |

Serves 4

1 cup dried yellow lentils, rinsed and drained
4 cups water
1 tablespoon olive oil
½ medium yellow onion, peeled and chopped
1 clove garlic, peeled and minced

½ teaspoon smoked paprika
½ teaspoon ground black pepper
1 (15-ounce / 425-g) can diced tomatoes, drained
10 ounces (283 g) baby spinach leaves
½ cup crumbled feta cheese

1. Add lentils and water to the Instant Pot®. Close lid, set steam release to Sealing, press the Manual button, and set time to 6 minutes. When the timer beeps, quick-release the pressure. Press the Cancel button and open lid. Drain lentils and set aside. Clean pot. 2. Press the Sauté button and heat oil. Add onion and cook until just tender, about 3 minutes. Add garlic, smoked paprika, and pepper, and cook for an additional 30 seconds. Stir in tomatoes, spinach, and lentils. Simmer for 10 minutes. Top with feta and serve.

Per Serving:

calories: 289 | fat: 8g | protein: 21g | carbs: 31g | fiber: 10g | sodium: 623mg

Garlic-Asparagus Israeli Couscous

Prep time: 5 minutes |Cook time: 25 minutes|

Serves: 6

1 cup garlic-and-herb goat cheese (about 4 ounces/ 113 g)
1½ pounds (680 g) asparagus spears, ends trimmed and stalks chopped into 1-inch pieces (about 2¾ to 3 cups chopped)
1 tablespoon extra-virgin olive oil
1 garlic clove, minced (about ½

teaspoon)
¼ teaspoon freshly ground black pepper
1¾ cups water
1 (8-ounce/ 227-g) box uncooked whole-wheat or regular Israeli couscous (about 1⅓ cups)
¼ teaspoon kosher or sea salt

1. Preheat the oven to 425°F (220ºC). Put the goat cheese on the counter to bring to room temperature. 2. In a large bowl, mix together the asparagus, oil, garlic, and pepper. Spread the asparagus on a large, rimmed baking sheet and roast for 10 minutes, stirring a few times. Remove the pan from the oven, and spoon the asparagus into a large serving bowl. 3. While the asparagus is roasting, in a medium saucepan, bring the water to a boil. Add the couscous and salt. Reduce the heat to medium-low, cover, and cook for 12 minutes, or until the water is absorbed. 4. Pour the hot couscous into the bowl with the asparagus. Add the goat cheese, mix thoroughly until completely melted, and serve.

Per Serving:

calories: 98 | fat: 1.3g | protein: 10.2g | carbs: 13.5g | fiber:3.67g | sodium: 262mg

Fava and Garbanzo Bean Fūl

Prep time: 10 minutes | Cook time: 10 minutes |

Serves 6

1 (16-ounce/ 454-g) can garbanzo beans, rinsed and drained
1 (15-ounce/ 425-g) can fava beans, rinsed and drained
3 cups water

½ cup lemon juice
3 cloves garlic, peeled and minced
1 teaspoon salt
3 tablespoons extra-virgin olive oil

1. In a 3-quart pot over medium heat, cook the garbanzo beans, fava beans, and water for 10 minutes. 2. Reserving 1 cup of the liquid from the cooked beans, drain the beans and put them in a bowl. 3. Mix the reserved liquid, lemon juice, minced garlic, and salt together and add to the beans in the bowl. Using a potato masher, mash up about half the beans in the bowl. 4. After mashing half the beans, give the mixture one more stir to make sure the beans are evenly mixed. 5. Drizzle the olive oil over the top. 6. Serve warm or cold with pita bread.

Per Serving:

calories: 199 | fat: 9g | protein: 10g | carbs: 25g | fiber: 9g | sodium: 395mg

Creamy Lima Bean Soup

Prep time: 10 minutes | Cook time: 17 minutes |

Serves 6

1 tablespoon olive oil	overnight and drained
1 small onion, peeled and diced	½ teaspoon salt
1 clove garlic, peeled and minced	½ teaspoon ground black pepper
2 cups vegetable stock	2 tablespoons thinly sliced chives
½ cup water	
2 cups dried lima beans, soaked	

1. Press the Sauté button on the Instant Pot® and heat oil. Add onion and cook until golden brown, about 10 minutes. Add garlic and cook until fragrant, about 30 seconds. Press the Cancel button. 2. Add stock, water, and lima beans. Close lid, set steam release to Sealing, press the Manual button, and set time to 6 minutes. When the timer beeps, let pressure release naturally, about 20 minutes. 3. Open lid and purée soup with an immersion blender or in batches in a blender. Season with salt and pepper, then sprinkle with chives before serving.

Per Serving:

calories: 67 | fat: 2g | protein: 2g | carbs: 9g | fiber: 2g | sodium: 394mg

South Indian Split Yellow Pigeon Peas with Mixed Vegetables

Prep time: 20 minutes | Cook time: 4½ to 6½ minutes | Serves 6

Sambar Masala:	chopped
1 teaspoon rapeseed oil	1 red potato, peeled and diced
3 tablespoons coriander seeds	1 white radish (mooli), peeled
2 tablespoons split gram	and chopped into 2¾-inch
1 teaspoon black peppercorns	sticks
½ teaspoon fenugreek seeds	1 tomato, roughly chopped
½ teaspoon mustard seeds	4 cups water
¼ teaspoon cumin seeds	2 to 3 moringa seed pods, or ⅓
12 whole dried red chiles	pound (151 g) green beans or
Sambar:	asparagus, chopped into 2¾-
1½ cups split yellow pigeon	inch lengths
peas, washed	2 tablespoons tamarind paste
2 fresh green chiles, sliced	½ teaspoon asafetida
lengthwise	2 teaspoons coconut oil
2 garlic cloves, chopped	1 teaspoon mustard seeds
6 pearl onions	20 curry leaves
4 to 5 tablespoons sambar	2 dried red chilies
masala	Handful fresh coriander leaves,
2 teaspoons salt	chopped (optional)
1 to 2 carrots, peeled and	

Make the Sambar Masala: 1. Add the oil to a medium nonstick skillet. Add all of the remaining ingredients and roast for a few minutes until fragrant. The spices will brown a little, but don't let them burn. 2. Remove from the heat and pour onto a plate to cool. Once cooled, place into your spice grinder or mortar and pestle and grind to a powder. Set aside. Make the Sambar: 3. Heat the slow cooker to high and add the pigeon peas, green chiles, garlic, pearl onions, sambar masala, salt, carrots, potatoes, radish, tomato, and water. 4. Cover and cook for 4 hours on high, or for 6 hours on low. 5. Add the moringa (or green beans or asparagus), tamarind paste, and asafetida. Cover and cook for another 30 minutes. 6. When you're ready to serve, heat the coconut oil in a frying pan and pop the mustard seeds with the curry leaves and dried chiles. Pour over the sambar. Top with coriander leaves (if using) and serve.

Per Serving:

calories: 312 | fat: 7g | protein: 12g | carbs: 59g | fiber: 16g | sodium: 852mg

Vegetable Risotto with Beet Greens

Prep time: 30 minutes | Cook time: 10 minutes |

Serves 6

¼ cup light olive oil	thickly sliced
1 clove garlic, peeled and minced	½ teaspoon salt
1 small Asian eggplant, sliced	½ teaspoon ground black pepper
1 small zucchini, trimmed and sliced	1 cup Arborio rice
1 large red bell pepper, seeded and cut in quarters	½ cup dry white wine
1 large portobello mushroom, gills and stem removed, cap sliced	2 cups low-sodium chicken broth
1 medium onion, peeled and	2 cups sliced young beet greens
	¼ cup sliced fresh basil
	½ cup grated Parmesan cheese

1. Combine oil and garlic in a small bowl. Stir to mix and set aside 10 minutes to infuse. 2. Preheat a grill or a grill pan over medium-high heat. 3. Brush all sides of eggplant slices, zucchini slices, bell pepper quarters, mushroom slices, and onion slices with garlic-infused oil, making sure to reserve 1 tablespoon of the oil. 4. Place vegetables on the grill rack or in the grill pan. Sprinkle with salt and black pepper. 5. Grill vegetables for several minutes on each side or until softened and slightly charred, about 1 minute per side. Set aside to cool, and then coarsely chop. 6. Press the Sauté button on the Instant Pot® and heat reserved 1 tablespoon garlic-infused oil. Add rice and stir it to coat it in oil. Stir in wine and broth. Press the Cancel button. 7. Close lid, set steam release to Sealing, press the Manual button, and set time to 7 minutes. When the timer beeps, quick-release the pressure until the float valve drops and open the lid. 8. Add chopped grilled vegetables, beet greens, and basil. Cover the Instant Pot® (but do not lock the lid into place). Set aside for 5 minutes or until greens are wilted. Stir in cheese and serve hot.

Per Serving:

calories: 261 | fat: 12g | protein: 9g | carbs: 30g | fiber: 5g | sodium: 544mg

Confetti Couscous

Prep time: 5 minutes | Cook time: 20 minutes | Serves 4 to 6

3 tablespoons extra-virgin olive oil	½ cup golden raisins
1 large onion, chopped	1 teaspoon salt
2 carrots, chopped	2 cups vegetable broth
1 cup fresh peas	2 cups couscous

1. In a medium pot over medium heat, gently toss the olive oil, onions, carrots, peas, and raisins together and let cook for 5 minutes. 2. Add the salt and broth, and stir to combine. Bring to a boil, and let ingredients boil for 5 minutes. 3. Add the couscous. Stir, turn the heat to low, cover, and let cook for 10 minutes. Fluff with a fork and serve.

Per Serving:

calories: 511 | fat: 12g | protein: 14g | carbs: 92g | fiber: 7g | sodium: 504mg

Moroccan White Beans with Lamb

Prep time: 25 minutes | Cook time: 22 minutes | Serves 6 to 8

1½ tablespoons table salt, for brining	1 red bell pepper, stemmed, seeded, and chopped
1 pound (454 g) dried great Northern beans, picked over and rinsed	2 tablespoons tomato paste
	3 garlic cloves, minced
1 (12-ounce/ 340-g) lamb shoulder chop (blade or round bone), ¾ to 1 inch thick, trimmed and halved	2 teaspoons paprika
	2 teaspoons ground cumin
	1½ teaspoons ground ginger
	¼ teaspoon cayenne pepper
½ teaspoon table salt	½ cup dry white wine
2 tablespoons extra-virgin olive oil, plus extra for serving	2 cups chicken broth
	2 tablespoons minced fresh parsley
1 onion, chopped	

1. Dissolve 1½ tablespoons salt in 2 quarts cold water in large container. Add beans and soak at room temperature for at least 8 hours or up to 24 hours. Drain and rinse well. 2. Pat lamb dry with paper towels and sprinkle with ½ teaspoon salt. Using highest sauté function, heat oil in Instant Pot for 5 minutes (or until just smoking). Brown lamb, about 5 minutes per side; transfer to plate. 3. Add onion and bell pepper to fat left in pot and cook, using highest sauté function, until softened, about 5 minutes. Stir in tomato paste, garlic, paprika, cumin, ginger, and cayenne and cook until fragrant, about 30 seconds. Stir in wine, scraping up any browned bits, then stir in broth and beans. 4. Nestle lamb into beans and add any accumulated juices. Lock lid in place and close pressure release valve. Select high pressure cook function and cook for 1 minute. Turn off Instant Pot and let pressure release naturally for 15 minutes. Quick-release any remaining pressure, then carefully remove lid, allowing steam to escape away from you. 5. Transfer lamb to cutting board, let cool slightly, then shred into bite-size pieces using 2 forks; discard excess fat and bones. Stir lamb and parsley into beans, and season with salt and pepper to taste. Drizzle individual portions with extra oil before serving.

Per Serving:

calories: 350 | fat: 12g | protein: 20g | carbs: 40g | fiber: 15g | sodium: 410mg

Moroccan Date Pilaf

Prep time: 10 minutes | Cook time: 30 minutes | Serves 4

3 tablespoons olive oil	¼ teaspoon ground cinnamon
1 onion, chopped	½ teaspoon ground turmeric
3 garlic cloves, minced	¼ teaspoon sea salt
1 cup uncooked long-grain rice	¼ teaspoon freshly ground black pepper
½ to 1 tablespoon harissa	
5 or 6 Medjool dates (or another variety), pitted and chopped	2 cups chicken broth
	¼ cup shelled whole pistachios, for garnish
¼ cup dried cranberries	

1. In a large stockpot, heat the olive oil over medium heat. Add the onion and garlic and sauté for 3 to 5 minutes, until the onion is soft. Add the rice and cook for 3 minutes, until the grains start to turn opaque. Add the harissa, dates, cranberries, cinnamon, turmeric, salt, and pepper and cook for 30 seconds. Add the broth and bring to a boil, then reduce the heat to low, cover, and simmer for 20 minutes, or until the liquid has been absorbed. 2. Remove the rice from the heat and stir in the nuts. Let stand for 10 minutes before serving.

Per Serving:

calories: 368 | fat: 15g | protein: 6g | carbs: 54g | fiber: 4g | sodium: 83mg

Couscous with Apricots

Prep time: 10 minutes | Cook time: 15 minutes | Serves 4

2 tablespoons olive oil	water overnight
1 small onion, diced	½ cup slivered almonds or pistachios
1 cup whole-wheat couscous	
2 cups water or broth	½ teaspoon dried mint
½ cup dried apricots, soaked in	½ teaspoon dried thyme

1. Heat the olive oil in a large skillet over medium-high heat. Add the onion and cook until translucent and soft. 2. Stir in the couscous and cook for 2–3 minutes. 3. Add the water or broth, cover, and cook for 8–10 minutes until the water is mostly absorbed. 4. Remove from the heat and let stand for a few minutes. 5. Fluff with a fork and fold in the apricots, nuts, mint, and thyme.

Per Serving:

calories: 294 | fat: 15g | protein: 8g | carbs: 38g | fiber: 6g | sodium: 6mg

Spanakorizo (Greek Spinach and Rice)

Prep time: 5 minutes | Cook time: 27 minutes | Serves 2

3½ tbsp extra virgin olive oil, divided
1lb (450g) fresh spinach, rinsed and torn into large pieces
2 tbsp fresh lemon juice plus juice of ½ lemon, for serving
1 medium red onion, chopped
1 tsp dried mint

2 tbsp chopped fresh dill
⅓ cup uncooked medium-grain rice
⅔ cup hot water
½ tsp fine sea salt
¼ tsp freshly ground black pepper

1. Add 1½ teaspoons of olive oil to a deep pan over medium heat. When the oils starts to shimmer, add the spinach and 2 tablespoons lemon juice. Using tongs, toss the spinach until it's wilted and develops a bright green color, about 2–3 minutes, then transfer to a colander and set aside to drain. 2. In a separate large pot placed over medium heat, combine the onions with 2 tablespoons of the olive oil. Sauté until the onions are soft, about 3 minutes. 3. Add the cooked spinach, mint, dill, and rice to the pot and then stir to coat the spinach and rice in the olive oil. Continue sautéing for 1 minute, then add the hot water, sea salt, and black pepper. Stir, then increase the heat slightly and bring the mixture to a boil. 4. Once the mixture comes to a boil, reduce the heat to low and simmer for 20 minutes or until the rice is soft, adding more warm water as needed if the rice becomes too dry. 5. Serve warm or at room temperature with a squeeze of lemon juice and 1½ teaspoons of the olive oil drizzled over each serving. Store covered in the refrigerator for up to 3 days.

Per Serving:

Calories 431 Total fat 25g Saturated fat 4g Carbohydrate 42g Protein 10g

Chapter 5 Beef, Pork, and Lamb

Beef and Mushroom Stroganoff

Prep time: 15 minutes | Cook time: 31 minutes |
Serves 6

2 tablespoons olive oil
1 medium onion, peeled and chopped
2 cloves garlic, peeled and minced
1 pound (454 g) beef stew meat, cut into 1" pieces
3 tablespoons all-purpose flour
¼ teaspoon salt

¼ teaspoon ground black pepper
2 cups beef broth
1 pound (454 g) sliced button mushrooms
1 pound (454 g) wide egg noodles
½ cup low-fat plain Greek yogurt

1. Press the Sauté button on the Instant Pot® and heat oil. Add onion and cook until soft, about 5 minutes. Add garlic and cook until fragrant, about 30 seconds. 2. Combine beef, flour, salt, and pepper in a medium bowl and toss to coat beef completely. Add beef to the pot and cook, stirring often, until browned, about 10 minutes. Stir in beef broth and scrape any brown bits from bottom of pot. Stir in mushrooms and press the Cancel button. 3. Close lid, set steam release to Sealing, press the Manual button, and set time to 10 minutes. When the timer beeps, quick-release the pressure until the float valve drops, open lid, and stir well. Press the Cancel button. 4. Add noodles and stir, making sure noodles are submerged in liquid. Close lid, set steam release to Sealing, press the Manual button, and set time to 5 minutes. 5. When the timer beeps, quick-release the pressure until the float valve drops. Open lid and stir well. Press the Cancel button and cool for 5 minutes, then stir in yogurt. Serve hot.

Per Serving:
calories: 446 | fat: 13g | protein: 19g | carbs: 63g | fiber: 4g | sodium: 721mg

Saucy Beef Fingers

Prep time: 30 minutes | Cook time: 14 minutes |
Serves 4

1½ pounds (680 g) sirloin steak
¼ cup red wine
¼ cup fresh lime juice
1 teaspoon garlic powder
1 teaspoon shallot powder
1 teaspoon celery seeds
1 teaspoon mustard seeds

Coarse sea salt and ground black pepper, to taste
1 teaspoon red pepper flakes
2 eggs, lightly whisked
1 cup Parmesan cheese
1 teaspoon paprika

1. Place the steak, red wine, lime juice, garlic powder, shallot

powder, celery seeds, mustard seeds, salt, black pepper, and red pepper in a large ceramic bowl; let it marinate for 3 hours. 2. Tenderize the cube steak by pounding with a mallet; cut into 1-inch strips. 3. In a shallow bowl, whisk the eggs. In another bowl, mix the Parmesan cheese and paprika. 4. Dip the beef pieces into the whisked eggs and coat on all sides. Now, dredge the beef pieces in the Parmesan mixture. 5. Cook at 400°F (204°C) for 14 minutes, flipping halfway through the cooking time. 6. Meanwhile, make the sauce by heating the reserved marinade in a saucepan over medium heat; let it simmer until thoroughly warmed. Serve the steak fingers with the sauce on the side. Enjoy!

Per Serving:
calories: 483 | fat: 29g | protein: 49g | carbs: 4g | fiber: 1g | sodium: 141mg

Spicy Lamb Burgers with Harissa Mayo

Prep timePrep Time: 15 minutes | Cook Time: 10
minutes | Serves 2

½ small onion, minced
1 garlic clove, minced
2 teaspoons minced fresh parsley
2 teaspoons minced fresh mint
¼ teaspoon salt
Pinch freshly ground black pepper
1 teaspoon cumin
1 teaspoon smoked paprika

¼ teaspoon coriander
8 ounces (227 g) lean ground lamb
2 tablespoons olive oil mayonnaise
½ teaspoon harissa paste (more or less to taste)
2 hamburger buns or pitas, fresh greens, tomato slices (optional, for serving)

1. Preheat the grill to medium-high and oil the grill grate. Alternatively, you can cook these in a heavy pan (cast iron is best) on the stovetop. 2. In a large bowl, combine the onion, garlic, parsley, mint, salt, pepper, cumin, paprika, and coriander. Add the lamb and, using your hands, combine the meat with the spices so they are evenly distributed. Form meat mixture into 2 patties. 3. Grill the burgers for 4 minutes per side, or until the internal temperature registers 160°F (71°C) for medium. 4. If cooking on the stovetop, heat the pan to medium-high and oil the pan. Cook the burgers for 5 to 6 minutes per side, or until the internal temperature registers 160°F(71°C). 5. While the burgers are cooking, combine the mayonnaise and harissa in a small bowl. 6. Serve the burgers with the harissa mayonnaise and slices of tomato and fresh greens on a bun or pita—or skip the bun altogether.

Per Serving:
calories: 381 | fat: 20g | protein: 22g | carbs: 27g | fiber: 2g | sodium: 653mg

Baked Lamb Kofta Meatballs

Prep timePrep Time: 15 minutes | Cook Time: 30 minutes | Serves 2

¼ cup walnuts
½ small onion
1 garlic clove
1 roasted piquillo pepper
2 tablespoons fresh parsley
2 tablespoons fresh mint
¼ teaspoon salt
¼ teaspoon cumin
¼ teaspoon allspice
Pinch cayenne pepper
8 ounces (227 g) lean ground lamb

1. Preheat the oven to 350°F (180°C) and set the rack to the middle position. Line a baking sheet with foil. 2. In the bowl of a food processor, combine the walnuts, onion, garlic, roasted pepper, parsley, mint, salt, cumin, allspice, and cayenne pepper. Pulse about 10 times to combine everything. 3. Transfer the spice mixture to the bowl and add the lamb. With your hands or a spatula, mix the spices into the lamb. 4. Roll into 1½-inch balls (about the size of golf balls). 5. Place the meatballs on the foil-lined baking sheet and bake for 30 minutes, or until cooked to an internal temperature of 160°F(71°C).

Per Serving:
calories: 408 | fat: 23g | protein: 22g | carbs: 7g | fiber: 3g | sodium: 429mg

Lebanese Ground Meat with Rice

Prep time: 10 minutes | Cook time: 35 minutes | Serves 6

3 tablespoons olive oil, divided
4 ounces (113 g) cremini (baby bella) mushrooms, sliced
½ red onion, finely chopped
2 garlic cloves, minced
1 pound (454 g) lean ground beef
¾ teaspoon ground cinnamon
¼ teaspoon ground cloves
¼ teaspoon ground nutmeg
Sea salt
Freshly ground black pepper
1½ cups basmati rice
2¾ cups chicken broth
½ cup pine nuts
½ cup coarsely chopped fresh Italian parsley

1. In a sauté pan, heat 2 tablespoons of olive oil over medium-high heat. Add the mushrooms, onion, and garlic and sauté until the mushrooms release their liquid and the onion becomes translucent, about 5 minutes. Add the ground beef, cinnamon, cloves, and nutmeg and season with salt and pepper. Reduce the heat to medium and cook, stirring often, for 5 to 7 minutes, until the meat is cooked through. Remove the beef mixture from the pan with a slotted spoon and set aside in a medium bowl. 2. In the same pan, heat the remaining 1 tablespoon of olive oil over medium-high heat. Add the rice and fry for about 5 minutes. Return the meat mixture to the pan and mix well to combine with the rice. Add the broth and bring to a boil, then reduce the heat to low, cover, and simmer for 15 minutes, or until you can fluff the rice with a fork. 3. Add the pine nuts and mix well. Garnish with the parsley and serve.

Per Serving:
calories: 422 | fat: 19g | protein: 22g | carbs: 43g | fiber: 2g | sodium: 81mg

Pork Souvlaki

Prep time: 1 hour 15 minutes | Cook time: 10 minutes | Serves 4

1 (1½-pound / 680-g) pork loin
2 tablespoons garlic, minced
⅓ cup extra-virgin olive oil
⅓ cup lemon juice
1 tablespoon dried oregano
1 teaspoon salt
Pita bread and tzatziki, for serving (optional)

1. Cut the pork into 1-inch cubes and put them into a bowl or plastic zip-top bag. 2. In a large bowl, mix together the garlic, olive oil, lemon juice, oregano, and salt. 3. Pour the marinade over the pork and let it marinate for at least 1 hour. 4. Preheat a grill, grill pan, or lightly oiled skillet to high heat. Using wood or metal skewers, thread the pork onto the skewers. 5. Cook the skewers for 3 minutes on each side, for 12 minutes in total. 6. Serve with pita bread and tzatziki sauce, if desired.

Per Serving:
calories: 393 | fat: 25g | protein: 38g | carbs: 3g | fiber: 0g | sodium: 666mg

Pan-Fried Pork Chops with Peppers and Onions

Prep time: 5 minutes | Cook time: 25 minutes | Serves 4

4 (4-ounce / 113-g) pork chops, untrimmed
1½ teaspoons salt, divided
1 teaspoon freshly ground black pepper, divided
½ cup extra-virgin olive oil, divided
1 red or orange bell pepper, thinly sliced
1 green bell pepper, thinly sliced
1 small yellow onion, thinly sliced
2 teaspoons dried Italian herbs (such as oregano, parsley, or rosemary)
2 garlic cloves, minced
1 tablespoon balsamic vinegar

1. Season the pork chops with 1 teaspoon salt and ½ teaspoon pepper. 2. In a large skillet, heat ¼ cup olive oil over medium-high heat. Fry the pork chops in the oil until browned and almost cooked through but not fully cooked, 4 to 5 minutes per side, depending on the thickness of chops. Remove from the skillet and cover to keep warm. 3. Pour the remaining ¼ cup olive oil in the skillet and sauté the sliced peppers, onions, and herbs over medium-high heat until tender, 6 to 8 minutes. Add the garlic, stirring to combine, and return the pork to skillet. Cover, reduce the heat to low, and cook for another 2 to 3 minutes, or until the pork is cooked through. 4. Turn off the heat. Using a slotted spoon, transfer the pork, peppers, and onions to a serving platter. Add the vinegar to the oil in the skillet and whisk to combine well. Drizzle the vinaigrette over the pork and serve warm.

Per Serving:
calories: 402 | fat: 31g | protein: 26g | carbs: 4g | fiber: 1g | sodium: 875mg

Seasoned Beef Kebabs

Prep time: 15 minutes | Cook time: 10 minutes |
Serves 6

2 pounds beef fillet
1½ teaspoons salt
1 teaspoon freshly ground black pepper
½ teaspoon ground allspice
½ teaspoon ground nutmeg

⅓ cup extra-virgin olive oil
1 large onion, cut into 8 quarters
1 large red bell pepper, cut into 1-inch cubes

1. Preheat a grill, grill pan, or lightly oiled skillet to high heat. 2. Cut the beef into 1-inch cubes and put them in a large bowl. 3. In a small bowl, mix together the salt, black pepper, allspice, and nutmeg. 4. Pour the olive oil over the beef and toss to coat the beef. Then evenly sprinkle the seasoning over the beef and toss to coat all pieces. 5. Skewer the beef, alternating every 1 or 2 pieces with a piece of onion or bell pepper. 6. To cook, place the skewers on the grill or skillet, and turn every 2 to 3 minutes until all sides have cooked to desired doneness, 6 minutes for medium-rare, 8 minutes for well done. Serve warm.

Per Serving:

calories: 326 | fat: 21g | protein: 32g | carbs: 4g | fiber: 1g | sodium: 714mg

Stuffed Flank Steak

Prep time: 20 minutes | Cook time: 6 hours | Serves 6

2 pounds (907 g) flank steak
Sea salt and freshly ground pepper, to taste
1 tablespoon olive oil
¼ cup onion, diced
1 clove garlic, minced
2 cups baby spinach, chopped

½ cup dried tomatoes, chopped
½ cup roasted red peppers, diced
½ cup almonds, toasted and chopped
Kitchen twine
½ cup chicken stock

1. Lay the flank steak out on a cutting board, and generously season with sea salt and freshly ground pepper 2. Heat the olive oil in a medium saucepan. Add the onion and garlic. 3. Cook 5 minutes on medium heat, or until onion is tender and translucent, stirring frequently. 4. Add the spinach, tomatoes, peppers, and chopped almonds, and cook an additional 3 minutes, or until the spinach wilts slightly. 5. Let the tomato and spinach mixture cool to room temperature. Spread the tomato and spinach mixture evenly over the flank steak. 6. Roll the flank steak up slowly, and tie it securely with kitchen twine on both ends and in the middle. 7. Brown the flank steak in the same pan for 5 minutes, turning it carefully to brown all sides. 8. Place steak in a slow cooker with the chicken stock. Cover and cook on low for 4–6 hours. 9. Cut into rounds, discarding the twine, and serve.

Per Serving:

calories: 287 | fat: 14g | protein: 35g | carbs: 4g | fiber: 2g | sodium: 95mg

Greek Lamb Chops

Prep time: 10 minutes | Cook time: 6 to 8 hours |
Serves 6

3 pounds (1.4 kg) lamb chops
½ cup low-sodium beef broth
Juice of 1 lemon
1 tablespoon extra-virgin olive oil

2 garlic cloves, minced
1 teaspoon dried oregano
1 teaspoon sea salt
½ teaspoon freshly ground black pepper

1. Put the lamb chops in a slow cooker. 2. In a small bowl, whisk together the beef broth, lemon juice, olive oil, garlic, oregano, salt, and pepper until blended. Pour the sauce over the lamb chops. 3. Cover the cooker and cook for 6 to 8 hours on Low heat.

Per Serving:

calories: 325 | fat: 13g | protein: 47g | carbs: 1g | fiber: 0g | sodium: 551mg

Slow-Cooked Pork and Potatoes

Prep time: 15 minutes | Cook time: 8 hours 10
minutes | Serves 8

1 teaspoon plus 2 tablespoons extra-virgin olive oil
2 pounds (907 g) small red and yellow new potatoes, halved (quartered if large)
1 small white onion, thinly sliced
4 pounds (1.8 kg) boneless, skinless pork shoulder (Boston butt)
5 cloves garlic, minced
1 tablespoon chopped fresh

oregano or 1 teaspoon dried
1 tablespoon chopped fresh rosemary or 1 teaspoon dried
1 tablespoon chopped fresh sage or 1 teaspoon dried
1 tablespoon chopped fresh thyme or 1 teaspoon dried
2 teaspoons kosher salt
1 teaspoon ground black pepper
1 cup low-sodium chicken broth

1. Brush the bottom of a 6-quart slow cooker with 1 teaspoon of the oil. Scatter the potatoes and onion on the bottom and place the pork on top. Using a sharp paring knife, poke holes throughout the entire pork shoulder. 2. In a small bowl, combine the remaining 2 tablespoons oil, the garlic, oregano, rosemary, sage, thyme, salt, and pepper. Pour over the pork. Using your fingers, poke some of the sauce into the holes. Pour in the broth around the pork. Cover and cook on low for about 8 hours or high for about 4 hours, occasionally turning the meat. 3. Remove the pork to a cutting board. Transfer the potatoes and onion to a serving platter and cover to keep warm. 4. Pour the juices from the slow cooker into a small saucepan and cook over medium-high heat until thickened and reduced, 8 to 10 minutes. 5. Break up the pork into large pieces and arrange on the platter with the potatoes. Pour the sauce over the pork or serve on the side.

Per Serving:

calories: 300 | fat: 12g | protein: 28g | carbs: 20g | fiber: 2g | sodium: 595mg

Greek-Style Ground Beef Pita Sandwiches

Prep timePrep Time: 15 minutes | Cook Time: 10 minutes | Serves 2

For the beef
1 tablespoon olive oil
½ medium onion, minced
2 garlic cloves, minced
6 ounces (170 g) lean ground beef
1 teaspoon dried oregano
For the yogurt sauce
⅓ cup plain Greek yogurt
1 ounce (28 g) crumbled feta cheese (about 3 tablespoons)
1 tablespoon minced fresh

parsley
1 tablespoon minced scallion
1 tablespoon freshly squeezed lemon juice
Pinch salt
For the sandwiches
2 large Greek-style pitas
½ cup cherry tomatoes, halved
1 cup diced cucumber
Salt
Freshly ground black pepper

Make the beef Heat the olive oil in a sauté pan over medium high-heat. Add the onion, garlic, and ground beef and sauté for 7 minutes, breaking up the meat well. When the meat is no longer pink, drain off any fat and stir in the oregano. Turn off the heat. Make the yogurt sauce In a small bowl, combine the yogurt, feta, parsley, scallion, lemon juice, and salt. To assemble the sandwiches 1. Warm the pitas in the microwave for 20 seconds each. 2. To serve, spread some of the yogurt sauce over each warm pita. Top with the ground beef, cherry tomatoes, and diced cucumber. Season with salt and pepper. Add additional yogurt sauce if desired.

Per Serving:

calories: 541 | fat: 21g | protein: 29g | carbs: 57g | fiber: 4g | sodium: 694mg

Greek Lamb Burgers

Prep time: 10 minutes | Cook time: 10 minutes | Serves 4

1 pound (454 g) ground lamb
½ teaspoon salt
½ teaspoon freshly ground black pepper

4 tablespoons feta cheese, crumbled
Buns, toppings, and tzatziki, for serving (optional)

1. Preheat a grill, grill pan, or lightly oiled skillet to high heat. 2. In a large bowl, using your hands, combine the lamb with the salt and pepper. 3. Divide the meat into 4 portions. Divide each portion in half to make a top and a bottom. Flatten each half into a 3-inch circle. Make a dent in the center of one of the halves and place 1 tablespoon of the feta cheese in the center. Place the second half of the patty on top of the feta cheese and press down to close the 2 halves together, making it resemble a round burger. 4. Cook the stuffed patty for 3 minutes on each side, for medium-well. Serve on a bun with your favorite toppings and tzatziki sauce, if desired.

Per Serving:

calories: 345 | fat: 29g | protein: 20g | carbs: 1g | fiber: 0g | sodium: 462mg

Baby Back Ribs

Prep time: 5 minutes | Cook time: 25 minutes | Serves 4

2 pounds (907 g) baby back ribs
2 teaspoons chili powder
1 teaspoon paprika
½ teaspoon onion powder
½ teaspoon garlic powder

¼ teaspoon ground cayenne pepper
½ cup low-carb, sugar-free barbecue sauce

1. Rub ribs with all ingredients except barbecue sauce. Place into the air fryer basket. 2. Adjust the temperature to 400ºF (204ºC) and roast for 25 minutes. 3. When done, ribs will be dark and charred with an internal temperature of at least 185ºF (85ºC). Brush ribs with barbecue sauce and serve warm.

Per Serving:

calories: 571 | fat: 36g | protein: 45g | carbs: 17g | fiber: 1g | sodium: 541mg

Herb-Crusted Lamb Chops

Prep time: 10 minutes | Cook time: 5 minutes | Serves 2

1 large egg
2 cloves garlic, minced
¼ cup pork dust
¼ cup powdered Parmesan cheese
1 tablespoon chopped fresh oregano leaves
1 tablespoon chopped fresh rosemary leaves
1 teaspoon chopped fresh thyme

leaves
½ teaspoon ground black pepper
4 (1-inch-thick) lamb chops
For Garnish/Serving (Optional):
Sprigs of fresh oregano
Sprigs of fresh rosemary
Sprigs of fresh thyme
Lavender flowers
Lemon slices

1. Spray the air fryer basket with avocado oil. Preheat the air fryer to 400ºF (204ºC). 2. Beat the egg in a shallow bowl, add the garlic, and stir well to combine. In another shallow bowl, mix together the pork dust, Parmesan, herbs, and pepper. 3. One at a time, dip the lamb chops into the egg mixture, shake off the excess egg, and then dredge them in the Parmesan mixture. Use your hands to coat the chops well in the Parmesan mixture and form a nice crust on all sides; if necessary, dip the chops again in both the egg and the Parmesan mixture. 4. Place the lamb chops in the air fryer basket, leaving space between them, and air fry for 5 minutes, or until the internal temperature reaches 145ºF (63ºC) for medium doneness. Allow to rest for 10 minutes before serving. 5. Garnish with sprigs of oregano, rosemary, and thyme, and lavender flowers, if desired. Serve with lemon slices, if desired. 6. Best served fresh. Store leftovers in an airtight container in the fridge for up to 4 days. Serve chilled over a salad, or reheat in a 350ºF (177ºC) air fryer for 3 minutes, or until heated through.

Per Serving:

calories: 510 | fat: 42g | protein: 30g | carbs: 3g | fiber: 1g | sodium: 380mg

Pork and Cabbage Egg Roll in a Bowl

Prep time: 10 minutes | Cook time: 10 minutes |

Serves 6

1 tablespoon light olive oil
1 pound (454 g) ground pork
1 medium yellow onion, peeled and chopped
1 clove garlic, peeled and minced
2 teaspoons minced fresh ginger

¼ cup low-sodium chicken broth
2 tablespoons soy sauce
2 (10-ounce/ 283-g) bags shredded coleslaw mix
1 teaspoon sesame oil
1 teaspoon garlic chili sauce

1. Press the Sauté button on the Instant Pot® and heat olive oil. Add pork and sauté until cooked through, about 8 minutes. Add onion, garlic, and ginger, and cook until fragrant, about 2 minutes. Stir in chicken broth and soy sauce. Press the Cancel button. 2. Spread coleslaw mix over pork, but do not mix. Close lid, set steam release to Sealing, press the Manual button, and set time to 0 minutes. 3. When the timer beeps, quick-release the pressure until the float valve drops and open lid. Stir in sesame oil and garlic chili sauce. Serve hot.

Per Serving:

calories: 283 | fat: 24g | protein: 12g | carbs: 5g | fiber: 2g | sodium: 507mg

Lamb Tagine

Prep time: 15 minutes | Cook time: 7 hours | Serves 6

1 navel orange
2 tablespoons all-purpose flour
2 pounds (907 g) boneless leg of lamb, trimmed and cut into 1½-inch cubes
½ cup chicken stock
2 large white onions, chopped
1 teaspoon pumpkin pie spice
1 teaspoon ground cumin
½ teaspoon sea salt

¼ teaspoon saffron threads, crushed in your palm
¼ teaspoon ground red pepper
1 cup pitted dates
2 tablespoons honey
3 cups hot cooked couscous, for serving
2 tablespoons toasted slivered almonds, for serving

1. Grate 2 teaspoons of zest from the orange into a small bowl. Squeeze ¼ cup juice from the orange into another small bowl. 2. Add the flour to the orange juice, stirring with a whisk until smooth. Stir in the orange zest. 3. Heat a large nonstick skillet over medium-high heat. Add the lamb and sauté 7 minutes or until browned. Stir in the stock, scraping the bottom of the pan with a wooden spoon to loosen the flavorful brown bits. Stir in the orange juice mixture. 4. Stir the onions into the lamb mixture. Add the pumpkin pie spice, cumin, salt, saffron, and ground red pepper. 5. Pour the lamb mixture into the slow cooker. Cover and cook on low for 6 hours or until the lamb is tender. 6. Stir the dates and honey into the lamb mixture. Cover and cook on low for 1 hour or until thoroughly heated. 7. Serve the lamb tagine over the couscous and sprinkle with the almonds.

Per Serving:

calories: 451 | fat: 11g | protein: 37g | carbs: 53g | fiber: 5g | sodium: 329mg

Spiced Lamb Stew with Fennel and Dates

Prep time: 10 minutes | Cook time: 3 hours | Serves 4

2 tablespoons olive oil, divided
1 fennel bulb, trimmed, cored, and thinly sliced
1 red onion, thinly sliced
2 cloves garlic, thinly sliced
1½ pounds (680 g) lamb shoulder, cut into 1½-inch cubes and dried with paper towels

1 teaspoon ground ginger
2 teaspoons ground cumin
2 teaspoons ground coriander
¼ teaspoon cayenne pepper
1 teaspoon salt
1 cup pitted chopped dates
2 cups water, divided
¼ cup chopped cilantro, for garnish

1. Heat 1 tablespoon of olive oil in a Dutch oven. Add the fennel, onion, and garlic and cook, stirring frequently, until softened and beginning to brown, about 7 minutes. Transfer the vegetables to a plate. 2. Add the remaining 1 tablespoon of olive oil to the pot and cook the lamb, turning every couple of minutes, until browned on all sides. 3. In a small bowl, combine the ginger, cumin, coriander, cayenne, and salt and mix well. Sprinkle the spice mixture over the meat in the pot and cook, stirring, for 1 minute. 4. Return the vegetables to the pot and add the dates and 1 cup of water. Reduce the heat to medium-low, cover, and cook, stirring occasionally and adding the remaining 1 cup of water as needed, for 2½ hours, until the lamb is very tender and the sauce has thickened. Serve immediately, garnished with cilantro.

Per Serving:

calories: 539 | fat: 20g | protein: 50g | carbs: 52g | fiber: 6g | sodium: 749mg

Southern Chili

Prep time: 20 minutes | Cook time: 25 minutes |

Serves 4

1 pound (454 g) ground beef (85% lean)
1 cup minced onion
1 (28-ounce / 794-g) can tomato purée
1 (15-ounce / 425-g) can diced

tomatoes with green chilies
1 (15-ounce / 425-g) can light red kidney beans, rinsed and drained
¼ cup Chili seasoning

1. Preheat the air fryer to 400ºF (204ºC). 2. In a baking pan, mix the ground beef and onion. Place the pan in the air fryer. 3. Cook for 4 minutes. Stir and cook for 4 minutes more until browned. Remove the pan from the fryer. Drain the meat and transfer to a large bowl. 4. Reduce the air fryer temperature to 350ºF (177ºC). 5. To the bowl with the meat, add in the tomato purée, diced tomatoes and green chilies, kidney beans, and Chili seasoning. Mix well. Pour the mixture into the baking pan. 6. Cook for 25 minutes, stirring every 10 minutes, until thickened.

Per Serving:

calories: 455 | fat: 18g | protein: 32g | carbs: 44g | fiber: 11g | sodium: 815mg

Garlic-Marinated Flank Steak

Prep time: 30 minutes | Cook time: 8 to 10 minutes |

Serves 6

½ cup avocado oil
¼ cup coconut aminos
1 shallot, minced
1 tablespoon minced garlic
2 tablespoons chopped fresh oregano, or 2 teaspoons dried

1½ teaspoons sea salt
1 teaspoon freshly ground black pepper
¼ teaspoon red pepper flakes
2 pounds (907 g) flank steak

1. In a blender, combine the avocado oil, coconut aminos, shallot, garlic, oregano, salt, black pepper, and red pepper flakes. Process until smooth. 2. Place the steak in a zip-top plastic bag or shallow dish with the marinade. Seal the bag or cover the dish and marinate in the refrigerator for at least 2 hours or overnight. 3. Remove the steak from the bag and discard the marinade. 4. Set the air fryer to 400°F (204°C). Place the steak in the air fryer basket (if needed, cut into sections and work in batches). Air fry for 4 to 6 minutes, flip the steak, and cook for another 4 minutes or until the internal temperature reaches 120°F (49°C) in the thickest part for medium-rare (or as desired).

Per Serving:

calories: 373 | fat: 26g | protein: 33g | carbs: 1g | fiber: 0g | sodium: 672mg

Poblano Pepper Cheeseburgers

Prep time: 5 minutes | Cook time: 30 minutes |

Serves 4

2 poblano chile peppers
1½ pounds (680 g) 85% lean ground beef
1 clove garlic, minced
1 teaspoon salt

½ teaspoon freshly ground black pepper
4 slices Cheddar cheese (about 3 ounces / 85 g)
4 large lettuce leaves

1. Preheat the air fryer to 400°F (204°C). 2. Arrange the poblano peppers in the basket of the air fryer. Pausing halfway through the cooking time to turn the peppers, air fry for 20 minutes, or until they are softened and beginning to char. Transfer the peppers to a large bowl and cover with a plate. When cool enough to handle, peel off the skin, remove the seeds and stems, and slice into strips. Set aside. 3. Meanwhile, in a large bowl, combine the ground beef with the garlic, salt, and pepper. Shape the beef into 4 patties. 4. Lower the heat on the air fryer to 360°F (182°C). Arrange the burgers in a single layer in the basket of the air fryer. Pausing halfway through the cooking time to turn the burgers, air fry for 10 minutes, or until a thermometer inserted into the thickest part registers 160°F (71°C). 5. Top the burgers with the cheese slices and continue baking for a minute or two, just until the cheese has melted. Serve the burgers on a lettuce leaf topped with the roasted poblano peppers.

Per Serving:

calories: 489 | fat: 35g | protein: 39g | carbs: 3g | fiber: 1g | sodium: 703mg

Spaghetti Zoodles and Meatballs

Prep time: 30 minutes | Cook time: 11 to 13 minutes

| Serves 6

1 pound (454 g) ground beef
1½ teaspoons sea salt, plus more for seasoning
1 large egg, beaten
1 teaspoon gelatin
¾ cup Parmesan cheese
2 teaspoons minced garlic
1 teaspoon Italian seasoning

Freshly ground black pepper, to taste
Avocado oil spray
Keto-friendly marinara sauce, for serving
6 ounces (170 g) zucchini noodles, made using a spiralizer or store-bought

1. Place the ground beef in a large bowl, and season with the salt. 2. Place the egg in a separate bowl and sprinkle with the gelatin. Allow to sit for 5 minutes. 3. Stir the gelatin mixture, then pour it over the ground beef. Add the Parmesan, garlic, and Italian seasoning. Season with salt and pepper. 4. Form the mixture into 1½-inch meatballs and place them on a plate; cover with plastic wrap and refrigerate for at least 1 hour or overnight. 5. Spray the meatballs with oil. Set the air fryer to 400°F (204°C) and arrange the meatballs in a single layer in the air fryer basket. Air fry for 4 minutes. Flip the meatballs and spray them with more oil. Air fry for 4 minutes more, until an instant-read thermometer reads 160°F (71°C). Transfer the meatballs to a plate and allow them to rest. 6. While the meatballs are resting, heat the marinara in a saucepan on the stove over medium heat. 7. Place the zucchini noodles in the air fryer, and cook at 400°F (204°C) for 3 to 5 minutes. 8. To serve, place the zucchini noodles in serving bowls. Top with meatballs and warm marinara.

Per Serving:

calories: 176 | fat: 8g | protein: 23g | carbs: 2g | fiber: 0g | sodium: 689mg

Mediterranean Beef Steaks

Prep time: 20 minutes | Cook time: 20 minutes |

Serves 4

2 tablespoons coconut aminos
3 heaping tablespoons fresh chives
2 tablespoons olive oil
3 tablespoons dry white wine
4 small-sized beef steaks
2 teaspoons smoked cayenne

pepper
½ teaspoon dried basil
½ teaspoon dried rosemary
1 teaspoon freshly ground black pepper
1 teaspoon sea salt, or more to taste

1. Firstly, coat the steaks with the cayenne pepper, black pepper, salt, basil, and rosemary. 2. Drizzle the steaks with olive oil, white wine, and coconut aminos. 3. Finally, roast in the air fryer for 20 minutes at 340°F (171°C). Serve garnished with fresh chives. Bon appétit!

Per Serving:

calories: 320 | fat: 17g | protein: 37g | carbs: 5g | fiber: 1g | sodium: 401mg

Roasted Pork with Apple-Dijon Sauce

Prep time: 15 minutes | Cook time: 40 minutes |

Serves 8

1½ tablespoons extra-virgin olive oil
1 (12-ounce/ 340-g) pork tenderloin
¼ teaspoon kosher salt
¼ teaspoon freshly ground black pepper

¼ cup apple jelly
¼ cup apple juice
2 to 3 tablespoons Dijon mustard
½ tablespoon cornstarch
½ tablespoon cream

1. Preheat the oven to 325°F(165°C). 2. In a large sauté pan or skillet, heat the olive oil over medium heat. 3. Add the pork to the skillet, using tongs to turn and sear the pork on all sides. Once seared, sprinkle pork with salt and pepper, and set it on a small baking sheet. 4. In the same skillet, with the juices from the pork, mix the apple jelly, juice, and mustard into the pan juices. Heat thoroughly over low heat, stirring consistently for 5 minutes. Spoon over the pork. 5. Put the pork in the oven and roast for 15 to 17 minutes, or 20 minutes per pound. Every 10 to 15 minutes, baste the pork with the apple-mustard sauce. 6. Once the pork tenderloin is done, remove it from the oven and let it rest for 15 minutes. Then, cut it into 1-inch slices. 7. In a small pot, blend the cornstarch with cream. Heat over low heat. Add the pan juices into the pot, stirring for 2 minutes, until thickened. Serve the sauce over the pork.

Per Serving:

calories: 146 | fat: 7g | protein: 13g | carbs: 8g | fiber: 0g | sodium: 192mg

Pork with Orzo

Prep time: 10 minutes | Cook time: 30 minutes |

Serves 4

2 tablespoons olive oil
2 yellow squash, diced
2 carrots, chopped
½ red onion, chopped
2 garlic cloves, minced
1 pound (454 g) boneless pork loin chops, cut into 2-inch pieces

1 teaspoon Italian seasoning
2 cups chicken broth
1 cup dried orzo
2 cups arugula
Sea salt
Freshly ground black pepper
Grated Parmesan cheese (optional)

1. In a Dutch oven, heat the olive oil over medium-high heat. Add the squash, carrots, onion, and garlic and sauté for 5 minutes, or until softened. Add the pork and Italian seasoning and sauté, stirring occasionally, for 3 to 5 minutes, until browned. 2. Increase the heat to high, add the broth, and bring to a boil. Add the orzo, reduce the heat to medium-low, and simmer, stirring occasionally, for 8 minutes. Add the arugula and stir until wilted. Turn off the heat, cover, and let sit for 5 minutes. 3. Season with salt and pepper and serve topped with Parmesan, if desired.

Per Serving:

calories: 423 | fat: 11g | protein: 31g | carbs: 48g | fiber: 4g | sodium: 127mg

Beef Bourguignon with Egg Noodles

Prep time: 15 minutes | Cook time: 8 hours | Serves 8

2 pounds (907 g) lean beef stew meat
6 tablespoons all-purpose flour
2 large carrots, cut into 1-inch slices
16 ounces (454 g) pearl onions, peeled fresh or frozen, thawed
8 ounces (227 g) mushrooms, stems removed
2 garlic cloves, minced
¾ cup beef stock

½ cup dry red wine
¼ cup tomato paste
1½ teaspoons sea salt
½ teaspoon dried rosemary
¼ teaspoon dried thyme
½ teaspoon black pepper
8 ounces (227 g) uncooked egg noodles
¼ cup chopped fresh thyme leaves

1. Place the beef in a medium bowl, sprinkle with the flour, and toss well to coat. 2. Place the beef mixture, carrots, onions, mushrooms, and garlic in the slow cooker. 3. Combine the stock, wine, tomato paste, salt, rosemary, thyme, and black pepper in a small bowl. Stir into the beef mixture. 4. Cover and cook on low for 8 hours. 5. Cook the noodles according to package directions, omitting any salt. 6. Serve the beef mixture over the noodles, sprinkled with the thyme.

Per Serving:

calories: 397 | fat: 6g | protein: 34g | carbs: 53g | fiber: 6g | sodium: 592mg

Italian Pot Roast

Prep time: 15 minutes | Cook time: 6 hours | Serves 8

1 (3-pound / 1.4-kg)beef chuck roast, trimmed and halved crosswise
4 cloves garlic, halved lengthwise
1½ teaspoons coarse sea salt
1 teaspoon black pepper
1 tablespoon olive oil
1 large yellow onion, cut into 8

wedges
1¼ pounds (567 g) small white potatoes
1 (28-ounce / 794-g) can whole tomatoes in purée
1 tablespoon chopped fresh rosemary leaves (or 1 teaspoon dried and crumbled rosemary)

1. With a sharp paring knife, cut four slits in each of the beef roast halves, and stuff the slits with one-half of the garlic halves. Generously season the beef with the salt and pepper. 2. In a large skillet, heat the olive oil over medium-high heat, swirling to coat the bottom of the pan. Cook the beef until browned on all sides, about 5 minutes. 3. Combine the beef, onion, potatoes, tomatoes, rosemary, and the remaining garlic in the slow cooker. 4. Cover and cook until the meat is fork-tender, on high for about 6 hours. 5. Transfer the meat to a cutting board. Thinly slice, and discard any fat or gristle. 6. Skim the fat from the top of the sauce in the slow cooker. 7. Serve hot, dividing the beef and vegetables among the eight bowls, and generously spooning the sauce over the top.

Per Serving:

calories: 317 | fat: 12g | protein: 37g | carbs: 17g | fiber: 4g | sodium: 605mg

Nigerian Peanut-Crusted Flank Steak

**Prep time: 30 minutes | Cook time: 8 minutes |
Serves 4**

Suya Spice Mix:
¼ cup dry-roasted peanuts
1 teaspoon cumin seeds
1 teaspoon garlic powder
1 teaspoon smoked paprika
½ teaspoon ground ginger

1 teaspoon kosher salt
½ teaspoon cayenne pepper
Steak:
1 pound (454 g) flank steak
2 tablespoons vegetable oil

1. For the spice mix: In a clean coffee grinder or spice mill, combine the peanuts and cumin seeds. Process until you get a coarse powder. (Do not overprocess or you will wind up with peanut butter! Alternatively, you can grind the cumin with ⅓ cup ready-made peanut powder, such as PB2, instead of the peanuts.) 2. Pour the peanut mixture into a small bowl, add the garlic powder, paprika, ginger, salt, and cayenne, and stir to combine. This recipe makes about ½ cup suya spice mix. Store leftovers in an airtight container in a cool, dry place for up to 1 month. 3. For the steak: Cut the flank steak into ½-inch-thick slices, cutting against the grain and at a slight angle. Place the beef strips in a resealable plastic bag and add the oil and 2½ to 3 tablespoons of the spice mixture. Seal the bag and massage to coat all of the meat with the oil and spice mixture. Marinate at room temperature for 30 minutes or in the refrigerator for up to 24 hours. 4. Place the beef strips in the air fryer basket. Set the air fryer to 400°F (204°C) for 8 minutes, turning the strips halfway through the cooking time. 5. Transfer the meat to a serving platter. Sprinkle with additional spice mix, if desired.

Per Serving:
calories: 275 | fat: 17g | protein: 27g | carbs: 3g | fiber: 1g | sodium: 644mg

Lamb Burger with Feta and Olives

**Prep time: 10 minutes | Cook time: 20 minutes |
Serves 3 to 4**

2 teaspoons olive oil
⅓ onion, finely chopped
1 clove garlic, minced
1 pound (454 g) ground lamb
2 tablespoons fresh parsley, finely chopped
1½ teaspoons fresh oregano, finely chopped

½ cup black olives, finely chopped
⅓ cup crumbled feta cheese
½ teaspoon salt
Freshly ground black pepper, to taste
4 thick pita breads

1. Preheat a medium skillet over medium-high heat on the stovetop. Add the olive oil and cook the onion until tender, but not browned, about 4 to 5 minutes. Add the garlic and cook for another minute. Transfer the onion and garlic to a mixing bowl and add the ground lamb, parsley, oregano, olives, feta cheese, salt and pepper. Gently mix the ingredients together. 2. Divide the mixture into 3 or 4 equal portions and then form the hamburgers, being careful not to over-handle the meat. One good way to do this is to throw the meat back and forth between your hands like a baseball, packing the

meat each time you catch it. Flatten the balls into patties, making an indentation in the center of each patty. Flatten the sides of the patties as well to make it easier to fit them into the air fryer basket. 3. Preheat the air fryer to 370°F (188°C). 4. If you don't have room for all four burgers, air fry two or three burgers at a time for 8 minutes at 370°F (188°C). Flip the burgers over and air fry for another 8 minutes. If you cooked your burgers in batches, return the first batch of burgers to the air fryer for the last two minutes of cooking to re-heat. This should give you a medium-well burger. If you'd prefer a medium-rare burger, shorten the cooking time to about 13 minutes. Remove the burgers to a resting plate and let the burgers rest for a few minutes before dressing and serving. 5. While the burgers are resting, toast the pita breads in the air fryer for 2 minutes. Tuck the burgers into the toasted pita breads, or wrap the pitas around the burgers and serve with a tzatziki sauce or some mayonnaise.

Per Serving:
calories: 380 | fat: 21g | protein: 28g | carbs: 20g | fiber: 2g | sodium: 745mg

Beef Stew with Red Wine

**Prep time: 15 minutes | Cook time: 46 minutes |
Serves 8**

1 pound (454 g) beef stew meat, cut into 1" pieces
2 tablespoons all-purpose flour
¼ teaspoon salt
¼ teaspoon ground black pepper
2 tablespoons olive oil, divided
1 pound (454 g) whole crimini mushrooms
2 cloves garlic, peeled and

minced
4 sprigs thyme
2 bay leaves
8 ounces (227 g) baby carrots
8 ounces (227 g) frozen pearl onions, thawed
1 cup red wine
½ cup beef broth
¼ cup chopped fresh parsley

1. In a medium bowl, toss beef with flour, salt, and pepper until thoroughly coated. Set aside. 2. Press the Sauté button on the Instant Pot® and heat 1 tablespoon oil. Add half of the beef pieces in a single layer, leaving space between each piece to prevent steaming, and brown well on all sides, about 3 minutes per side. Transfer beef to a medium bowl and repeat with remaining 1 tablespoon oil and beef. Press the Cancel button. 3. Add mushrooms, garlic, thyme, bay leaves, carrots, onions, wine, and broth to the Instant Pot®. Stir well. Close lid, set steam release to Sealing, press the Stew button, and set time to 40 minutes. When the timer beeps, quick-release the pressure until the float valve drops, open lid, and stir well. Remove and discard thyme and bay leaves. Sprinkle with parsley and serve hot.

Per Serving:
calories: 206 | fat: 13g | protein: 12g | carbs: 6g | fiber: 1g | sodium: 186mg

Chapter 6 Poultry

Chicken Cutlets with Greek Salsa

Prep time: 15 minutes | Cook time: 15 minutes |
Serves 2

2 tablespoons olive oil, divided
¼ teaspoon salt, plus additional to taste
Zest of ½ lemon
Juice of ½ lemon
8 ounces (227 g) chicken cutlets, or chicken breast sliced through the middle to make 2 thin pieces
1 cup cherry or grape tomatoes, halved or quartered (about 4 ounces / 113 g)
½ cup minced red onion (about ⅓ medium onion)

1 medium cucumber, peeled, seeded and diced (about 1 cup)
5 to 10 pitted Greek olives, minced (more or less depending on size and your taste)
1 tablespoon minced fresh parsley
1 tablespoon minced fresh oregano
1 tablespoon minced fresh mint
1 ounce (28 g) crumbled feta cheese
1 tablespoon red wine vinegar

1. In a medium bowl, combine 1 tablespoon of olive oil, the salt, lemon zest, and lemon juice. Add the chicken and let it marinate while you make the salsa. 2. In a small bowl, combine the tomatoes, onion, cucumber, olives, parsley, oregano, mint, feta cheese, and red wine vinegar, and toss lightly. Cover and let rest in the refrigerator for at least 30 minutes. Taste the salsa before serving and add a pinch of salt or extra herbs if desired. 3. To cook the chicken, heat the remaining 1 tablespoon of olive oil in a large nonstick skillet over medium-high heat. Add the chicken pieces and cook for 3 to 6 minutes on each side, depending on the thickness. If the chicken sticks to the pan, it's not quite ready to flip. 4. When chicken is cooked through, top with the salsa and serve.

Per Serving:
calories: 357 | fat: 23g | protein: 31g | carbs: 8g | fiber: 2g | sodium: 202mg

Simply Terrific Turkey Meatballs

Prep time: 10 minutes | Cook time: 7 to 10 minutes |
Serves 4

1 red bell pepper, seeded and coarsely chopped
2 cloves garlic, coarsely chopped
¼ cup chopped fresh parsley
1½ pounds (680 g) 85% lean

ground turkey
1 egg, lightly beaten
½ cup grated Parmesan cheese
1 teaspoon salt
½ teaspoon freshly ground black pepper

1. Preheat the air fryer to 400ºF (204ºC). 2. In a food processor fitted with a metal blade, combine the bell pepper, garlic, and parsley. Pulse until finely chopped. Transfer the vegetables to a large mixing bowl. 3. Add the turkey, egg, Parmesan, salt, and black pepper. Mix gently until thoroughly combined. Shape the mixture into 1¼-inch meatballs. 4. Working in batches if necessary, arrange the meatballs in a single layer in the air fryer basket; coat lightly with olive oil spray. Pausing halfway through the cooking time to shake the basket, air fry for 7 to 10 minutes, until lightly browned and a thermometer inserted into the center of a meatball registers 165ºF (74ºC).

Per Serving:
calories: 388 | fat: 25g | protein: 34g | carbs: 5g | fiber: 1g | sodium: 527mg

Tahini Chicken Rice Bowls

Prep time: 10 minutes |Cook time: 15 minutes|
Serves: 4

1 cup uncooked instant brown rice
¼ cup tahini or peanut butter (tahini for nut-free)
¼ cup 2% plain Greek yogurt
2 tablespoons chopped scallions, green and white parts (2 scallions)
1 tablespoon freshly squeezed lemon juice (from ½ medium lemon)
1 tablespoon water

1 teaspoon ground cumin
¾ teaspoon ground cinnamon
¼ teaspoon kosher or sea salt
2 cups chopped cooked chicken breast (about 1 pound / 454 g)
½ cup chopped dried apricots
2 cups peeled and chopped seedless cucumber (1 large cucumber)
4 teaspoons sesame seeds
Fresh mint leaves, for serving (optional)

1. Cook the brown rice according to the package instructions. 2. While the rice is cooking, in a medium bowl, mix together the tahini, yogurt, scallions, lemon juice, water, cumin, cinnamon, and salt. Transfer half the tahini mixture to another medium bowl. Mix the chicken into the first bowl. 3. When the rice is done, mix it into the second bowl of tahini (the one without the chicken). 4. To assemble, divide the chicken among four bowls. Spoon the rice mixture next to the chicken in each bowl. Next to the chicken, place the dried apricots, and in the remaining empty section, add the cucumbers. Sprinkle with sesame seeds, and top with mint, if desired, and serve.

Per Serving:
calories: 448 | fat: 13g | protein: 30g | carbs: 53g | fiber: 5g | sodium: 243mg

Chicken Pesto Parmigiana

Prep time: 10 minutes | Cook time: 23 minutes |

Serves 4

2 large eggs
1 tablespoon water
Fine sea salt and ground black pepper, to taste
1 cup powdered Parmesan cheese (about 3 ounces / 85 g)
2 teaspoons Italian seasoning
4 (5-ounce / 142-g) boneless, skinless chicken breasts or

thighs, pounded to ¼ inch thick
1 cup pesto
1 cup shredded Mozzarella cheese (about 4 ounces / 113 g)
Finely chopped fresh basil, for garnish (optional)
Grape tomatoes, halved, for serving (optional)

1. Spray the air fryer basket with avocado oil. Preheat the air fryer to 400ºF (204ºC). 2. Crack the eggs into a shallow baking dish, add the water and a pinch each of salt and pepper, and whisk to combine. In another shallow baking dish, stir together the Parmesan and Italian seasoning until well combined. 3. Season the chicken breasts well on both sides with salt and pepper. Dip one chicken breast in the eggs and let any excess drip off, then dredge both sides of the breast in the Parmesan mixture. Spray the breast with avocado oil and place it in the air fryer basket. Repeat with the remaining 3 chicken breasts. 4. Air fry the chicken in the air fryer for 20 minutes, or until the internal temperature reaches 165ºF (74ºC) and the breading is golden brown, flipping halfway through. 5. Dollop each chicken breast with ¼ cup of the pesto and top with the Mozzarella. Return the breasts to the air fryer and cook for 3 minutes, or until the cheese is melted. Garnish with basil and serve with halved grape tomatoes on the side, if desired. 6. Store leftovers in an airtight container in the refrigerator for up to 4 days. Reheat in a preheated 400ºF (204ºC) air fryer for 5 minutes, or until warmed through.

Per Serving:

calories: 631 | fat: 45g | protein: 52g | carbs: 4g | fiber: 0g | sodium: 607mg

Skillet Creamy Tarragon Chicken and Mushrooms

Prep time: 10 minutes | Cook time: 20 minutes |

Serves 2

2 tablespoons olive oil, divided
½ medium onion, minced
4 ounces (113 g) baby bella (cremini) mushrooms, sliced
2 small garlic cloves, minced
8 ounces (227 g) chicken cutlets
2 teaspoons tomato paste
2 teaspoons dried tarragon

2 cups low-sodium chicken stock
6 ounces (170 g) pappardelle pasta
¼ cup plain full-fat Greek yogurt
Salt
Freshly ground black pepper

1. Heat 1 tablespoon of the olive oil in a sauté pan over medium-high heat. Add the onion and mushrooms and sauté for 5 minutes. Add the garlic and cook for 1 minute more. 2. Move the vegetables to the edges of the pan and add the remaining 1 tablespoon of olive oil to the center of the pan. Place the cutlets in the center and let them cook for about 3 minutes, or until they lift up easily and are golden brown on the bottom. 3. Flip the chicken and cook for another 3 minutes. 4. Mix in the tomato paste and tarragon. Add the chicken stock and stir well to combine everything. Bring the stock to a boil. 5. Add the pappardelle. Break up the pasta if needed to fit into the pan. Stir the noodles so they don't stick to the bottom of the pan. 6. Cover the sauté pan and reduce the heat to medium-low. Let the chicken and noodles simmer for 15 minutes, stirring occasionally, until the pasta is cooked and the liquid is mostly absorbed. If the liquid absorbs too quickly and the pasta isn't cooked, add more water or chicken stock, about ¼ cup at a time as needed. 7. Remove the pan from the heat. 8. Stir 2 tablespoons of the hot liquid from the pan into the yogurt. Pour the tempered yogurt into the pan and stir well to mix it into the sauce. Season with salt and pepper. 9. The sauce will tighten up as it cools, so if it seems too thick, add a few tablespoons of water.

Per Serving:

calories: 556 | fat: 18g | protein: 42g | carbs: 56g | fiber: 2g | sodium: 190mg

Roast Chicken

Prep time: 20 minutes | Cook time: 55 minutes |

Serves 4

¼ cup white wine
2 tablespoons olive oil, divided
1 tablespoon Dijon mustard
1 garlic clove, minced
1 teaspoon dried rosemary
Juice and zest of 1 lemon
Sea salt and freshly ground pepper, to taste

1 large roasting chicken, giblets removed
3 large carrots, peeled and cut into chunks
1 fennel bulb, peeled and cut into ½-inch cubes
2 celery stalks, cut into chunks

1. Preheat the oven to 400ºF (205ºC). 2. Combine the white wine, 1 tablespoon of olive oil, mustard, garlic, rosemary, lemon juice and zest, sea salt, and freshly ground pepper in a small bowl. 3. Place the chicken in a shallow roasting pan on a roasting rack. 4. Rub the entire chicken, including the cavity, with the wine and mustard mixture. 5. Place the chicken in the oven and roast for 15 minutes. 6. Toss the vegetables with the remaining tablespoon of olive oil, and place around the chicken. 7. Turn the heat down to 375ºF (190ºC). 8. Roast an additional 40–60 minutes, basting the chicken every 15 minutes with the drippings in the bottom of the pan. 9. Cook chicken until internal temperature reaches 180ºF (82ºC) in between the thigh and the body of the chicken. When you remove the instant-read thermometer, the juices should run clear. 10. Let the chicken rest for at least 10–15 minutes before serving.

Per Serving:

calories: 387 | fat: 14g | protein: 50g | carbs: 12g | fiber: 4g | sodium: 306mg

Sheet Pan Pesto Chicken with Crispy Garlic Potatoes

Prep time: 15 minutes | Cook time: 50 minutes |

Serves 2

12 ounces (340 g) small red potatoes (3 or 4 potatoes)
1 tablespoon olive oil
¼ teaspoon salt

½ teaspoon garlic powder
1 (8-ounce / 227-g) boneless, skinless chicken breast
3 tablespoons prepared pesto

1. Preheat the oven to 425°F (220°C) and set the rack to the bottom position. Line a baking sheet with parchment paper. (Do not use foil, as the potatoes will stick.) 2. Scrub the potatoes and dry them well, then dice into 1-inch pieces. 3. In a medium bowl, combine the potatoes, olive oil, salt, and garlic powder. Toss well to coat. 4. Place the potatoes on the parchment paper and roast for 10 minutes. Flip the potatoes and return to the oven for another 10 minutes. 5. While the potatoes are roasting, place the chicken in the same bowl and toss with the pesto, coating the chicken evenly. 6. Check the potatoes to make sure they are golden brown on the top and bottom. Toss them again and add the chicken breast to the pan. 7. Turn the heat down to 350°F (180°C) and let the chicken and potatoes roast for 30 minutes. Check to make sure the chicken reaches an internal temperature of 165°F (74°C) and the potatoes are tender inside.

Per Serving:

calories: 377 | fat: 16g | protein: 30g | carbs: 31g | fiber: 4g | sodium: 426mg

Herb-Marinated Chicken Breasts

Prep time: 10 minutes | Cook time: 10 minutes |

Serves 4

½ cup fresh lemon juice
¼ cup extra-virgin olive oil
4 cloves garlic, minced
2 tablespoons chopped fresh basil
1 tablespoon chopped fresh oregano
1 tablespoon chopped fresh

mint
2 pounds (907 g) chicken breast tenders
½ teaspoon unrefined sea salt or salt
¼ teaspoon freshly ground black pepper

1. In a small bowl, whisk the lemon juice, olive oil, garlic, basil, oregano, and mint well to combine. Place the chicken breasts in a large shallow bowl or glass baking pan, and pour dressing over the top. 2. Cover, place in the refrigerator, and allow to marinate for 1 to 2 hours. Remove from the refrigerator, and season with salt and pepper. 3. Heat a large, wide skillet over medium-high heat. Using tongs, place chicken tenders evenly in the bottom of the skillet. Pour the remaining marinade over the chicken. 4. Allow to cook for 3 to 5 minutes each side, or until chicken is golden, juices have been absorbed, and meat is cooked to an internal temperature of 160°F (71°C).

Per Serving:

calories: 521 | fat: 35g | protein: 48g | carbs: 3g | fiber: 0g | sodium: 435mg

Chicken Thighs with Cilantro

Prep time: 15 minutes | Cook time: 25 minutes |

Serves 4

1 tablespoon olive oil
Juice of ½ lime
1 tablespoon coconut aminos
1½ teaspoons Montreal chicken seasoning

8 bone-in chicken thighs, skin on
2 tablespoons chopped fresh cilantro

1. In a gallon-size resealable bag, combine the olive oil, lime juice, coconut aminos, and chicken seasoning. Add the chicken thighs, seal the bag, and massage the bag to ensure the chicken is thoroughly coated. Refrigerate for at least 2 hours, preferably overnight. 2. Preheat the air fryer to 400°F (204°C). 3. Remove the chicken from the marinade (discard the marinade) and arrange in a single layer in the air fryer basket. Pausing halfway through the cooking time to flip the chicken, air fry for 20 to 25 minutes, until a thermometer inserted into the thickest part registers 165°F (74°C). 4. Transfer the chicken to a serving platter and top with the cilantro before serving.

Per Serving:

calories: 692 | fat: 53g | protein: 49g | carbs: 2g | fiber: 0g | sodium: 242mg

Pesto Chicken and Potatoes

Prep time: 15 minutes | Cook time: 6 to 8 hours |

Serves 6

For the Pesto:
1 cup fresh basil leaves
1 garlic clove, crushed
¼ cup pine nuts
¼ cup grated Parmesan cheese
2 tablespoons extra-virgin olive oil, plus more as needed
1 teaspoon sea salt
½ teaspoon freshly ground

black pepper
For the Chicken:
Nonstick cooking spray
2 pounds (907 g) red potatoes, quartered
3 pounds (1.4 kg) boneless, skinless chicken thighs
½ cup low-sodium chicken broth

Make the Pesto: In a food processor, combine the basil, garlic, pine nuts, Parmesan cheese, olive oil, salt, and pepper. Pulse until smooth, adding more olive oil ½ teaspoon at a time if needed until any clumps are gone. Set aside. Make the Chicken: 1. Coat a slow-cooker insert with cooking spray and put the potatoes into the prepared slow cooker. 2. Place the chicken on top of the potatoes. 3. In a medium bowl, whisk together the pesto and broth until combined and pour the mixture over the chicken. 4. Cover the cooker and cook for 6 to 8 hours on Low heat.

Per Serving:

calories: 467 | fat: 24g | protein: 38g | carbs: 25g | fiber: 3g | sodium: 819mg

Cajun-Breaded Chicken Bites

Prep time: 10 minutes | Cook time: 12 minutes |
Serves 4

1 pound (454 g) boneless, skinless chicken breasts, cut into 1-inch cubes
½ cup heavy whipping cream
½ teaspoon salt
¼ teaspoon ground black

pepper
1 ounce (28 g) plain pork rinds, finely crushed
¼ cup unflavored whey protein powder
½ teaspoon Cajun seasoning

1. Place chicken in a medium bowl and pour in cream. Stir to coat. Sprinkle with salt and pepper. 2. In a separate large bowl, combine pork rinds, protein powder, and Cajun seasoning. Remove chicken from cream, shaking off any excess, and toss in dry mix until fully coated. 3. Place bites into ungreased air fryer basket. Adjust the temperature to 400ºF (204ºC) and air fry for 12 minutes, shaking the basket twice during cooking. Bites will be done when golden brown and have an internal temperature of at least 165ºF (74ºC). Serve warm.

Per Serving:

calories: 272 | fat: 13g | protein: 35g | carbs: 2g | fiber: 1g | sodium: 513mg

Deconstructed Greek Chicken Kebabs

Prep time: 20 minutes | Cook time: 6 to 8 hours |
Serves 4

2 pounds (907 g) boneless, skinless chicken thighs, cut into 1-inch cubes
2 zucchini (nearly 1 pound / 454 g), cut into 1-inch pieces
1 green bell pepper, seeded and cut into 1-inch pieces
1 red bell pepper, seeded and cut into 1-inch pieces
1 large red onion, chopped
2 tablespoons extra-virgin olive

oil
2 tablespoons freshly squeezed lemon juice
1 tablespoon red wine vinegar
2 garlic cloves, minced
1 teaspoon sea salt
1 teaspoon dried oregano
½ teaspoon dried basil
½ teaspoon dried thyme
¼ teaspoon freshly ground black pepper

1. In a slow cooker, combine the chicken, zucchini, green and red bell peppers, onion, olive oil, lemon juice, vinegar, garlic, salt, oregano, basil, thyme, and black pepper. Stir to mix well. 2. Cover the cooker and cook for 6 to 8 hours on Low heat.

Per Serving:

calories: 372 | fat: 17g | protein: 47g | carbs: 8g | fiber: 2g | sodium: 808mg

Mediterranean Roasted Turkey Breast

Prep time: 15 minutes | Cook time: 6 to 8 hours |
Serves 4

3 garlic cloves, minced
1 teaspoon sea salt
1 teaspoon dried oregano
½ teaspoon freshly ground black pepper
½ teaspoon dried basil
½ teaspoon dried parsley
½ teaspoon dried rosemary
½ teaspoon dried thyme
¼ teaspoon dried dill
¼ teaspoon ground nutmeg
2 tablespoons extra-virgin olive oil

2 tablespoons freshly squeezed lemon juice
1 (4- to 6-pound / 1.8- to 2.7-kg) boneless or bone-in turkey breast
1 onion, chopped
½ cup low-sodium chicken broth
4 ounces (113 g) whole Kalamata olives, pitted
1 cup sun-dried tomatoes (packaged, not packed in oil), chopped

1. In a small bowl, stir together the garlic, salt, oregano, pepper, basil, parsley, rosemary, thyme, dill, and nutmeg. 2. Drizzle the olive oil and lemon juice all over the turkey breast and generously season it with the garlic-spice mix. 3. In a slow cooker, combine the onion and chicken broth. Place the seasoned turkey breast on top of the onion. Top the turkey with the olives and sun-dried tomatoes. 4. Cover the cooker and cook for 6 to 8 hours on Low heat. 5. Slice or shred the turkey for serving.

Per Serving:

calories: 676 | fat: 19g | protein: 111g | carbs: 14g | fiber: 3g | sodium: 626mg

Punjabi Chicken Curry

Prep time: 20 minutes | Cook time: 4 to 6 hours |
Serves 6

2 tablespoons vegetable oil
3 onions, finely diced
6 garlic cloves, finely chopped
1 heaped tablespoon freshly grated ginger
1 (14-ounce / 397-g) can plum tomatoes
1 teaspoon salt
1 teaspoon turmeric
1 teaspoon chili powder
Handful coriander stems, finely

chopped
3 fresh green chiles, finely chopped
12 pieces chicken, mixed thighs and drumsticks, or a whole chicken, skinned, trimmed, and chopped
2 teaspoons garam masala
Handful fresh coriander leaves, chopped

1. Heat the oil in a frying pan (or in the slow cooker if you have a sear setting). Add the diced onions and cook for 5 minutes. Add the garlic and continue to cook for 10 minutes until the onions are brown. 2. Heat the slow cooker to high and add the onion-and-garlic mixture. Stir in the ginger, tomatoes, salt, turmeric, chili powder, coriander stems, and chiles. 3. Add the chicken pieces. Cover and cook on low for 6 hours, or on high for 4 hours. 4. Once cooked, check the seasoning, and then stir in the garam masala and coriander leaves.

Per Serving:

calories: 298 | fat: 9g | protein: 35g | carbs: 19g | fiber: 3g | sodium: 539mg

Chicken and Olives with Couscous

Prep time: 15 minutes | Cook time: 1 hour | Serves 6

2 tablespoons olive oil, divided
8 bone-in, skin-on chicken thighs
½ teaspoon kosher salt
¼ teaspoon ground black pepper
2 cloves garlic, chopped
1 small red onion, chopped
1 red bell pepper, seeded and chopped
1 green bell pepper, seeded and chopped

1 tablespoon fresh thyme leaves
2 teaspoons fresh oregano leaves
1 (28-ounce / 794-g) can no-salt-added diced tomatoes
1 cup low-sodium chicken broth
1 cup pitted green olives, coarsely chopped
2 cups whole wheat couscous
Chopped flat-leaf parsley, for garnish

1. Preheat the oven to 350°F(180°C). 2. In a large ovenproof or cast-iron skillet over medium heat, warm 1 tablespoon of the oil. Pat the chicken thighs dry with a paper towel, season with the salt and black pepper, and cook, turning once, until golden and crisp, 8 to 10 minutes per side. Remove the chicken from the skillet and set aside. 3. Add the remaining 1 tablespoon oil to the skillet. Cook the garlic, onion, bell peppers, thyme, and oregano until softened, about 5 minutes. Add the tomatoes and broth and bring to a boil. Return the chicken to the skillet, add the olives, cover, and place the skillet in the oven. Roast until the chicken is tender and a thermometer inserted in the thickest part registers 165°F(74°C), 40 to 50 minutes. 4. While the chicken is cooking, prepare the couscous according to package directions. 5. To serve, pile the couscous on a serving platter and nestle the chicken on top. Pour the vegetables and any pan juices over the chicken and couscous. Sprinkle with the parsley and serve.

Per Serving:

calories: 481 | fat: 15g | protein: 29g | carbs: 61g | fiber: 11g | sodium: 893mg

Baked Chicken Caprese

Prep time: 5minutes |Cook time: 25 minutes|
Serves: 4

Nonstick cooking spray
1 pound (454 g) boneless, skinless chicken breasts
2 tablespoons extra-virgin olive oil
¼ teaspoon freshly ground black pepper
¼ teaspoon kosher or sea salt
1 large tomato, sliced thinly

1 cup shredded mozzarella or 4 ounces (113 g) fresh mozzarella cheese, diced
1 (14½-ounce / 411-g) can low-sodium or no-salt-added crushed tomatoes
2 tablespoons fresh torn basil leaves
4 teaspoons balsamic vinegar

1. Set one oven rack about 4 inches below the broiler element. Preheat the oven to 450°F(235°C). Line a large, rimmed baking sheet with aluminum foil. Place a wire cooling rack on the aluminum foil, and spray the rack with nonstick cooking spray. Set aside. 2. Cut the chicken into 4 pieces (if they aren't already). Put the chicken breasts in a large zip-top plastic bag. With a rolling pin or meat mallet, pound the chicken so it is evenly flattened, about ¼-inch thick. Add the oil, pepper, and salt to the bag. Reseal the bag, and massage the ingredients into the chicken. Take the chicken out of the bag and place it on the prepared wire rack. 3. Cook the chicken for 15 to 18 minutes, or until the internal temperature of the chicken is 165°F(74°C) on a meat thermometer and the juices run clear. Turn the oven to the high broiler setting. Layer the tomato slices on each chicken breast, and top with the mozzarella. Broil the chicken for another 2 to 3 minutes, or until the cheese is melted (don't let the chicken burn on the edges). Remove the chicken from the oven. 4. While the chicken is cooking, pour the crushed tomatoes into a small, microwave-safe bowl. Cover the bowl with a paper towel, and microwave for about 1 minute on high, until hot. When you're ready to serve, divide the tomatoes among four dinner plates. Place each chicken breast on top of the tomatoes. Top with the basil and a drizzle of balsamic vinegar.

Per Serving:

calories: 304 | fat: 15g | protein: 34g | carbs: 7g | fiber: 3g | sodium: 215mg

Chettinad Chicken

Prep time: 15 minutes | Cook time: 4 to 6 hours |
Serves 6

1 tablespoon white poppy seeds
1 teaspoon coriander seeds
2 teaspoons cumin seeds
1 teaspoon fennel seeds
4 to 5 dried red chiles
2-inch piece cinnamon stick
6 green cardamom pods
4 cloves
1½ cups grated coconut
4 garlic cloves
1 tablespoon freshly grated ginger
2 tablespoons coconut oil

20 curry leaves
3 onions, finely sliced
2 star anise
4 tomatoes
1 teaspoon turmeric
Sea salt
1 teaspoon chili powder
12 chicken thighs on the bone, skinned and trimmed
Juice of 2 or 3 limes
Handful fresh coriander leaves, chopped

1. In a frying pan, toast the poppy seeds, coriander seeds, cumin seeds, fennel seeds, dried red chiles, cinnamon, green cardamom pods, and cloves until fragrant, about 1 minute. Remove from the pan and set aside to cool. Once cooled, grind to a fine powder in a spice grinder. 2. In the same pan, toast the grated coconut for 3 to 4 minutes until it just starts to turn golden. Remove from the pan and spread on a plate to cool. Once cooled, grind and mix with the ground spices. 3. Crush the garlic and ginger in a mortar and pestle and set aside. 4. Either heat the slow cooker to sauté or use a pan on the stove. Heat the coconut oil and add the curry leaves, when they stop spluttering, add the sliced onions and fry them until they are light brown. Stir in the crushed garlic and ginger, and stir for a minute or two. 5. Add to the slow cooker along with the ground spices and anise. Chop and add the tomatoes, the turmeric, and the salt, and stir in the chili powder. 6. Place the chicken pieces in the cooker, cover and cook on low for 6 hours, or on high for 4 hours, until tender and cooked through. 7. Check the seasoning and adjust if needed, squeeze in the lime juice, and serve topped with fresh coriander leaves.

Per Serving:

calories: 628 | fat: 28g | protein: 79g | carbs: 13g | fiber: 4g | sodium: 393mg

Stuffed Turkey Roulade

Prep time: 10 minutes | Cook time: 45 minutes | Serves 4

1 (2-pound / 907-g) boneless turkey breast, skin removed
1 teaspoon salt
½ teaspoon black pepper
4 ounces (113 g) goat cheese
1 tablespoon fresh thyme
1 tablespoon fresh sage
2 garlic cloves, minced
2 tablespoons olive oil
Fresh chopped parsley, for garnish

1. Preheat the air fryer to 380°F(193°C). 2. Using a sharp knife, butterfly the turkey breast, and season both sides with salt and pepper and set aside. 3. In a small bowl, mix together the goat cheese, thyme, sage, and garlic. 4. Spread the cheese mixture over the turkey breast, then roll it up tightly, tucking the ends underneath. 5. Place the turkey breast roulade onto a piece of aluminum foil, wrap it up, and place it into the air fryer. 6. Bake for 30 minutes. Remove the foil from the turkey breast and brush the top with oil, then continue cooking for another 10 to 15 minutes, or until the outside has browned and the internal temperature reaches 165°F(74°C). 7. Remove and cut into 1-inch-wide slices and serve with a sprinkle of parsley on top.

Per Serving:

calories: 452 | fat: 20g | protein: 62g | carbs: 2g | fiber: 0g | sodium: 702mg

Hot Goan-Style Coconut Chicken

Prep time: 20 minutes | Cook time: 4 to 6 hours | Serves 6

Spice Paste:
8 dried Kashmiri chiles, broken into pieces
2 tablespoons coriander seeds
2-inch piece cassia bark, broken into pieces
1 teaspoon black peppercorns
1 teaspoon cumin seeds
1 teaspoon fennel seeds
4 cloves
2 star anise
1 tablespoon poppy seeds
1 cup freshly grated coconut, or desiccated coconut shreds
6 garlic cloves
⅓ cup water
Chicken:
12 chicken thigh and drumstick pieces, on the bone, skinless
1 teaspoon salt (or to taste)
1 teaspoon turmeric
2 tablespoons coconut oil
2 medium onions, finely sliced
⅓ cup water
½ teaspoon ground nutmeg
2 teaspoons tamarind paste
Handful fresh coriander leaves, chopped for garnish
1 or 2 fresh red chiles, for garnish

Make the Spice Paste: 1. In a dry frying pan, roast the Kashmiri chiles, coriander seeds, cassia bark, peppercorns, cumin seeds, fennel seeds, cloves, and star anise until fragrant, about 1 minute. Add the poppy seeds and continue roasting for a few minutes. Then remove from the heat and leave to cool. 2. Once cooled, grind the toasted spices in your spice grinder and set aside. 3. In the same pan, add the dried coconut and toast it for 5 to 7 minutes, until it just starts to turn golden. 4. Transfer to a blender with the garlic, and add the water. Blend to make a thick, wet paste. 5. Add the ground spices and blend again to mix together. Make the Chicken: 6. In a large bowl, toss the chicken with the salt and turmeric. Marinate for 15 to 20 minutes. In the meantime, heat the slow cooker to high. 7. Heat the oil in a frying pan (or in the slow cooker if you have a sear setting). Cook the sliced onions for 10 minutes, and then add the spice and coconut paste. Cook until it becomes fragrant. 8. Transfer everything to the slow cooker. Add the chicken, then the water. Cover and cook on low for 6 hours, or on high for 4 hours. 9. Sprinkle in the nutmeg and stir in the tamarind paste. Cover and cook for another 5 minutes. 10. Garnish with fresh coriander leaves and whole red chiles to serve.

Per Serving:

calories: 583 | fat: 26g | protein: 77g | carbs: 7g | fiber: 3g | sodium: 762mg

Chicken Cacciatore with Wild Mushrooms and Fresh Fennel

Prep time: 10 minutes | Cook time: 1 hour and 10 minutes | Serves 6 to 8

½ ounce (14 g) dried porcini mushrooms
1 cup boiling water
2 tablespoons olive oil
12 boneless, skinless chicken thighs (about 3 pounds / 1.4 kg), trimmed of fat
1 large green bell pepper, seeded and cut into rings
1 large onion, halved and thinly sliced
1 large fennel bulb, trimmed,
halved, cored and thinly sliced
3 cloves garlic, minced
1 tablespoon minced fresh rosemary
2 teaspoons freshly grated orange zest
1 teaspoon fresh thyme leaves
3 tablespoons red wine vinegar
¾ cup dry white wine
2 tablespoons tomato paste
1 teaspoon salt

1. Preheat the oven to 350°F (180°C) . 2. Soak the porcinis in the boiling water for about 20 minutes. 3. While the mushrooms are soaking, heat the olive oil in a large skillet over medium-high heat. Brown the chicken pieces on all sides, working in batches if needed. Transfer the chicken to a 9-by-13-inch baking dish as the pieces are browned. 4. Reduce the heat under the skillet to medium. Add the pepper, onion, and fennel and cook, stirring frequently, until softened, about 5 minutes. Stir in the garlic, rosemary, orange zest, and thyme and cook, stirring, for another 30 seconds. Add the vinegar and cook, stirring, 1 minute longer. Remove from the heat. 5. Remove the mushrooms from the water, reserving the soaking water, and chop them coarsely. Add the chopped mushrooms and the soaking water to the pan along with the wine, tomato paste, and salt. 6. Bring to a simmer over medium heat, then add the hot mixture to the baking dish, pouring it over the chicken legs. Cover with aluminum foil and bake in the preheated oven for 45 minutes. Remove from the oven and let it rest for 5 to 10 minutes before serving. Serve hot.

Per Serving:

calories: 468 | fat: 19g | protein: 58g | carbs: 9g | fiber: 3g | sodium: 527mg

Chicken Patties

Prep time: 15 minutes | Cook time: 12 minutes |
Serves 4

1 pound (454 g) ground chicken thigh meat
½ cup shredded Mozzarella cheese
1 teaspoon dried parsley
½ teaspoon garlic powder
¼ teaspoon onion powder
1 large egg
2 ounces (57 g) pork rinds, finely ground

1. In a large bowl, mix ground chicken, Mozzarella, parsley, garlic powder, and onion powder. Form into four patties. 2. Place patties in the freezer for 15 to 20 minutes until they begin to firm up. 3. Whisk egg in a medium bowl. Place the ground pork rinds into a large bowl. 4. Dip each chicken patty into the egg and then press into pork rinds to fully coat. Place patties into the air fryer basket. 5. Adjust the temperature to 360ºF (182ºC) and air fry for 12 minutes. 6. Patties will be firm and cooked to an internal temperature of 165ºF (74ºC) when done. Serve immediately.

Per Serving:
calories: 265 | fat: 15g | protein: 29g | carbs: 1g | fiber: 0g | sodium: 285mg

Broccoli Cheese Chicken

Prep time: 10 minutes | Cook time: 19 to 24 minutes | Serves 6

1 tablespoon avocado oil
¼ cup chopped onion
½ cup finely chopped broccoli
4 ounces (113 g) cream cheese, at room temperature
2 ounces (57 g) Cheddar cheese, shredded
1 teaspoon garlic powder
½ teaspoon sea salt, plus
additional for seasoning, divided
¼ freshly ground black pepper, plus additional for seasoning, divided
2 pounds (907 g) boneless, skinless chicken breasts
1 teaspoon smoked paprika

1. Heat a medium skillet over medium-high heat and pour in the avocado oil. Add the onion and broccoli and cook, stirring occasionally, for 5 to 8 minutes, until the onion is tender. 2. Transfer to a large bowl and stir in the cream cheese, Cheddar cheese, and garlic powder, and season to taste with salt and pepper. 3. Hold a sharp knife parallel to the chicken breast and cut a long pocket into one side. Stuff the chicken pockets with the broccoli mixture, using toothpicks to secure the pockets around the filling. 4. In a small dish, combine the paprika, ½ teaspoon salt, and ¼ teaspoon pepper. Sprinkle this over the outside of the chicken. 5. Set the air fryer to 400ºF (204ºC). Place the chicken in a single layer in the air fryer basket, cooking in batches if necessary, and cook for 14 to 16 minutes, until an instant-read thermometer reads 160ºF (71ºC). Place the chicken on a plate and tent a piece of aluminum foil over the chicken. Allow to rest for 5 to 10 minutes before serving.

Per Serving:
calorie: 287 | fat: 16g | protein: 32g | carbs: 1g | sugars: 0g | fiber: 0g | sodium: 291mg

Chicken Shawarma

Prep time: 30 minutes | Cook time: 15 minutes |
Serves 4

Shawarma Spice:
2 teaspoons dried oregano
1 teaspoon ground cinnamon
1 teaspoon ground cumin
1 teaspoon ground coriander
1 teaspoon kosher salt
½ teaspoon ground allspice
½ teaspoon cayenne pepper
Chicken:
1 pound (454 g) boneless, skinless chicken thighs, cut into large bite-size chunks
2 tablespoons vegetable oil
For Serving:
Tzatziki
Pita bread

1. For the shawarma spice: In a small bowl, combine the oregano, cayenne, cumin, coriander, salt, cinnamon, and allspice. 2. For the chicken: In a large bowl, toss together the chicken, vegetable oil, and shawarma spice to coat. Marinate at room temperature for 30 minutes or cover and refrigerate for up to 24 hours. 3. Place the chicken in the air fryer basket. Set the air fryer to 350ºF (177ºC) for 15 minutes, or until the chicken reaches an internal temperature of 165ºF (74ºC). 4. Transfer the chicken to a serving platter. Serve with tzatziki and pita bread.

Per Serving:
calories: 202 | fat: 12g | protein: 23g | carbs: 1g | fiber: 1g | sodium: 690mg

Jerk Chicken Kebabs

Prep time: 10 minutes | Cook time: 14 minutes |
Serves 4

8 ounces (227 g) boneless, skinless chicken thighs, cut into 1-inch cubes
2 tablespoons jerk seasoning
2 tablespoons coconut oil
½ medium red bell pepper,
seeded and cut into 1-inch pieces
¼ medium red onion, peeled and cut into 1-inch pieces
½ teaspoon salt

1. Place chicken in a medium bowl and sprinkle with jerk seasoning and coconut oil. Toss to coat on all sides. 2. Using eight (6-inch) skewers, build skewers by alternating chicken, pepper, and onion pieces, about three repetitions per skewer. 3. Sprinkle salt over skewers and place into ungreased air fryer basket. Adjust the temperature to 370ºF (188ºC) and air fry for 14 minutes, turning skewers halfway through cooking. Chicken will be golden and have an internal temperature of at least 165ºF (74ºC) when done. Serve warm.

Per Serving:
calories: 142 | fat: 9g | protein: 12g | carbs: 4g | fiber: 1g | sodium: 348mg

Citrus and Spice Chicken

Prep time: 15 minutes | Cook time: 17 minutes | Serves 8

2 tablespoons olive oil
3 pounds (1.4 kg) boneless, skinless chicken thighs
1 teaspoon smoked paprika
½ teaspoon salt
⅛ teaspoon ground cinnamon
⅛ teaspoon ground ginger
⅛ teaspoon ground nutmeg
½ cup golden raisins
½ cup slivered almonds
1 cup orange juice
⅛ cup lemon juice
⅛ cup lime juice
1 pound (454 g) carrots, peeled and chopped
2 tablespoons water
1 tablespoon arrowroot powder

1. Press the Sauté button on the Instant Pot® and heat oil. Fry chicken thighs for 2 minutes on each side until browned. 2. Add paprika, salt, cinnamon, ginger, nutmeg, raisins, almonds, orange juice, lemon juice, lime juice, and carrots. Press the Cancel button. 3. Close lid, set steam release to Sealing, press the Manual button, and set time to 10 minutes. When the timer beeps, let pressure release naturally for 5 minutes. Quick-release any remaining pressure until the float valve drops and then open lid. Check chicken using a meat thermometer to make sure the internal temperature is at least 165°F (74°C). 4. Use a slotted spoon to remove chicken, carrots, and raisins, and transfer to a serving platter. Press the Cancel button. 5. In a small bowl, whisk together water and arrowroot to create a slurry. Add to liquid in the Instant Pot® and stir to combine. Press the Sauté button, press the Adjust button to change the temperature to Less, and simmer uncovered for 3 minutes until sauce is thickened. Pour sauce over chicken and serve.

Per Serving:

calories: 332 | fat: 14g | protein: 36g | carbs: 14g | fiber: 3g | sodium: 337mg

Lemon Chicken

Prep time: 5 minutes | Cook time: 20 to 25 minutes | Serves 4

8 bone-in chicken thighs, skin on
1 tablespoon olive oil
1½ teaspoons lemon-pepper seasoning
½ teaspoon paprika
½ teaspoon garlic powder
¼ teaspoon freshly ground black pepper
Juice of ½ lemon

1. Preheat the air fryer to 360°F (182°C). 2. Place the chicken in a large bowl and drizzle with the olive oil. Top with the lemon-pepper seasoning, paprika, garlic powder, and freshly ground black pepper. Toss until thoroughly coated. 3. Working in batches if necessary, arrange the chicken in a single layer in the basket of the air fryer. Pausing halfway through the cooking time to turn the chicken, air fry for 20 to 25 minutes, until a thermometer inserted into the thickest piece registers 165°F (74°C). 4. Transfer the chicken to a serving platter and squeeze the lemon juice over the top.

Per Serving:

calories: 399 | fat: 19g | protein: 56g | carbs: 1g | fiber: 0g | sodium: 367mg

Chicken and Potato Tagine

Prep time: 20 minutes | Cook time: 55 minutes | Serves 6

1 chicken, cut up into 8 pieces
1 medium onion, thinly sliced
3 cloves garlic, minced
¼ cup olive oil
½ teaspoon ground cumin
½ teaspoon freshly ground pepper
¼ teaspoon ginger
Pinch saffron threads
1 teaspoon paprika
Sea salt, to taste
2 cups water
3 cups potatoes, peeled and diced
½ cup flat-leaf parsley, chopped
½ cup fresh cilantro, chopped
1 cup fresh or frozen green peas

1. Place the chicken, onion, garlic, olive oil, and seasonings into a Dutch oven. Add about 2 cups water and bring to a boil over medium-high heat. Reduce heat and cover. Simmer for 30 minutes. 2. Add the potatoes, parsley, and cilantro, and simmer an additional 20 minutes, or until the potatoes are almost tender. 3. Add the peas at the last moment, simmering for an additional 5 minutes. Serve hot.

Per Serving:

calories: 345 | fat: 14g | protein: 36g | carbs: 19g | fiber: 3g | sodium: 155mg

Chicken Breasts Stuffed with Feta and Spinach

Prep time: 10 minutes | Cook time: 14 minutes | Serves 4

1 cup chopped frozen spinach, thawed and drained well
½ cup crumbled feta cheese
4 (6-ounce / 170-g) boneless, skinless chicken breasts
¼ teaspoon salt
¼ teaspoon ground black pepper
2 tablespoons light olive oil, divided
1 cup water

1. In a small bowl, combine spinach and feta. Slice a pocket into each chicken breast along one side. Stuff one-quarter of the spinach and feta mixture into the pocket of each breast. Season chicken on all sides with salt and pepper. Set aside. 2. Press the Sauté button on the Instant Pot® and add 1 tablespoon oil. Add two chicken breasts and brown on both sides, about 3 minutes per side. Transfer to a plate and repeat with remaining 1 tablespoon oil and chicken. 3. Add water to pot and place rack inside. Place chicken breasts on rack. Close lid, set steam release to Sealing, press the Manual button, and set time to 8 minutes. 4. When the timer beeps, quick-release the pressure until the float valve drops. Press the Cancel button and open lid. Transfer chicken to a serving platter. Serve hot.

Per Serving:

calories: 304 | fat: 17g | protein: 40g | carbs: 2g | fiber: 1g | sodium: 772mg

Chicken Korma

Prep time: 20 minutes | Cook time: 3 to 4 hours | Serves 6

Marinade:
1 tablespoon coriander seeds, ground
1 teaspoon salt
6 whole black peppercorns
1-inch piece fresh ginger, roughly chopped
3 garlic cloves, roughly chopped
12 boneless chicken thighs, skinned and chopped into chunks
1 cup Greek yogurt
1 heaped teaspoon gram flour
1 teaspoon turmeric
Korma:
1 tablespoon ghee or vegetable oil
3 cloves

3 green cardamom pods
1-inch piece cassia bark
1 to 3 dried red chiles
2 onions, minced
⅓ cup creamed coconut
2 heaped tablespoons ground almonds
1 teaspoon ground white poppy seeds
Pinch of saffron
2 tablespoons milk
1 teaspoon garam masala
Handful fresh coriander leaves, finely chopped
1 tablespoon chopped toasted almonds
Squeeze of lemon juice

Make the Marinade: 1. Place the coriander seeds, salt, and peppercorns into a mortar and pestle and crush, or grind them in a spice grinder. Then add the roughly chopped ginger and garlic, and pound (or grind) to create an aromatic paste. 2. Place the chicken in a large bowl and add the yogurt, gram flour, turmeric, and spice paste. Stir thoroughly, cover, and leave to marinate for an hour, or longer if possible, in the refrigerator. Make the Korma: 3. Heat the slow cooker to high and add the oil. Add the cloves, cardamom pods, cassia bark, and the dried red chiles, and toast until fragrant, about 1 minute. 4. Add the minced onions, and then add the marinated chicken. Cover and cook for 2 hours on low, or for 1 hour on high. 5. Pour in the creamed coconut, ground almonds, and poppy seeds, then stir. Cover and cook on low for 2 more hours. 6. Crumble the saffron into a small bowl, add the milk, and leave to steep for 20 minutes. 7. Once cooked through and the sauce has thickened, pour in the saffron milk for added decadence, if using. Then add the garam masala. Garnish with the fresh coriander leaves and chopped almonds. You can also add a squeeze of lemon juice for added freshness, then serve.

Per Serving:
calories: 568 | fat: 23g | protein: 79g | carbs: 9g | fiber: 2g | sodium: 779mg

Chicken and Broccoli Casserole

Prep time: 5 minutes | Cook time: 20 to 25 minutes | Serves 4

½ pound (227 g) broccoli, chopped into florets
2 cups shredded cooked chicken
4 ounces (113 g) cream cheese
⅓ cup heavy cream
1½ teaspoons Dijon mustard

½ teaspoon garlic powder
Salt and freshly ground black pepper, to taste
2 tablespoons chopped fresh basil
1 cup shredded Cheddar cheese

1. Preheat the air fryer to 390ºF (199ºC). Lightly coat a casserole dish that will fit in air fryer, with olive oil and set aside. 2. Place the broccoli in a large glass bowl with 1 tablespoon of water and cover with a microwavable plate. Microwave on high for 2 to 3 minutes until the broccoli is bright green but not mushy. Drain if necessary and add to another large bowl along with the shredded chicken. 3. In the same glass bowl used to microwave the broccoli, combine the cream cheese and cream. Microwave for 30 seconds to 1 minute on high and stir until smooth. Add the mustard and garlic powder and season to taste with salt and freshly ground black pepper. Whisk until the sauce is smooth. 4. Pour the warm sauce over the broccoli and chicken mixture and then add the basil. Using a silicone spatula, gently fold the mixture until thoroughly combined. 5. Transfer the chicken mixture to the prepared casserole dish and top with the cheese. Air fry for 20 to 25 minutes until warmed through and the cheese has browned.

Per Serving:
calories: 503 | fat: 39g | protein: 32g | carbs: 7g | fiber: 2g | sodium: 391mg

Chapter 7 Fish and Seafood

Salmon with Cauliflower

Prep time: 10 minutes | Cook time: 25 minutes |
Serves 4

1 pound (454 g) salmon fillet, diced
1 cup cauliflower, shredded
1 tablespoon dried cilantro
1 tablespoon coconut oil, melted
1 teaspoon ground turmeric
¼ cup coconut cream

1. Mix salmon with cauliflower, dried cilantro, ground turmeric, coconut cream, and coconut oil. 2. Transfer the salmon mixture into the air fryer and cook the meal at 350ºF (177ºC) for 25 minutes. Stir the meal every 5 minutes to avoid the burning.

Per Serving:

calories: 232 | fat: 14g | protein: 24g | carbs: 3g | fiber: 1g | sodium: 94mg

Italian Fish

Prep time: 10 minutes | Cook time: 3 minutes |
Serves 4

1 (14½-ounce / 411-g) can diced tomatoes
¼ teaspoon dried minced onion
¼ teaspoon onion powder
¼ teaspoon dried minced garlic
¼ teaspoon garlic powder
¼ teaspoon dried basil
¼ teaspoon dried parsley
⅛ teaspoon dried oregano
¼ teaspoon sugar
⅛ teaspoon dried lemon granules, crushed
⅛ teaspoon chili powder
⅛ teaspoon dried red pepper flakes
1 tablespoon grated Parmesan cheese
4 (4-ounce / 113-g) cod fillets, rinsed and patted dry

1. Add tomatoes, minced onion, onion powder, minced garlic, garlic powder, basil, parsley, oregano, sugar, lemon granules, chili powder, red pepper flakes, and cheese to the Instant Pot® and stir to mix. Arrange the fillets over the tomato mixture, folding thin tail ends under to give the fillets even thickness. Spoon some of the tomato mixture over the fillets. 2. Close lid, set steam release to Sealing, press the Manual button, and set time to 3 minutes. When the timer beeps, quick-release the pressure until the float valve drops and open lid. Serve immediately.

Per Serving:

calories: 116 | fat: 3g | protein: 20g | carbs: 5g | fiber: 2g | sodium: 400mg

Citrus-Marinated Scallops

Prep time: 10 minutes | Cook time: 10 minutes |
Serves 4

Juice and zest of 2 lemons
¼ cup extra-virgin olive oil
Unrefined sea salt or salt, to taste
Freshly ground black pepper, to
taste
1 clove garlic, minced
1½ pounds (680 g) dry scallops, side muscle removed

1. In a large shallow bowl or baking dish, combine the lemon juice and zest, olive oil, salt, pepper, and garlic. Mix well to combine. Add the scallops to the marinade; cover and refrigerate 1 hour. 2. Heat a large skillet over medium-high heat. Drain the scallops and place them in skillet. Cook 4 to 5 minutes per side, until cooked through.

Per Serving:

calories: 243 | fat: 14g | protein: 21g | carbs: 7g | fiber: 0g | sodium: 567mg

Roasted Branzino with Lemon and Herbs

Prep time: 10 minutes | Cook time: 20 minutes |
Serves 2

1 to 1½ pounds (454 to 680 g) branzino, scaled and gutted
Salt
Freshly ground black pepper
1 tablespoon olive oil
1 lemon, sliced
3 garlic cloves, minced
¼ cup chopped fresh herbs (any mixture of oregano, thyme, parsley, and rosemary)

1. Preheat the oven to 425ºF (220ºC) and set the rack to the middle position. 2. Lay the cleaned fish in a baking dish and make 4 to 5 slits in it, about 1½ inches apart. 3. Season the inside of the branzino with salt and pepper and drizzle with olive oil. 4. Fill the cavity of the fish with lemon slices. Sprinkle the chopped garlic and herbs over the lemon and close the fish. 5. Roast the fish for 15 to 20 minutes, or until the flesh is opaque and it flakes apart easily. 6. Before eating, open the fish, remove the lemon slices, and carefully pull out the bone.

Per Serving:

calories: 287 | fat: 12g | protein: 42g | carbs: 2g | fiber: 0g | sodium: 151mg

Grilled Salmon

Prep time: 5 minutes | Cook time: 10 minutes | Serves 4

1 teaspoon garlic powder	½ teaspoon salt
1 teaspoon onion powder	4 (5- to 6-ounce / 142- to 170-g) salmon fillets with skin on
1 teaspoon freshly ground black pepper	½ cup lemon juice

1. In a small bowl, mix together the garlic powder, onion powder, black pepper, and salt. 2. Put the salmon in a large dish; pour the lemon juice over the salmon. 3. Season the salmon with the seasoning mix. 4. Preheat a grill, grill pan, or lightly oiled skillet to high heat. Place the salmon on the grill or skillet, skin-side down first. 5. Cook each side for 4 minutes. Serve immediately.

Per Serving:

calories: 238 | fat: 13g | protein: 29g | carbs: 4g | fiber: 0g | sodium: 360mg

Pesto Shrimp with Wild Rice Pilaf

Prep time: 5 minutes | Cook time: 5 minutes | Serves 4

1 pound (454 g) medium shrimp, peeled and deveined	1 lemon, sliced
¼ cup pesto sauce	2 cups cooked wild rice pilaf

1. Preheat the air fryer to 360°F(182°C). 2. In a medium bowl, toss the shrimp with the pesto sauce until well coated. 3. Place the shrimp in a single layer in the air fryer basket. Put the lemon slices over the shrimp and roast for 5 minutes. 4. Remove the lemons and discard. Serve a quarter of the shrimp over ½ cup wild rice with some favorite steamed vegetables.

Per Serving:

calories: 265 | fat: 9g | protein: 28g | carbs: 19g | fiber: 2g | sodium: 277mg

Friday Night Fish Fry

Prep time: 10 minutes | Cook time: 10 minutes | Serves 4

1 large egg	pepper
½ cup powdered Parmesan cheese (about 1½ ounces / 43 g)	4 (4-ounce / 113-g) cod fillets
1 teaspoon smoked paprika	Chopped fresh oregano or parsley, for garnish (optional)
¼ teaspoon celery salt	Lemon slices, for serving (optional)
¼ teaspoon ground black	

1. Spray the air fryer basket with avocado oil. Preheat the air fryer to 400°F (204°C). 2. Crack the egg in a shallow bowl and beat it lightly with a fork. Combine the Parmesan cheese, paprika, celery salt, and pepper in a separate shallow bowl. 3. One at a time, dip the fillets into the egg, then dredge them in the Parmesan mixture.

Using your hands, press the Parmesan onto the fillets to form a nice crust. As you finish, place the fish in the air fryer basket. 4. Air fry the fish in the air fryer for 10 minutes, or until it is cooked through and flakes easily with a fork. Garnish with fresh oregano or parsley and serve with lemon slices, if desired. 5. Store leftovers in an airtight container in the refrigerator for up to 3 days. Reheat in a preheated 400°F (204°C) air fryer for 5 minutes, or until warmed through.

Per Serving:

calories: 165 | fat: 6g | protein: 25g | carbs: 2g | fiber: 0g | sodium: 392mg

Salmon with Provolone Cheese

Prep time: 5 minutes | Cook time: 15 minutes | Serves 4

1 pound (454 g) salmon fillet, chopped	grated
2 ounces (57 g) Provolone,	1 teaspoon avocado oil
	¼ teaspoon ground paprika

1. Sprinkle the salmon fillets with avocado oil and put in the air fryer. 2. Then sprinkle the fish with ground paprika and top with Provolone cheese. 3. Cook the fish at 360°F (182°C) for 15 minutes.

Per Serving:

calories: 204 | fat: 10g | protein: 27g | carbs: 0g | fiber: 0g | sodium: 209mg

Lemon Pesto Salmon

Prep time: 5 minutes | Cook time: 10 minutes | Serves 2

10 ounces (283 g) salmon fillet (1 large piece or 2 smaller ones)	2 tablespoons prepared pesto sauce
Salt	1 large fresh lemon, sliced
Freshly ground black pepper	

1. Oil the grill grate and heat the grill to medium-high heat. Alternatively, you can roast the salmon in a 350°F (180°C) oven. 2. Prepare the salmon by seasoning with salt and freshly ground black pepper, and then spread the pesto sauce on top. 3. Make a bed of fresh lemon slices about the same size as your fillet on the hot grill (or on a baking sheet if roasting), and rest the salmon on top of the lemon slices. Place any additional lemon slices on top of the salmon. 4. Grill the salmon for 6 to 10 minutes, or until it's opaque and flakes apart easily. If roasting, it will take about 20 minutes. There is no need to flip the fish over.

Per Serving:

calories: 315 | fat: 21g | protein: 29g | carbs: 1g | fiber: 0g | sodium: 176mg

Nut-Crusted Baked Fish

Prep time: 10 minutes | Cook time: 20 minutes |

Serves 4

½ cup extra-virgin olive oil, divided
1 pound (454 g) flaky white fish (such as cod, haddock, or halibut), skin removed
½ cup shelled finely chopped pistachios
½ cup ground flaxseed

Zest and juice of 1 lemon, divided
1 teaspoon ground cumin
1 teaspoon ground allspice
½ teaspoon salt (use 1 teaspoon if pistachios are unsalted)
¼ teaspoon freshly ground black pepper

1. Preheat the oven to 400°F(205°C). 2. Line a baking sheet with parchment paper or aluminum foil and drizzle 2 tablespoons olive oil over the sheet, spreading to evenly coat the bottom. 3. Cut the fish into 4 equal pieces and place on the prepared baking sheet. 4. In a small bowl, combine the pistachios, flaxseed, lemon zest, cumin, allspice, salt, and pepper. Drizzle in ¼ cup olive oil and stir well. 5. Divide the nut mixture evenly atop the fish pieces. Drizzle the lemon juice and remaining 2 tablespoons oil over the fish and bake until cooked through, 15 to 20 minutes, depending on the thickness of the fish.

Per Serving:

calories: 499 | fat: 41g | protein: 26g | carbs: 41g | fiber: 6g | sodium: 358mg

Italian Tuna Roast

Prep time: 15 minutes | Cook time: 21 to 24 minutes

| Serves 8

Cooking spray
1 tablespoon Italian seasoning
⅛ teaspoon ground black pepper
1 tablespoon extra-light olive

oil
1 teaspoon lemon juice
1 tuna loin (approximately 2 pounds / 907 g, 3 to 4 inches thick)

1. Spray baking dish with cooking spray and place in air fryer basket. Preheat the air fryer to 390ºF (199ºC). 2. Mix together the Italian seasoning, pepper, oil, and lemon juice. 3. Using a dull table knife or butter knife, pierce top of tuna about every half inch: Insert knife into top of tuna roast and pierce almost all the way to the bottom. 4. Spoon oil mixture into each of the holes and use the knife to push seasonings into the tuna as deeply as possible. 5. Spread any remaining oil mixture on all outer surfaces of tuna. 6. Place tuna roast in baking dish and roast at 390ºF (199ºC) for 20 minutes. Check temperature with a meat thermometer. Cook for an additional 1 to 4 minutes or until temperature reaches 145ºF (63ºC). 7. Remove basket from the air fryer and let tuna sit in the basket for 10 minutes.

Per Serving:

calories: 178 | fat: 7g | protein: 26g | carbs: 0g | fiber: 0g | sodium: 44mg

Swordfish in Tarragon-Citrus Butter

Prep time: 5 minutes | Cook time: 20 minutes |

Serves 4

1 pound (454 g) swordfish steaks, cut into 2-inch pieces
1 teaspoon salt
¼ teaspoon freshly ground black pepper
¼ cup extra-virgin olive oil, plus 2 tablespoons, divided
2 tablespoons unsalted butter

Zest and juice of 2 clementines
Zest and juice of 1 lemon
2 tablespoons chopped fresh tarragon
Sautéed greens, riced cauliflower, or zucchini noodles, for serving

1. In a bowl, toss the swordfish with salt and pepper. 2. In a large skillet, heat ¼ cup olive oil over medium-high heat. Add the swordfish chunks to the hot oil and sear on all sides, 2 to 3 minutes per side, until they are lightly golden brown. Using a slotted spoon, remove the fish from the pan and keep warm. 3. Add the remaining 2 tablespoons olive oil and butter to the oil already in the pan and return the heat to medium-low. Once the butter has melted, whisk in the clementine and lemon zests and juices, along with the tarragon. Season with salt. Return the fish pieces to the pan and toss to coat in the butter sauce. Serve the fish drizzled with sauce over sautéed greens, riced cauliflower, or zucchini noodles.

Per Serving:

calories: 330 | fat: 26g | protein: 23g | carbs: 1g | fiber: 0g | sodium: 585mg

Baked Monkfish

Prep time: 20 minutes | Cook time: 12 minutes |

Serves 2

2 teaspoons olive oil
1 cup celery, sliced
2 bell peppers, sliced
1 teaspoon dried thyme
½ teaspoon dried marjoram
½ teaspoon dried rosemary
2 monkfish fillets

1 tablespoon coconut aminos
2 tablespoons lime juice
Coarse salt and ground black pepper, to taste
1 teaspoon cayenne pepper
½ cup Kalamata olives, pitted and sliced

1. In a nonstick skillet, heat the olive oil for 1 minute. Once hot, sauté the celery and peppers until tender, about 4 minutes. Sprinkle with thyme, marjoram, and rosemary and set aside. 2. Toss the fish fillets with the coconut aminos, lime juice, salt, black pepper, and cayenne pepper. Place the fish fillets in the lightly greased air fryer basket and bake at 390ºF (199ºC) for 8 minutes. 3. Turn them over, add the olives, and cook an additional 4 minutes. Serve with the sautéed vegetables on the side. Bon appétit!

Per Serving:

calories: 263 | fat: 11g | protein: 27g | carbs: 13g | fiber: 5g | sodium: 332mg

Shrimp with Marinara Sauce

Prep time: 15 minutes | Cook time: 6 to 7 hours |
Serves 4

1 (15-ounce / 425-g) can diced tomatoes, with the juice
1 (6-ounce / 170-g) can tomato paste
1 clove garlic, minced
2 tablespoons minced fresh flat-leaf parsley
½ teaspoon dried basil
1 teaspoon dried oregano

1 teaspoon garlic powder
1½ teaspoons sea salt
¼ teaspoon black pepper
1 pound (454 g) cooked shrimp, peeled and deveined
2 cups hot cooked spaghetti or linguine, for serving
½ cup grated parmesan cheese, for serving

1. Combine the tomatoes, tomato paste, and minced garlic in the slow cooker. Sprinkle with the parsley, basil, oregano, garlic powder, salt, and pepper. 2. Cover and cook on low for 6 to 7 hours. 3. Turn up the heat to high, stir in the cooked shrimp, and cover and cook on high for about 15 minutes longer. 4. Serve hot over the cooked pasta. Top with Parmesan cheese.

Per Serving:

calories: 313 | fat: 5g | protein: 39g | carbs: 32g | fiber: 7g | sodium: 876mg

Bouillabaisse

Prep time: 30 minutes | Cook time: 50 minutes |
Serves 8

½ cup olive oil
2 onions, diced
4 tomatoes, peeled and chopped
5 cloves garlic, minced
3 pints low-salt fish stock
8 small red potatoes, cubed and cooked
1 cup white wine
1 bunch basil leaves, finely chopped
1 tablespoon Tabasco or other hot sauce

1 teaspoon dried thyme
½ teaspoon saffron
10 clams, scrubbed
10 mussels, scrubbed
1 pound (454 g) shrimp, peeled, deveined, and tails removed
1 pound (454 g) fresh monkfish fillets, cut into chunks
1 pound (454 g) fresh cod, cut into chunks
½ cup flat-leaf parsley, chopped

1. Heat the olive oil in a large stockpot over medium-high heat. 2. Add the onions and cook for 5 minutes, or until the onions are soft and translucent. 3. Add the tomatoes and garlic, and simmer 5 minutes more. 4. Add the fish stock, potatoes, wine, basil, hot sauce, thyme, and saffron, and simmer for 20 minutes. 5. Purée half of this mixture in the blender, then return to stockpot. 6. Add the shellfish, shrimp, fish, and parsley, and simmer 20 minutes. Serve with brown rice.

Per Serving:

calories: 458 | fat: 16g | protein: 39g | carbs: 35g | fiber: 4g | sodium: 344mg

Cod with Tomatoes and Garlic

Prep time: 10 minutes | Cook time: 20 minutes |
Serves 4

1 pound (454 g) cod or your favorite white-fleshed fish
Sea salt
Freshly ground black pepper
2 tablespoons olive oil
2 garlic cloves, minced

1 (15-ounce / 425-g) can diced tomatoes, with their juices
¼ cup white wine
¼ cup chopped fresh Italian parsley

1. Pat the fish dry with paper towels and season with salt and pepper. 2. In a large skillet, heat the olive oil over medium heat. Add the cod and cook for 3 to 5 minutes on each side, or until cooked through. Transfer the fish to a plate, cover loosely with aluminum foil, and set aside. 3. Add the garlic to the skillet and sauté until fragrant, about 3 minutes. Add the tomatoes and wine and increase the heat to medium-high. Cook the tomato mixture for about 4 minutes. Season with salt and pepper. 4. Return the fish to the skillet and spoon the tomato mixture over it. Serve garnished with the parsley.

Per Serving:

calories: 170 | fat: 7g | protein: 18g | carbs: 5g | fiber: 2g | sodium: 507mg

Fish Chili

Prep time: 10 minutes | Cook time: 5 to 7 hours |
Serves 6

1 (28-ounce / 794-g) can no-salt-added diced tomatoes
1 (15-ounce / 425-g) can reduced sodium white beans, drained and rinsed
1 (10-ounce / 283-g) can no-salt-added diced tomatoes with green chiles
1 (8-ounce / 227-g) can no-salt-added tomato sauce
3 garlic cloves, minced

1 small onion, diced
1 bell pepper, any color, seeded and diced
2 tablespoons chili powder
2 teaspoons ground cumin
1½ teaspoons paprika
1 teaspoon sea salt
1 teaspoon dried oregano
2 pounds (907 g) fresh or frozen fish fillets of your choice, cut into 2-inch pieces

1. In a slow cooker, combine the tomatoes, beans, tomatoes with green chiles, tomato sauce, garlic, onion, bell pepper, chili powder, cumin, paprika, salt, and oregano. Stir to mix well. 2. Cover the cooker and cook for 5 to 7 hours on Low heat. 3. Stir in the fish, replace the cover on the cooker, and cook for 30 minutes on Low heat.

Per Serving:

calories: 292 | fat: 2g | protein: 41g | carbs: 27g | fiber: 9g | sodium: 611mg

Steamed Cod with Garlic and Swiss Chard

Prep time: 5 minutes | Cook time: 12 minutes | Serves 4

1 teaspoon salt
½ teaspoon dried oregano
½ teaspoon dried thyme
½ teaspoon garlic powder
4 cod fillets

½ white onion, thinly sliced
2 cups Swiss chard, washed, stemmed, and torn into pieces
¼ cup olive oil
1 lemon, quartered

1. Preheat the air fryer to 380°F(193ºC). 2. In a small bowl, whisk together the salt, oregano, thyme, and garlic powder. 3. Tear off four pieces of aluminum foil, with each sheet being large enough to envelop one cod fillet and a quarter of the vegetables. 4. Place a cod fillet in the middle of each sheet of foil, then sprinkle on all sides with the spice mixture. 5. In each foil packet, place a quarter of the onion slices and ½ cup Swiss chard, then drizzle 1 tablespoon olive oil and squeeze ¼ lemon over the contents of each foil packet. 6. Fold and seal the sides of the foil packets and then place them into the air fryer basket. Steam for 12 minutes. 7. Remove from the basket, and carefully open each packet to avoid a steam burn.

Per Serving:
calories: 324 | fat: 15g | protein: 42g | carbs: 4g | fiber: 1g | sodium: 746mg

Olive Oil–Poached Fish over Citrus Salad

Prep time: 10 minutes | Cook time: 25 minutes | Serves 4

Fish
4 skinless white fish fillets (1¼ to 1½ pounds / 567 to 680 g total), such as halibut, sole, or cod, ¾'–1' thick
¼ teaspoon kosher salt
¼ teaspoon ground black pepper
5–7 cups olive oil
1 lemon, thinly sliced
Salad
¼ cup white wine vinegar
1 Earl Grey tea bag
2 blood oranges or tangerines

1 ruby red grapefruit or pomelo
6 kumquats, thinly sliced, or 2 clementines, peeled and sectioned
4 cups baby arugula
½ cup pomegranate seeds
¼ cup extra-virgin olive oil
2 teaspoons minced shallot
½ teaspoon kosher salt
¼ teaspoon ground black pepper
¼ cup mint leaves, coarsely chopped

1. Make the fish: Season the fish with the salt and pepper and set aside for 30 minutes. 2. Preheat the oven to 225°F. 3. In a large high-sided ovenproof skillet or roasting pan over medium heat, warm 1' to 1½' of the oil and the lemon slices until the temperature reaches 120°F (use a candy thermometer). Add the fish fillets to the oil, without overlapping, making sure they're completely submerged. 4. Transfer the skillet or pan to the oven, uncovered. Bake for 25 minutes. Transfer the fish to a rack to drain for 5 minutes. 5. Make the salad: In a small saucepan, heat the vinegar until almost boiling. Add the tea bag and set aside to steep for 10 minutes. 6. Meanwhile, with a paring knife, cut off enough of the top and bottom of 1 of the oranges or tangerines to reveal the flesh. Cut along the inside of the peel, between the pith and the flesh, taking off as much pith as possible. Over a large bowl, hold the orange in 1 hand. With the paring knife, cut along the membranes between each section, allowing the fruit to fall into the bowl. Once all the fruit segments have been released, squeeze the remaining membranes over a small bowl. Repeat with the second orange and the grapefruit or pomelo. 7. In the large bowl with the segmented fruit, add the kumquats or clementines, arugula, and pomegranate seeds. Gently toss to distribute. 8. Remove the tea bag from the vinegar and squeeze out as much liquid as possible. Discard the bag and add the vinegar to the small bowl with the citrus juice. Slowly whisk in the oil, shallot, salt, and pepper. Drizzle 3 to 4 tablespoons over the salad and gently toss. (Store the remaining vinaigrette in the refrigerator for up to 1 week.) 9. Sprinkle the salad with the mint and serve with the fish.

Per Serving:
calories: 280 | fat: 7g | protein: 29g | carbs: 25g | fiber: 6g | sodium: 249mg

Parchment-Baked Halibut with Fennel and Carrots

Prep time: 10 minutes | Cook time: 25 minutes | Serves 4

1 bulb fennel, cored, thinly sliced, and fronds reserved
1 bunch young carrots, quartered and tops removed
1 small shallot, sliced
4 skinless halibut fillets (6 ounces / 170 geach)

½ teaspoon kosher salt
¼ teaspoon ground black pepper
4 slices orange
8 sprigs thyme
4 leaves fresh sage, sliced
½ cup white wine

1. Preheat the oven to 425°F(220ºC). Tear 4 squares of parchment paper, about 15' × 15'. 2. In the middle of a piece of parchment, set ¼ of the fennel, carrots, and shallot, topped by 1 piece of fish. Sprinkle with ⅛ teaspoon of the salt and a pinch of the pepper. Lay 1 slice of the orange, 2 sprigs of the thyme, ¼ of the sage, and a bit of fennel frond on top. Drizzle 2 tablespoons of the wine around the fish. 3. Bring up the opposite sides of the parchment and fold them together, like you're folding the top of a paper bag, to seal all the edges. Set the packet on a baking sheet, and repeat with the remaining ingredients. 4. Bake until the packets are slightly browned and puffed, about 13 minutes. Allow to rest for 2 to 3 minutes. Set individual packets on plates and with kitchen shears or a small knife, carefully cut open at the table. (Caution: The escaping steam will be hot.)

Per Serving:
calories: 253 | fat: 3g | protein: 34g | carbs: 18g | fiber: 5g | sodium: 455mg

Tuna Steaks with Olive Tapenade

Prep time: 10 minutes | Cook time: 10 minutes | Serves 4

4 (6-ounce / 170-g) ahi tuna steaks
1 tablespoon olive oil
Salt and freshly ground black pepper, to taste
½ lemon, sliced into 4 wedges
Olive Tapenade:
½ cup pitted kalamata olives
1 tablespoon olive oil
1 tablespoon chopped fresh parsley
1 clove garlic
2 teaspoons red wine vinegar
1 teaspoon capers, drained

1. Preheat the air fryer to 400°F (204°C). 2. Drizzle the tuna steaks with the olive oil and sprinkle with salt and black pepper. Arrange the tuna steaks in a single layer in the air fryer basket. Pausing to turn the steaks halfway through the cooking time, air fry for 10 minutes until the fish is firm. 3. To make the tapenade: In a food processor fitted with a metal blade, combine the olives, olive oil, parsley, garlic, vinegar, and capers. Pulse until the mixture is finely chopped, pausing to scrape down the sides of the bowl if necessary. Spoon the tapenade over the top of the tuna steaks and serve with lemon wedges.

Per Serving:

calories: 269 | fat: 9g | protein: 42g | carbs: 2g | fiber: 1g | sodium: 252mg

Quick Seafood Paella

Prep time: 20 minutes | Cook time: 20 minutes | Serves 4

¼ cup plus 1 tablespoon extra-virgin olive oil
1 large onion, finely chopped
2 tomatoes, peeled and chopped
1½ tablespoons garlic powder
1½ cups medium-grain Spanish paella rice or arborio rice
2 carrots, finely diced
Salt
1 tablespoon sweet paprika
8 ounces (227 g) lobster meat or canned crab
½ cup frozen peas
3 cups chicken stock, plus more if needed
1 cup dry white wine
6 jumbo shrimp, unpeeled
⅓ pound calamari rings
1 lemon, halved

1. In a large sauté pan or skillet (16-inch is ideal), heat the oil over medium heat until small bubbles start to escape from oil. Add the onion and cook for about 3 minutes, until fragrant, then add tomatoes and garlic powder. Cook for 5 to 10 minutes, until the tomatoes are reduced by half and the consistency is sticky. 2. Stir in the rice, carrots, salt, paprika, lobster, and peas and mix well. In a pot or microwave-safe bowl, heat the chicken stock to almost boiling, then add it to the rice mixture. Bring to a simmer, then add the wine. 3. Smooth out the rice in the bottom of the pan. Cover and cook on low for 10 minutes, mixing occasionally, to prevent burning. 4. Top the rice with the shrimp, cover, and cook for 5 more minutes. Add additional broth to the pan if the rice looks dried out. 5. Right before removing the skillet from the heat, add the calamari rings. Toss the ingredients frequently. In about 2 minutes, the rings will look opaque. Remove the pan from the heat immediately—you don't want the paella to overcook). Squeeze fresh lemon juice over the dish.

Per Serving:

calories: 613 | fat: 15g | protein: 26g | carbs: 86g | fiber: 7g | sodium: 667mg

Pecan-Crusted Catfish

Prep time: 5 minutes | Cook time: 12 minutes | Serves 4

½ cup pecan meal
1 teaspoon fine sea salt
¼ teaspoon ground black pepper
4 (4-ounce / 113-g) catfish
fillets
For Garnish (Optional):
Fresh oregano
Pecan halves

1. Spray the air fryer basket with avocado oil. Preheat the air fryer to 375°F (191°C). 2. In a large bowl, mix the pecan meal, salt, and pepper. One at a time, dredge the catfish fillets in the mixture, coating them well. Use your hands to press the pecan meal into the fillets. Spray the fish with avocado oil and place them in the air fryer basket. 3. Air fry the coated catfish for 12 minutes, or until it flakes easily and is no longer translucent in the center, flipping halfway through. 4. Garnish with oregano sprigs and pecan halves, if desired. 5. Store leftovers in an airtight container in the fridge for up to 3 days. Reheat in a preheated 350°F (177°C) air fryer for 4 minutes, or until heated through.

Per Serving:

calories: 165 | fat: 3g | protein: 20g | carbs: 12g | fiber: 1g | sodium: 485mg

Oven-Poached Cod

Prep time: 5 minutes | Cook time: 30 minutes | Serves 4

4 (6-ounce / 170-g) cod filets
½ teaspoon salt
½ teaspoon freshly ground black pepper
½ cup dry white wine
½ cup seafood or vegetable
stock
2 garlic cloves, minced
1 bay leaf
1 teaspoon chopped fresh sage
4 rosemary sprigs for garnish

1. Preheat the oven to 375°F (190°C). 2. Season each filet with salt and pepper and place in a large ovenproof skillet or baking pan. Add the wine, stock, garlic, bay leaf, and sage and cover. Bake until the fish flakes easily with a fork, about 20 minutes. 3. Use a spatula to remove the filet from the skillet. Place the poaching liquid over high heat and cook, stirring frequently, until reduced by half, about 10 minutes. (Do this in a small saucepan if you used a baking pan.) 4. To serve, place a filet on each plate and drizzle with the reduced poaching liquid. Garnish each with a fresh rosemary sprig.

Per Serving:

calories: 168 | fat: 1g | protein: 39g | carbs: 2g | fiber: 0g | sodium: 500mg

One-Pot Shrimp Fried Rice

Prep time: 10 minutes | Cook time: 25 minutes |

Serves 4

Shrimp:
1 teaspoon cornstarch
½ teaspoon kosher salt
¼ teaspoon black pepper
1 pound (454 g) jumbo raw shrimp (21 to 25 count), peeled and deveined
Rice:
2 cups cold cooked rice
1 cup frozen peas and carrots, thawed

¼ cup chopped green onions (white and green parts)
3 tablespoons toasted sesame oil
1 tablespoon soy sauce
½ teaspoon kosher salt
1 teaspoon black pepper
Eggs:
2 large eggs, beaten
¼ teaspoon kosher salt
¼ teaspoon black pepper

1. For the shrimp: In a small bowl, whisk together the cornstarch, salt, and pepper until well combined. Place the shrimp in a large bowl and sprinkle the seasoned cornstarch over. Toss until well coated; set aside. 2. For the rice: In a baking pan, combine the rice, peas and carrots, green onions, sesame oil, soy sauce, salt, and pepper. Toss and stir until well combined. 3. Place the pan in the air fryer basket. Set the air fryer to 350ºF (177ºC) for 15 minutes, stirring and tossing the rice halfway through the cooking time. 4. Place the shrimp on top of the rice. Set the air fryer to 350ºF (177ºC) for 5 minutes. 5. Meanwhile, for the eggs: In a medium bowl, beat the eggs with the salt and pepper. 6. Open the air fryer and pour the eggs over the shrimp and rice mixture. Set the air fryer to 350ºF (177ºC) for 5 minutes. 7. Remove the pan from the air fryer. Stir to break up the rice and mix in the eggs and shrimp.

Per Serving:

calories: 364 | fat: 15g | protein: 30g | carbs: 28g | fiber: 3g | sodium: 794mg

Mediterranean Grilled Shrimp

Prep time: 20 minutes | Cook time: 5 minutes |

Serves 4 to 6

2 tablespoons garlic, minced
½ cup lemon juice
3 tablespoons fresh Italian parsley, finely chopped

¼ cup extra-virgin olive oil
1 teaspoon salt
2 pounds (907 g) jumbo shrimp (21-25), peeled and deveined

1. In a large bowl, mix the garlic, lemon juice, parsley, olive oil, and salt. 2. Add the shrimp to the bowl and toss to make sure all the pieces are coated with the marinade. Let the shrimp sit for 15 minutes. 3. Preheat a grill, grill pan, or lightly oiled skillet to high heat. While heating, thread about 5 to 6 pieces of shrimp onto each skewer. 4. Place the skewers on the grill, grill pan, or skillet and cook for 2 to 3 minutes on each side until cooked through. Serve warm.

Per Serving:

calories: 217 | fat: 10g | protein: 31g | carbs: 2g | fiber: 0g | sodium: 569mg

Baked Spanish Salmon

Prep time: 10 minutes | Cook time: 20 minutes |

Serves 4

2 small red onions, thinly sliced
1 cup shaved fennel bulbs
1 cup cherry tomatoes
15 green pimiento-stuffed olives
Salt
Freshly ground black pepper
1 teaspoon cumin seeds

½ teaspoon smoked paprika
4 (8-ounce / 227-g) salmon fillets
½ cup low-sodium chicken broth
2 to 4 tablespoons extra-virgin olive oil
2 cups cooked couscous

1. Put the oven racks in the middle of the oven and preheat the oven to 375ºF. 2. On 2 baking sheets, spread out the onions, fennel, tomatoes, and olives. Season them with salt, pepper, cumin, and paprika. 3. Place the fish over the vegetables, season with salt, and gently pour the broth over the 2 baking sheets. Drizzle a light stream of olive oil over baking sheets before popping them in the oven. 4. Bake the vegetables and fish for 20 minutes, checking halfway to ensure nothing is burning. Serve over couscous.

Per Serving:

calories: 476 | fat: 18g | protein: 50g | carbs: 26g | fiber: 3g | sodium: 299mg

Moroccan Braised Halibut with Cinnamon and Capers

Prep time: 5 minutes | Cook time: 20 minutes |

Serves 4

¼ cup olive oil
¾ teaspoon ground cumin
1 (15-ounce / 425-g) can diced tomatoes, drained
1½ tablespoons drained capers
½ teaspoon cinnamon

½ teaspoon salt, divided
½ teaspoon freshly ground black pepper, divided
4 halibut fillets, about 6 ounces (170 g) each and 1-inch-thick

1. Heat the olive oil in a large skillet over medium heat. Add the cumin and cook, stirring, for 1 minute. Add the tomatoes, capers, cinnamon, ¼ teaspoon of salt, and ¼ teaspoon of pepper and cook for about 10 minutes, until the mixture is thickened. 2. Dry the fish well with paper towels and then season all over with the remaining ¼ teaspoon of salt and ¼ teaspoon of pepper. Add the fish to the sauce in the pan, cover, and simmer for 8 to 10 minutes, until the fish is cooked through. Serve immediately.

Per Serving:

calories: 309 | fat: 14g | protein: 40g | carbs: 5g | fiber: 2g | sodium: 525mg

Baked Salmon with Tomatoes and Olives

Prep time: 5 minutes | Cook time: 8 minutes | Serves 4

2 tablespoons olive oil
4 (1½-inch-thick) salmon fillets
½ teaspoon salt
¼ teaspoon cayenne

1 teaspoon chopped fresh dill
2 Roma tomatoes, diced
¼ cup sliced Kalamata olives
4 lemon slices

1. Preheat the air fryer to 380°F(193°C). 2. Brush the olive oil on both sides of the salmon fillets, and then season them lightly with salt, cayenne, and dill. 3. Place the fillets in a single layer in the basket of the air fryer, then layer the tomatoes and olives over the top. Top each fillet with a lemon slice. 4. Bake for 8 minutes, or until the salmon has reached an internal temperature of 145°F(63°C).

Per Serving:

calories: 483 | fat: 22g | protein: 66g | carbs: 3g | fiber: 1g | sodium: 593mg

Lemon Pepper Shrimp

Prep time: 15 minutes | Cook time: 8 minutes | Serves 2

Oil, for spraying
12 ounces (340 g) medium raw shrimp, peeled and deveined
3 tablespoons lemon juice

1 tablespoon olive oil
1 teaspoon lemon pepper
¼ teaspoon paprika
¼ teaspoon granulated garlic

1. Preheat the air fryer to 400°F (204°C). Line the air fryer basket with parchment and spray lightly with oil. 2. In a medium bowl, toss together the shrimp, lemon juice, olive oil, lemon pepper, paprika, and garlic until evenly coated. 3. Place the shrimp in the prepared basket. 4. Cook for 6 to 8 minutes, or until pink and firm. Serve immediately.

Per Serving:

calories: 211 | fat: 8g | protein: 34g | carbs: 2g | fiber: 0g | sodium: 203mg

Poached Salmon

Prep time: 10 minutes | Cook time: 5 minutes | Serves 4

1 lemon, sliced ¼ inch thick
4 (6-ounce / 170-g) skinless salmon fillets, 1½ inches thick

½ teaspoon table salt
¼ teaspoon pepper

1. Add ½ cup water to Instant Pot. Fold sheet of aluminum foil into 16 by 6-inch sling. Arrange lemon slices widthwise in 2 rows across center of sling. Sprinkle flesh side of salmon with salt and pepper, then arrange skinned side down on top of lemon slices. 2. Using sling, lower salmon into Instant Pot; allow narrow edges

of sling to rest along sides of insert. Lock lid in place and close pressure release valve. Select high pressure cook function and cook for 3 minutes. 3. Turn off Instant Pot and quick-release pressure. Carefully remove lid, allowing steam to escape away from you. Using sling, transfer salmon to large plate. Gently lift and tilt fillets with spatula to remove lemon slices. Serve.

Per Serving:

calories: 350 | fat: 23g | protein: 35g | carbs: 0g | fiber: 0g | sodium: 390mg

White Wine–Sautéed Mussels

Prep time: 10 minutes | Cook time: 10 minutes | Serves 4

3 pounds (1.4 kg) live mussels, cleaned
4 tablespoons (½ stick) salted butter

2 shallots, finely chopped
2 tablespoons garlic, minced
2 cups dry white wine

1. Scrub the mussel shells to make sure they are clean; trim off any that have a beard (hanging string). Put the mussels in a large bowl of water, discarding any that are not tightly closed. 2. In a large pot over medium heat, cook the butter, shallots, and garlic for 2 minutes. 3. Add the wine to the pot, and cook for 1 minute. 4. Add the mussels to the pot, toss with the sauce, and cover with a lid. Let cook for 7 minutes. Discard any mussels that have not opened. 5. Serve in bowls with the wine broth.

Per Serving:

calories: 468 | fat: 15g | protein: 41g | carbs: 21g | fiber: 0g | sodium: 879mg

Spicy Steamed Chili Crab

Prep time: 10 minutes | Cook time: 3 minutes | Serves 2

2 tablespoons garlic chili sauce
1 tablespoon hoisin sauce
1 tablespoon minced fresh ginger
1 teaspoon fish sauce
2 cloves garlic, peeled and

minced
2 small bird's eye chilies, minced
2 (2-pound / 907-g) Dungeness crabs
1 cup water

1. In a medium bowl, combine garlic chili sauce, hoisin sauce, ginger, fish sauce, garlic, and chilies. Mix well. Coat crabs in chili mixture. 2. Add water to the Instant Pot® and insert steamer basket. Add crabs to basket. Close lid, set steam release to Sealing, press the Manual button, and set time to 3 minutes. 3. When the timer beeps, quick-release the pressure until the float valve drops. Press the Cancel button and open lid. Transfer crabs to a serving platter. Serve hot.

Per Serving:

calories: 128 | fat: 1g | protein: 25g | carbs: 1g | fiber: 0g | sodium: 619mg

Southern Italian Seafood Stew in Tomato Broth

Prep time: 15 minutes | Cook time: 1 hour 20 minutes | Serves 6

½ cup olive oil
1 fennel bulb, cored and finely chopped
2 stalks celery, finely chopped
1 medium onion, finely chopped
1 tablespoon dried oregano
½ teaspoon crushed red pepper flakes
1½ pounds (680 g) cleaned squid, bodies cut into ½-inch rings, tentacles halved
2 cups dry white wine
1 (28-ounce / 794-g) can tomato
purée
1 bay leaf
1 teaspoon salt
½ teaspoon freshly ground black pepper
1 cup bottled clam juice
1 pound (454 g) whole head-on prawns
1½ pounds (680 g) mussels, scrubbed
1 lemon, cut into wedges, for serving

1. In a large Dutch oven, heat the olive oil over medium-high heat. Add the fennel, celery, onion, oregano, and red pepper flakes and reduce the heat to medium. Cook, stirring occasionally, for about 15 minutes, until the vegetables soften. Stir in the squid, reduce the heat to low, and simmer for 15 minutes. 2. Add the wine to the pot, raise the heat to medium-high, and bring to a boil. Cook, stirring occasionally, until the wine has evaporated. Reduce the heat again to low and add the tomato purée, bay leaf, salt, and pepper. Cook gently, stirring every once in a while, for about 40 minutes, until the mixture becomes very thick. 3. Stir in 2 cups of water and the clam juice, raise the heat again to medium-high, and bring to a boil. 4. Add the shrimp and mussels and cook, covered, for 5 minutes or so, until the shells of the mussels have opened and the prawns are pink and cooked through. 5. To serve, ladle the seafood and broth into bowls and garnish with the lemon wedges. Serve hot.

Per Serving:

calories: 490 | fat: 23g | protein: 48g | carbs: 22g | fiber: 5g | sodium: 899mg

Shrimp and Fish Chowder

Prep time: 20 minutes | Cook time: 4 to 6 hours | Serves 4

3 cups low-sodium vegetable broth
1 (28-ounce / 794-g) can no-salt-added crushed tomatoes
1 large bell pepper, any color, seeded and diced
1 large onion, diced
2 zucchini, chopped
3 garlic cloves, minced
1 teaspoon dried thyme
1 teaspoon dried basil
½ teaspoon sea salt
¼ teaspoon freshly ground black pepper
¼ teaspoon red pepper flakes
8 ounces (227 g) whole raw medium shrimp, peeled and deveined
8 ounces (227 g) fresh cod fillets, cut into 1-inch pieces

1. In a slow cooker, combine the vegetable broth, tomatoes, bell pepper, onion, zucchini, garlic, thyme, basil, salt, black pepper, and red pepper flakes. Stir to mix well. 2. Cover the cooker and cook for 4 to 6 hours on Low heat. 3. Stir in the shrimp and cod. Replace the cover on the cooker and cook for 15 to 30 minutes on Low heat, or until the shrimp have turned pink and the cod is firm and flaky.

Per Serving:

calories: 201 | fat: 1g | protein: 26g | carbs: 24g | fiber: 7g | sodium: 598mg

Steamed Clams

Prep time: 10 minutes | Cook time: 8 minutes | Serves 4

2 pounds (907 g) fresh clams, rinsed
1 tablespoon olive oil
1 small white onion, peeled and diced
1 clove garlic, peeled and quartered
½ cup Chardonnay
½ cup water

1. Place clams in the Instant Pot® steamer basket. Set aside. 2. Press the Sauté button and heat oil. Add onion and cook until tender, about 3 minutes. Add garlic and cook about 30 seconds. Pour in Chardonnay and water. Insert steamer basket with clams. Press the Cancel button. 3. Close lid, set steam release to Sealing, press the Manual button, and set time to 4 minutes. When the timer beeps, quick-release the pressure until the float valve drops. Open lid. 4. Transfer clams to four bowls and top with a generous scoop of cooking liquid.

Per Serving:

calories: 205 | fat: 6g | protein: 30g | carbs: 7g | fiber: 0g | sodium: 135mg

Marinated Swordfish Skewers

Prep time: 30 minutes | Cook time: 6 to 8 minutes | Serves 4

1 pound (454 g) filleted swordfish
¼ cup avocado oil
2 tablespoons freshly squeezed lemon juice
1 tablespoon minced fresh
parsley
2 teaspoons Dijon mustard
Sea salt and freshly ground black pepper, to taste
3 ounces (85 g) cherry tomatoes

1. Cut the fish into 1½-inch chunks, picking out any remaining bones. 2. In a large bowl, whisk together the oil, lemon juice, parsley, and Dijon mustard. Season to taste with salt and pepper. Add the fish and toss to coat the pieces. Cover and marinate the fish chunks in the refrigerator for 30 minutes. 3. Remove the fish from the marinade. Thread the fish and cherry tomatoes on 4 skewers, alternating as you go. 4. Set the air fryer to 400ºF (204ºC). Place the skewers in the air fryer basket and air fry for 3 minutes. Flip the skewers and cook for 3 to 5 minutes longer, until the fish is cooked through and an instant-read thermometer reads 140ºF (60ºC).

Per Serving:

calories: 291 | fat: 21g | protein: 23g | carbs: 2g | fiber: 0g | sodium: 121mg

Chopped Tuna Salad

Prep time: 15 minutes | Cook time: 0 minutes | Serves 4

2 tablespoons extra-virgin olive oil
2 tablespoons lemon juice
2 teaspoons Dijon mustard
½ teaspoon kosher salt
¼ teaspoon freshly ground black pepper
12 olives, pitted and chopped
½ cup celery, diced

½ cup red onion, diced
½ cup red bell pepper, diced
½ cup fresh parsley, chopped
2 (6-ounce / 170-g) cans no-salt-added tuna packed in water, drained
6 cups baby spinach

1. In a medium bowl, whisk together the olive oil, lemon juice, mustard, salt, and black pepper. Add in the olives, celery, onion, bell pepper, and parsley and mix well. Add the tuna and gently incorporate. 2. Divide the spinach evenly among 4 plates or bowls. Spoon the tuna salad evenly on top of the spinach.

Per Serving:

calories: 220 | fat: 11g | protein: 25g | carbs: 7g | fiber: 2g | sodium: 396mg

Grilled Halibut Steaks with Romesco Sauce

Prep time: 20 minutes | Cook time: 10 minutes | Serves 2

For the Romesco Sauce:
½ cup jarred roasted piquillo peppers
2 tablespoons sun-dried tomatoes in olive oil with herbs
2 small garlic cloves
¼ cup raw, unsalted almonds
2 tablespoons red wine vinegar
Pinch salt
¼ teaspoon smoked paprika (or more to taste)

¼ cup olive oil
1 to 2 tablespoons water
For the Halibut:
2 (5-ounce / 142-g) halibut steaks
1 tablespoon olive oil
Salt
Freshly ground black pepper

Make the Romesco Sauce: 1. Combine the piquillo peppers, sun-dried tomatoes, garlic, almonds, vinegar, salt, and paprika in a food processor or a blender and blend until mostly smooth. While the mixture is blending, drizzle in the olive oil. 2. Taste and adjust seasonings. If you prefer a smoother sauce, add water, 1 tablespoon at a time, until sauce reaches your desired consistency. Make the Salmon: 1. Heat the grill to medium-high and oil the grill grates. 2. Brush the fish with olive oil, and season with salt and pepper. 3. When the grill is hot, grill the fish for about 5 minutes per side, or until it's opaque and flakes easily. Serve topped with a few tablespoons of the romesco sauce. 4. Store any remaining sauce in an airtight container in the refrigerator for up to a week.

Per Serving:

calories: 264 | fat: 13g | protein: 31g | carbs: 3g | fiber: 1g | sodium: 109mg

Chili Tilapia

Prep time: 5 minutes | Cook time: 20 minutes | Serves 4

4 tilapia fillets, boneless
1 teaspoon chili flakes
1 teaspoon dried oregano

1 tablespoon avocado oil
1 teaspoon mustard

1. Rub the tilapia fillets with chili flakes, dried oregano, avocado oil, and mustard and put in the air fryer. 2. Cook it for 10 minutes per side at 360ºF (182ºC).

Per Serving:

calories: 146 | fat: 6g | protein: 23g | carbs: 1g | fiber: 0g | sodium: 94mg

Chapter 8 Snacks and Appetizers

Taco-Spiced Chickpeas

Prep time: 5 minutes | Cook time: 17 minutes | Serves 3

Oil, for spraying
1 (15½-ounce / 439-g) can chickpeas, drained
1 teaspoon chili powder
½ teaspoon ground cumin
½ teaspoon salt
½ teaspoon granulated garlic
2 teaspoons lime juice

1. Line the air fryer basket with parchment and spray lightly with oil. Place the chickpeas in the prepared basket. 2. Air fry at 390ºF (199ºC) for 17 minutes, shaking or stirring the chickpeas and spraying lightly with oil every 5 to 7 minutes. 3. In a small bowl, mix together the chili powder, cumin, salt, and garlic. 4. When 2 to 3 minutes of cooking time remain, sprinkle half of the seasoning mix over the chickpeas. Finish cooking. 5. Transfer the chickpeas to a medium bowl and toss with the remaining seasoning mix and the lime juice. Serve immediately.

Per Serving:

calories: 208 | fat: 4g | protein: 11g | carbs: 34g | fiber: 10g | sodium: 725mg

Baked Eggplant Baba Ganoush

Prep time: 10 minutes | Cook time: 1 hour | Makes about 4 cups

2 pounds (907 g, about 2 medium to large) eggplant
3 tablespoons tahini
Zest of 1 lemon
2 tablespoons lemon juice
¾ teaspoon kosher salt
½ teaspoon ground sumac, plus more for sprinkling (optional)
⅓ cup fresh parsley, chopped
1 tablespoon extra-virgin olive oil

1. Preheat the oven to 350ºF (180ºC). Place the eggplants directly on the rack and bake for 60 minutes, or until the skin is wrinkly. 2. In a food processor add the tahini, lemon zest, lemon juice, salt, and sumac. Carefully cut open the baked eggplant and scoop the flesh into the food processor. Process until the ingredients are well blended. 3. Place in a serving dish and mix in the parsley. Drizzle with the olive oil and sprinkle with sumac, if desired.

Per Serving:

calories: 50 | fat: 16g | protein: 4g | carbs: 2g | fiber: 1g | sodium: 110mg

Crispy Chili Chickpeas

Prep time: 5 minutes | Cook time: 15 minutes | Serves 4

1 (15-ounce / 425-g) can cooked chickpeas, drained and rinsed
1 tablespoon olive oil
¼ teaspoon salt
⅛ teaspoon chili powder
⅛ teaspoon garlic powder
⅛ teaspoon paprika

1. Preheat the air fryer to 380ºF(193ºC). 2. In a medium bowl, toss all of the ingredients together until the chickpeas are well coated. 3. Pour the chickpeas into the air fryer and spread them out in a single layer. 4. Roast for 15 minutes, stirring once halfway through the cook time.

Per Serving:

calories: 177 | fat: 6g | protein: 8g | carbs: 24g | fiber: 7g | sodium: 374mg

Pesto Cucumber Boats

Prep time: 10 minutes | Cook time: 0 minutes | Serves 4 to 6

3 medium cucumbers
¼ teaspoon salt
1 packed cup fresh basil leaves
1 garlic clove, minced
¼ cup walnut pieces
¼ cup grated Parmesan cheese
¼ cup extra-virgin olive oil
½ teaspoon paprika

1. Cut each cucumber in half lengthwise and again in half crosswise to make 4 stocky pieces. Use a spoon to remove the seeds and hollow out a shallow trough in each piece. Lightly salt each piece and set aside on a platter. 2. In a blender or food processor, combine the basil, garlic, walnuts, Parmesan cheese, and olive oil and blend until smooth. 3. Use a spoon to spread pesto into each cucumber "boat" and sprinkle each with paprika. Serve.

Per Serving:

calories: 143 | fat: 14g | protein: 3g | carbs: 4g | fiber: 1g | sodium: 175mg

Halloumi, Watermelon, Tomato Kebabs with Basil Oil Drizzle

Prep time: 20 minutes | Cook time: 10 minutes |
Serves 8

¼ cup coarsely chopped fresh basil
3 tablespoons extra-virgin olive oil
1 small clove garlic, chopped
¼ teaspoon kosher salt
¼ teaspoon ground black pepper

32 cubes watermelon (from 1 melon)
32 cherry tomatoes (about 1½ pints)
1 package (8 to 10 ounces / 227 to 283 g) Halloumi cheese, cut into 32 cubes

1. Soak 16 skewers in water. 2. In a blender or food processor, combine the basil, oil, garlic, salt, and pepper. Blend until the basil is finely chopped and the mixture is well combined. 3. Alternately thread the watermelon, tomatoes, and cheese onto the skewers. Brush with half the basil oil. Coat a grill rack or grill pan with olive oil and prepare the grill to medium-high heat. 4. Grill the kebabs, covered, until good grill marks form on the cheese, about 8 minutes, turning once. 5. Set kebabs on a platter and drizzle with the remaining basil oil.

Per Serving:

calories: 178 | fat: 15g | protein: 7g | carbs: 6g | fiber: 1g | sodium: 365mg

Fig-Pecan Energy Bites

Prep time: 20 minutes |Cook time: 0 minutes|
Serves: 6

¾ cup diced dried figs (6 to 8)
½ cup chopped pecans
¼ cup rolled oats (old-fashioned or quick oats)
2 tablespoons ground flaxseed

or wheat germ (flaxseed for gluten-free)
2 tablespoons powdered or regular peanut butter
2 tablespoons honey

1. In a medium bowl, mix together the figs, pecans, oats, flaxseed, and peanut butter. Drizzle with the honey, and mix everything together. A wooden spoon works well to press the figs and nuts into the honey and powdery ingredients. (If you're using regular peanut butter instead of powdered, the dough will be stickier to handle, so freeze the dough for 5 minutes before making the bites.) 2. Divide the dough evenly into four sections in the bowl. Dampen your hands with water—but don't get them too wet or the dough will stick to them. Using your hands, roll three bites out of each of the four sections of dough, making 12 total energy bites. 3. Enjoy immediately or chill in the freezer for 5 minutes to firm up the bites before serving. The bites can be stored in a sealed container in the refrigerator for up to 1 week.

Per Serving:

calories: 196 | fat: 10g | protein: 4g | carbs: 26g | fiber: 4g | sodium: 13mg

Bravas-Style Potatoes

Prep time: 15 minutes | Cook time: 50 minutes |
Serves 8

4 large russet potatoes (about 2½ pounds / 1.1 kg), scrubbed and cut into 1' cubes
1 teaspoon kosher salt, divided
½ teaspoon ground black pepper
¼ teaspoon red-pepper flakes

½ small yellow onion, chopped
1 large tomato, chopped
1 tablespoon sherry vinegar
1 teaspoon hot paprika
1 tablespoon chopped fresh flat-leaf parsley Hot sauce (optional)

1. Preheat the oven to 450°F(235°C). Bring a large pot of well-salted water to a boil. 2. Boil the potatoes until just barely tender, 5 to 8 minutes. Drain and transfer the potatoes to a large rimmed baking sheet. Add 1 tablespoon of the oil, ½ teaspoon of the salt, the black pepper, and pepper flakes. With 2 large spoons, toss very well to coat the potatoes in the oil. Spread the potatoes out on the baking sheet. Roast until the bottoms are starting to brown and crisp, 20 minutes. Carefully flip the potatoes and roast until the other side is golden and crisp, 15 to 20 minutes. 3. Meanwhile, in a small skillet over medium heat, warm the remaining 1 teaspoon oil. Cook the onion until softened, 3 to 4 minutes. Add the tomato and cook until it's broken down and saucy, 5 minutes. Stir in the vinegar, paprika, and the remaining ½ teaspoon salt. Cook for 30 seconds, remove from the heat, and cover to keep warm. 4. Transfer the potatoes to a large serving bowl. Drizzle the tomato mixture over the potatoes. Sprinkle with the parsley. Serve with hot sauce, if using.

Per Serving:

calories: 173 | fat: 2g | protein: 4g | carbs: 35g | fiber: 3g | sodium: 251mg

Red Pepper Tapenade

Prep time: 5 minutes | Cook time: 5 minutes | Serves 4

1 large red bell pepper
2 tablespoons plus 1 teaspoon olive oil, divided
½ cup Kalamata olives, pitted

and roughly chopped
1 garlic clove, minced
½ teaspoon dried oregano
1 tablespoon lemon juice

1. Preheat the air fryer to 380°F(193°C). 2. Brush the outside of a whole red pepper with 1 teaspoon olive oil and place it inside the air fryer basket. Roast for 5 minutes. 3. Meanwhile, in a medium bowl combine the remaining 2 tablespoons of olive oil with the olives, garlic, oregano, and lemon juice. 4. Remove the red pepper from the air fryer, then gently slice off the stem and remove the seeds. Roughly chop the roasted pepper into small pieces. 5. Add the red pepper to the olive mixture and stir all together until combined. 6. Serve with pita chips, crackers, or crusty bread.

Per Serving:

calories: 94 | fat: 9g | protein: 1g | carbs: 4g | fiber: 2g | sodium: 125mg

Whole Wheat Pitas

Prep time: 5 minutes | Cook time: 30 minutes |

Makes 8 pitas

2 cups whole wheat flour
1¼ cups all-purpose flour
1¼ teaspoons table salt
1¼ cup warm water (105°–

110°F)
1 (¼-ounce / 7-g) package
active dry yeast (2½ teaspoons)
1 teaspoon olive oil

1. In the bowl of an electric stand mixer (or a large bowl), whisk together the flours and salt. In a small bowl or glass measuring cup, whisk together the water and yeast until the yeast is dissolved. Let sit until foamy, about 5 minutes. Add the yeast mixture to the flour mixture. Fit the mixer with the dough hook and mix on low (or stir) until it forms a shaggy dough. 2. Increase the speed to medium and knead until the dough is smooth and elastic, 2 to 3 minutes. If kneading by hand, turn the dough out onto a lightly floured work surface and knead about 10 minutes. 3. Form the dough into a ball and return it to the bowl. Pour in the oil, turning the dough to coat. Cover the bowl with a kitchen towel and let the dough rise until doubled in size, about 1 hour. 4. Preheat the oven to 475°F(245°C). Place a baking sheet on the lowest rack of the oven. 5. When the dough has risen, take it out of the bowl and give it a few gentle kneads. Divide the dough into 8 equal portions and shape into balls. Place on a lightly floured surface and cover with the kitchen towel. 6. Roll out each dough ball to form a 6" circle. Place on the heated baking sheet. Bake until puffed up and beginning to turn color, 6 to 7 minutes. Remove with a metal spatula or tongs and place in a bread basket or on a serving platter. Repeat with the remaining dough balls. 7. To make a pocket in the pita, allow it to cool. Slice off ¼ of the pita from 1 edge, and then carefully insert the knife into the pita to cut the pocket. Gently pull the sides apart to make the pocket larger.

Per Serving:

calories: 181 | fat: 2g | protein: 6g | carbs: 37g | fiber: 4g | sodium: 366mg

Red Lentils with Sumac

Prep time: 5 minutes | Cook time: 20 minutes |

Serves 6 to 8

1 cup red lentils, picked through and rinsed
1 teaspoon ground sumac

½ teaspoon salt
Pita chips, warm pita bread, or raw vegetables, for serving

1. In a medium saucepan, combine the lentils, sumac, and 2 cups water. Bring the water to a boil. Reduce the heat to maintain a simmer and cook for 15 minutes, or until the lentils are softened and most of the water has been absorbed. Stir in the salt and cook until the lentils have absorbed all the water, about 5 minutes more. 2. Serve with pita chips, warm pita bread, or as a dip for raw vegetables.

Per Serving:

1 cup: calories: 162 | fat: 1g | protein: 11g | carbs: 30g | fiber: 9g | sodium: 219mg

Stuffed Dates with Feta, Parmesan, and Pine Nuts

Prep time: 5 minutes | Cook time: 10 minutes |

Serves 4

1 ounce (28 g) feta
1 ounce (28 g) Parmesan cheese
12 dried dates, pitted

½ tablespoon raw pine nuts
1 teaspoon extra virgin olive oil

1. Preheat the oven to 425°F (220ºC). Line a small baking pan with parchment paper. 2. Cut the feta and Parmesan into 12 small thin sticks, each about ¾ inch long and ¼ inch thick. 3. Use a sharp knife to cut a small slit lengthwise into each date. Insert a piece of the Parmesan followed by a piece of the feta, and then press 2–3 pine nuts slightly into the feta. 4. Transfer the dates to the prepared baking pan and place in the oven to roast for 10 minutes. (The edges of the dates should begin to brown.) 5. Remove the dates from the oven and drizzle a few drops of the olive oil over each date. Serve promptly. (These do not store well and are best enjoyed fresh.)

Per Serving:

calories: 126 | fat: 5g | protein: 4g | carbs: 17g | fiber: 2g | sodium: 194mg

Black-Eyed Pea "Caviar"

Prep time: 10 minutes | Cook time: 30 minutes |

Makes 5 cups

1 cup dried black-eyed peas
4 cups water
1 pound (454 g) cooked corn kernels
½ medium red onion, peeled and diced
½ medium green bell pepper, seeded and diced
2 tablespoons minced pickled jalapeño pepper

1 medium tomato, diced
2 tablespoons chopped fresh cilantro
¼ cup red wine vinegar
2 tablespoons extra-virgin olive oil
1 teaspoon salt
½ teaspoon ground black pepper
½ teaspoon ground cumin

1. Add black-eyed peas and water to the Instant Pot®. Close lid, set steam release to Sealing, press the Manual button, and set time to 30 minutes. 2. When the timer beeps, let pressure release naturally, about 25 minutes, and open lid. Drain peas and transfer to a large mixing bowl. Add all remaining ingredients and stir until thoroughly combined. Cover and refrigerate for 2 hours before serving.

Per Serving:

½ cup: calories: 28 | fat: 1g | protein: 1g | carbs: 4 | fiber: 1g | sodium: 51mg

Sweet Potato Fries

Prep time: 15 minutes | Cook time: 40 minutes | Serves 4

4 large sweet potatoes, peeled and cut into finger-like strips
2 tablespoons extra-virgin olive oil
½ teaspoon salt
½ teaspoon freshly ground black pepper

1. Preheat the oven to 350°F(180°C). Line a baking sheet with aluminum foil. Toss the potatoes in a large bowl with the olive oil, salt, and pepper. 2. Arrange the potatoes in a single layer on the baking sheet and bake until brown at the edges, about 40 minutes. Serve piping hot.

Per Serving:

calories: 171 | fat: 7g | protein: 2g | carbs: 26g | fiber: 4g | sodium: 362mg

Loaded Vegetable Pita Pizzas with Tahini Sauce

Prep time: 5 minutes | Cook time: 12 minutes | Serves 2

2 (6-inch) pita breads
4 canned artichoke hearts, chopped
¼ cup chopped tomato (any variety)
¼ cup chopped onion (any variety)
4 Kalamata olives, pitted and sliced
4 green olives, pitted and sliced
2 teaspoons pine nuts
2 teaspoons extra virgin olive oil
Pinch of kosher salt
Juice of 1 lemon
Tahini Sauce:
2 tablespoons tahini
2 tablespoons fresh lemon juice
1 tablespoon water
1 garlic clove, minced
Pinch of freshly ground black pepper

1. Preheat the oven to 400°F (205°C) and line a large baking sheet with wax paper. 2. Make the tahini sauce by combining the tahini and lemon juice in a small bowl. While stirring rapidly, begin adding the water, garlic, and black pepper. Continue stirring rapidly until the ingredients are well combined and smooth. 3. Place the pita breads on the prepared baking sheet. Spread about 1 tablespoon of the tahini sauce over the top of each pita and then top each pita with the chopped artichoke hearts, 2 tablespoons of the tomatoes, 2 tablespoons of the onions, half of the sliced Kalamata olives, half of the green olives, and 1 teaspoon of the pine nuts. 4. Transfer the pizzas to the oven and bake for 12 minutes or until the edges of the pita breads turn golden and crunchy. 5. Drizzle 1 teaspoon of the olive oil over each pizza, then sprinkle a pinch of kosher salt over the top followed by a squeeze of lemon. Cut the pizzas into quarters. Store covered in the refrigerator for up to 2 days.

Per Serving:

calories: 381 | fat: 17g | protein: 15g | carbs: 52g | fiber: 19g | sodium: 553mg

White Bean Harissa Dip

Prep time: 10 minutes | Cook time: 1 hour | Makes 1½ cups

1 whole head of garlic
½ cup olive oil, divided
1 (15-ounce / 425-g) can cannellini beans, drained and
rinsed
1 teaspoon salt
1 teaspoon harissa paste (or more to taste)

1. Preheat the oven to 350°F(180°C). 2. Cut about ½ inch off the top of a whole head of garlic and lightly wrap it in foil. Drizzle 1 to 2 teaspoons of olive oil over the top of the cut side. Place it in an oven-safe dish and roast it in the oven for about 1 hour or until the cloves are soft and tender. 3. Remove the garlic from the oven and let it cool. The garlic can be roasted up to 2 days ahead of time. 4. Remove the garlic cloves from their skin and place them in the bowl of a food processor along with the beans, salt, and harissa. Purée, drizzling in as much olive oil as needed until the beans are smooth. If the dip seems too stiff, add additional olive oil to loosen the dip. 5. Taste the dip and add additional salt, harissa, or oil as needed. 6. Store in the refrigerator for up to a week. 7. Portion out ¼ cup of dip and serve with a mixture of raw vegetables and mini pita breads.

Per Serving:

¼ cup: calories: 209 | fat: 17g | protein: 4g | carbs: 12g | fiber: 3g | sodium: 389mg

Asian Five-Spice Wings

Prep time: 30 minutes | Cook time: 13 to 15 minutes | Serves 4

2 pounds (907 g) chicken wings
½ cup Asian-style salad dressing
2 tablespoons Chinese five-spice powder

1. Cut off wing tips and discard or freeze for stock. Cut remaining wing pieces in two at the joint. 2. Place wing pieces in a large sealable plastic bag. Pour in the Asian dressing, seal bag, and massage the marinade into the wings until well coated. Refrigerate for at least an hour. 3. Remove wings from bag, drain off excess marinade, and place wings in air fryer basket. 4. Air fry at 360°F (182°C) for 13 to 15 minutes or until juices run clear. About halfway through cooking time, shake the basket or stir wings for more even cooking. 5. Transfer cooked wings to plate in a single layer. Sprinkle half of the Chinese five-spice powder on the wings, turn, and sprinkle other side with remaining seasoning.

Per Serving:

calories: 357 | fat: 12g | protein: 51g | carbs: 9g | fiber: 2g | sodium: 591mg

Steamed Artichokes with Herbs and Olive Oil

Prep time: 10 minutes | Cook time: 10 minutes | Serves 6

3 medium artichokes with stems cut off
1 medium lemon, halved
1 cup water
¼ cup lemon juice
⅓ cup extra-virgin olive oil
1 clove garlic, peeled and minced
¼ teaspoon salt
1 teaspoon chopped fresh oregano
1 teaspoon chopped fresh rosemary
1 teaspoon chopped fresh flat-leaf parsley
1 teaspoon fresh thyme leaves

1. Run artichokes under running water, making sure water runs between leaves to flush out any debris. Slice off top ⅓ of artichoke and pull away any tough outer leaves. Rub all cut surfaces with lemon. 2. Add water and lemon juice to the Instant Pot®, then add rack. Place artichokes upside down on rack. Close lid, set steam release to Sealing, press the Manual button, and set time to 10 minutes. When the timer beeps, let pressure release naturally, about 20 minutes. 3. Press the Cancel button and open lid. Remove artichokes, transfer to a cutting board, and slice in half. Place halves on a serving platter. 4. In a small bowl, combine oil, garlic, salt, oregano, rosemary, parsley, and thyme. Drizzle half of mixture over artichokes, then serve remaining mixture in a small bowl for dipping. Serve warm.

Per Serving:

calories: 137 | fat: 13g | protein: 2g | carbs: 7g | fiber: 4g | sodium: 158mg

Greens Chips with Curried Yogurt Sauce

Prep time: 10 minutes | Cook time: 5 to 6 minutes | Serves 4

1 cup low-fat Greek yogurt
1 tablespoon freshly squeezed lemon juice
1 tablespoon curry powder
½ bunch curly kale, stemmed, ribs removed and discarded,
leaves cut into 2- to 3-inch pieces
½ bunch chard, stemmed, ribs removed and discarded, leaves cut into 2- to 3-inch pieces
1½ teaspoons olive oil

1. In a small bowl, stir together the yogurt, lemon juice, and curry powder. Set aside. 2. In a large bowl, toss the kale and chard with the olive oil, working the oil into the leaves with your hands. This helps break up the fibers in the leaves so the chips are tender. 3. Air fry the greens in batches at 390°F (199°C) for 5 to 6 minutes, until crisp, shaking the basket once during cooking. Serve with the yogurt sauce.

Per Serving:

calories: 98 | fat: 4g | protein: 7g | carbs: 13g | fiber: 4g | sodium: 186mg

Savory Mackerel & Goat'S Cheese "Paradox" Balls

Prep time: 10 minutes | Cook time: 0 minutes | Makes 10 fat bombs

2 smoked or cooked mackerel fillets, boneless, skin removed
4.4 ounces (125 g) soft goat's cheese
1 tablespoon fresh lemon juice
1 teaspoon Dijon or yellow
mustard
1 small red onion, finely diced
2 tablespoons chopped fresh chives or herbs of choice
¾ cup pecans, crushed
10 leaves baby gem lettuce

1. In a food processor, combine the mackerel, goat's cheese, lemon juice, and mustard. Pulse until smooth. Transfer to a bowl, add the onion and herbs, and mix with a spoon. Refrigerate for 20 to 30 minutes, or until set. 2. Using a large spoon or an ice cream scoop, divide the mixture into 10 balls, about 40 g/1.4 ounces each. Roll each ball in the crushed pecans. Place each ball on a small lettuce leaf and serve. Keep the fat bombs refrigerated in a sealed container for up to 5 days.

Per Serving:

1 fat bomb: calories: 165 | fat: 12g | protein: 12g | carbs: 2g | fiber: 1g | sodium: 102mg

Crispy Spiced Chickpeas

Prep time: 5 minutes | Cook time: 25 minutes | Serves 6

3 cans (15 ounces / 425 g each) chickpeas, drained and rinsed
1 cup olive oil
1 teaspoon paprika
½ teaspoon ground cumin
½ teaspoon kosher salt
¼ teaspoon ground cinnamon
¼ teaspoon ground black pepper

1. Spread the chickpeas on paper towels and pat dry. 2. In a large saucepan over medium-high heat, warm the oil until shimmering. Add 1 chickpea; if it sizzles right away, the oil is hot enough to proceed. 3. Add enough chickpeas to form a single layer in the saucepan. Cook, occasionally gently shaking the saucepan until golden brown, about 8 minutes. With a slotted spoon, transfer to a paper towel–lined plate to drain. Repeat with the remaining chickpeas until all the chickpeas are fried. Transfer to a large bowl. 4. In a small bowl, combine the paprika, cumin, salt, cinnamon, and pepper. Sprinkle all over the fried chickpeas and toss to coat. The chickpeas will crisp as they cool.

Per Serving:

calories: 175 | fat: 9g | protein: 6g | carbs: 20g | fiber: 5g | sodium: 509mg

Salted Almonds

Prep time: 5 minutes | Cook time: 25 minutes |
Makes 1 cup

1 cup raw almonds
1 egg white, beaten

½ teaspoon coarse sea salt

1. Preheat oven to 350ºF (180ºC). 2. Spread the almonds in an even layer on a baking sheet. Bake for 20 minutes until lightly browned and fragrant. 3. Coat the almonds with the egg white and sprinkle with the salt. Put back in the oven for about 5 minutes until they have dried. Cool completely before serving.

Per Serving:

calories: 211 | fat: 18g | protein: 8g | carbs: 8g | fiber: 5g | sodium: 305mg

Stuffed Figs with Goat Cheese and Honey

Prep time: 5 minutes | Cook time: 10 minutes |
Serves 4

8 fresh figs
2 ounces (57 g) goat cheese
¼ teaspoon ground cinnamon

1 tablespoon honey, plus more for serving
1 tablespoon olive oil

1. Preheat the air fryer to 360°F(182ºC). 2. Cut the stem off of each fig. 3. Cut an X into the top of each fig, cutting halfway down the fig. Leave the base intact. 4. In a small bowl, mix together the goat cheese, cinnamon, and honey. 5. Spoon the goat cheese mixture into the cavity of each fig. 6. Place the figs in a single layer in the air fryer basket. Drizzle the olive oil over top of the figs and roast for 10 minutes. 7. Serve with an additional drizzle of honey.

Per Serving:

calories: 152 | fat: 9g | protein: 5g | carbs: 16g | fiber: 2g | sodium: 62mg

Sfougato

Prep time: 10 minutes | Cook time: 8 minutes |
Serves 4

½ cup crumbled feta cheese
¼ cup bread crumbs
1 medium onion, peeled and minced
4 tablespoons all-purpose flour
2 tablespoons minced fresh mint

½ teaspoon salt
½ teaspoon ground black pepper
1 tablespoon dried thyme
6 large eggs, beaten
1 cup water

1. In a medium bowl, mix cheese, bread crumbs, onion, flour, mint, salt, pepper, and thyme. Stir in eggs. 2. Spray an 8" round baking dish with nonstick cooking spray. Pour egg mixture into dish. 3.

Place rack in the Instant Pot® and add water. Fold a long piece of foil in half lengthwise. Lay foil over rack to form a sling and top with dish. Cover loosely with foil. Close lid, set steam release to Sealing, press the Manual button, and set time to 8 minutes. 4. When the timer beeps, quick-release the pressure until the float valve drops. Open lid. Let stand 5 minutes, then remove dish from pot.

Per Serving:

calories: 226 | fat: 12g | protein: 14g | carbs: 15g | fiber: 1g | sodium: 621mg

Sea Salt Potato Chips

Prep time: 30 minutes | Cook time: 27 minutes |
Serves 4

Oil, for spraying
4 medium yellow potatoes

1 tablespoon oil
⅛ to ¼ teaspoon fine sea salt

1. Line the air fryer basket with parchment and spray lightly with oil. 2. Using a mandoline or a very sharp knife, cut the potatoes into very thin slices. 3. Place the slices in a bowl of cold water and let soak for about 20 minutes. 4. Drain the potatoes, transfer them to a plate lined with paper towels, and pat dry. 5. Drizzle the oil over the potatoes, sprinkle with the salt, and toss to combine. Transfer to the prepared basket. 6. Air fry at 200ºF (93ºC) for 20 minutes. Toss the chips, increase the heat to 400ºF (204ºC), and cook for another 5 to 7 minutes, until crispy.

Per Serving:

calories: 194 | fat: 4g | protein: 4g | carbs: 37g | fiber: 5g | sodium: 90mg

Spanish Home Fries with Spicy Tomato Sauce

Prep time: 5 minutes | Cook time: 1 hour | Serves 6

4 russet potatoes, peeled, cut into large dice
¼ cup olive oil plus 1 tablespoon, divided
½ cup crushed tomatoes
1½ teaspoons red wine

1 teaspoon hot smoked paprika
1 serrano chile, seeded and chopped
½ teaspoon salt
¼ teaspoon freshly ground black pepper

1. Preheat the oven to 425°F(220ºC). 2. Toss the potatoes with ¼ cup of olive oil and spread on a large baking sheet. Season with salt and pepper and roast in the preheated oven for about 50 to 60 minutes, turning once in the middle, until the potatoes are golden brown and crisp. 3. Meanwhile, make the sauce by combining the tomatoes, the remaining 1 tablespoon olive oil, wine, paprika, chile, salt, and pepper in a food processor or blender and process until smooth. 4. Serve the potatoes hot with the sauce on the side for dipping or spooned over the top.

Per Serving:

calories: 201 | fat: 11g | protein: 3g | carbs: 25g | fiber: 4g | sodium: 243mg

Kale Chips

Prep time: 5 minutes | Cook time: 30 minutes | Serves 2 to 4

2 large bunches kale, ribs removed
1 tablespoon extra-virgin olive

oil
1 teaspoon salt

1. Arrange the oven racks in the upper and middle positions. Preheat the oven to 250°F(120°C). Line 2 baking sheets with aluminum foil. 2. Rinse the kale and dry very well with a towel or salad spinner. Tear into large pieces. 3. Toss the kale with the olive oil and arrange in a single layer on the baking sheets. Sprinkle with salt. 4. Bake for 20 minutes and then use tongs to gently turn each leaf over. Bake until dry and crisp, another 10 to 15 minutes. Serve warm.

Per Serving:

calories: 141 | fat: 6g | protein: 10g | carbs: 20g | fiber: 8g | sodium: 668mg

Roasted Za'atar Chickpeas

Prep time: 5 minutes | Cook time: 1 hour | Serves 8

3 tablespoons za'atar
2 tablespoons extra-virgin olive oil
½ teaspoon kosher salt
¼ teaspoon freshly ground

black pepper
4 cups cooked chickpeas, or 2 (15-ounce / 425-g) cans, drained and rinsed

1. Preheat the oven to 400°F (205°C). Line a baking sheet with foil or parchment paper. 2. In a large bowl, combine the za'atar, olive oil, salt, and black pepper. Add the chickpeas and mix thoroughly. 3. Spread the chickpeas in a single layer on the prepared baking sheet. Bake for 45 to 60 minutes, or until golden brown and crispy. Cool and store in an airtight container at room temperature for up to 1 week.

Per Serving:

calories: 150 | fat: 6g | protein: 6g | carbs: 17g | fiber: 6g | sodium: 230mg

Roasted Rosemary Olives

Prep time: 5 minutes | Cook time: 25 minutes | Serves 4

1 cup mixed variety olives, pitted and rinsed
2 tablespoons lemon juice
1 tablespoon extra-virgin olive

oil
6 garlic cloves, peeled
4 rosemary sprigs

1. Preheat the oven to 400°F (205°C). Line the baking sheet with parchment paper or foil. 2. Combine the olives, lemon juice, olive oil, and garlic in a medium bowl and mix together. Spread in a single layer on the prepared baking sheet. Sprinkle on the rosemary. Roast for 25 minutes, tossing halfway through. 3. Remove the rosemary leaves from the stem and place in a serving bowl. Add the olives and mix before serving.

Per Serving:

calories: 100 | fat: 9g | protein: 0g | carbs: 4g | fiber: 0g | sodium: 260mg

Savory Mediterranean Popcorn

Prep time: 5 minutes | Cook time: 2 minutes | Serves 4 to 6

3 tablespoons extra-virgin olive oil
¼ teaspoon garlic powder
¼ teaspoon freshly ground black pepper

¼ teaspoon sea salt
⅛ teaspoon dried thyme
⅛ teaspoon dried oregano
12 cups plain popped popcorn

1. In a large sauté pan or skillet, heat the oil over medium heat, until shimmering, and then add the garlic powder, pepper, salt, thyme, and oregano until fragrant. 2. In a large bowl, drizzle the oil over the popcorn, toss, and serve.

Per Serving:

calories: 183 | fat: 12g | protein: 3g | carbs: 19g | fiber: 4g | sodium: 146mg

Roasted Chickpeas with Herbs and Spices

Prep time: 5 minutes | Cook time: 22 minutes | Serves 4

1 (15-ounce / 425-g) can chickpeas, drained and rinsed
1 tablespoon olive oil
1 teaspoon za'atar
½ teaspoon ground sumac

1 teaspoon Aleppo pepper
1 teaspoon brown sugar
½ teaspoon kosher salt
2 tablespoons chopped fresh parsley

1. Preheat the oven to 350°F (180°C). 2. Spread the chickpeas in an even layer on an ungreased rimmed baking sheet and bake for 10 minutes, or until they are dried. Remove from the oven; keep the oven on. 3. Meanwhile, in a medium bowl, whisk together the olive oil, za'atar, sumac, Aleppo pepper, brown sugar, and salt until well combined. 4. Add the warm chickpeas to the oil-spice mixture and stir until they are completely coated. Return the chickpeas to the baking sheet and spread them into an even layer. Bake for 10 to 12 minutes more, until fragrant. 5. Transfer the chickpeas to a serving bowl, toss with the parsley, and serve.

Per Serving:

1 cup: calories: 122 | fat: 5g | protein: 5g | carbs: 16g | fiber: 4g | sodium: 427mg

Shrimp Pirogues

Prep time: 15 minutes | Cook time: 4 to 5 minutes |

Serves 8

12 ounces (340 g) small, peeled, and deveined raw shrimp
3 ounces (85 g) cream cheese, room temperature
2 tablespoons plain yogurt
1 teaspoon lemon juice

1 teaspoon dried dill weed, crushed
Salt, to taste
4 small hothouse cucumbers, each approximately 6 inches long

1. Pour 4 tablespoons water in bottom of air fryer drawer. 2. Place shrimp in air fryer basket in single layer and air fry at 390°F (199°C) for 4 to 5 minutes, just until done. Watch carefully because shrimp cooks quickly, and overcooking makes it tough. 3. Chop shrimp into small pieces, no larger than ½ inch. Refrigerate while mixing the remaining ingredients. 4. With a fork, mash and whip the cream cheese until smooth. 5. Stir in the yogurt and beat until smooth. Stir in lemon juice, dill weed, and chopped shrimp. 6. Taste for seasoning. If needed, add ¼ to ½ teaspoon salt to suit your taste. 7. Store in refrigerator until serving time. 8. When ready to serve, wash and dry cucumbers and split them lengthwise. Scoop out the seeds and turn cucumbers upside down on paper towels to drain for 10 minutes. 9. Just before filling, wipe centers of cucumbers dry. Spoon the shrimp mixture into the pirogues and cut in half crosswise. Serve immediately.

Per Serving:
calories: 85 | fat: 4g | protein: 10g | carbs: 2g | fiber: 1g | sodium: 93mg

Greek Yogurt Deviled Eggs

Prep time: 15 minutes | Cook time: 15 minutes |

Serves 4

4 eggs
¼ cup nonfat plain Greek yogurt
1 teaspoon chopped fresh dill
⅛ teaspoon salt

⅛ teaspoon paprika
⅛ teaspoon garlic powder
Chopped fresh parsley, for garnish

1. Preheat the air fryer to 260°F(127°C). 2. Place the eggs in a single layer in the air fryer basket and cook for 15 minutes. 3. Quickly remove the eggs from the air fryer and place them into a cold water bath. Let the eggs cool in the water for 10 minutes before removing and peeling them. 4. After peeling the eggs, cut them in half. 5. Spoon the yolk into a small bowl. Add the yogurt, dill, salt, paprika, and garlic powder and mix until smooth. 6. Spoon or pipe the yolk mixture into the halved egg whites. Serve with a sprinkle of fresh parsley on top.

Per Serving:
calories: 74 | fat: 4g | protein: 7g | carbs: 2g | fiber: 0g | sodium: 152mg

Feta and Quinoa Stuffed Mushrooms

Prep time: 5 minutes | Cook time: 8 minutes | Serves 6

2 tablespoons finely diced red bell pepper
1 garlic clove, minced
¼ cup cooked quinoa
⅛ teaspoon salt
¼ teaspoon dried oregano

24 button mushrooms, stemmed
2 ounces (57 g) crumbled feta
3 tablespoons whole wheat bread crumbs
Olive oil cooking spray

1. Preheat the air fryer to 360°F(182°C). 2. In a small bowl, combine the bell pepper, garlic, quinoa, salt, and oregano. 3. Spoon the quinoa stuffing into the mushroom caps until just filled. 4. Add a small piece of feta to the top of each mushroom. 5. Sprinkle a pinch bread crumbs over the feta on each mushroom. 6. Spray the basket of the air fryer with olive oil cooking spray, then gently place the mushrooms into the basket, making sure that they don't touch each other. (Depending on the size of the air fryer, you may have to cook them in two batches.) 7. Place the basket into the air fryer and bake for 8 minutes. 8. Remove from the air fryer and serve.

Per Serving:
calories: 65 | fat: 3g | protein: 4g | carbs: 7g | fiber: 1g | sodium: 167mg

Pita Pizza with Olives, Feta, and Red Onion

Prep time: 15 minutes | Cook time: 10 minutes |

Serves 4

4 (6-inch) whole-wheat pitas
1 tablespoon extra-virgin olive oil
½ cup hummus
½ bell pepper, julienned
½ red onion, julienned
¼ cup olives, pitted and

chopped
¼ cup crumbled feta cheese
¼ teaspoon red pepper flakes
¼ cup fresh herbs, chopped (mint, parsley, oregano, or a mix)

1. Preheat the broiler to low. Line a baking sheet with parchment paper or foil. 2. Place the pitas on the prepared baking sheet and brush both sides with the olive oil. Broil 1 to 2 minutes per side until starting to turn golden brown. 3. Spread 2 tablespoons hummus on each pita. Top the pitas with bell pepper, onion, olives, feta cheese, and red pepper flakes. Broil again until the cheese softens and starts to get golden brown, 4 to 6 minutes, being careful not to burn the pitas. 4. Remove from broiler and top with the herbs.

Per Serving:
calories: 185 | fat: 11g | protein: 5g | carbs: 17g | fiber: 3g | sodium: 285mg

Lemon Shrimp with Garlic Olive Oil

Prep time: 5 minutes | Cook time: 6 minutes | Serves 4

1 pound (454 g) medium shrimp, cleaned and deveined	½ teaspoon salt
¼ cup plus 2 tablespoons olive oil, divided	¼ teaspoon red pepper flakes
Juice of ½ lemon	Lemon wedges, for serving (optional)
3 garlic cloves, minced and divided	Marinara sauce, for dipping (optional)

1. Preheat the air fryer to 380°F(193ºC). 2. In a large bowl, combine the shrimp with 2 tablespoons of the olive oil, as well as the lemon juice, ⅓ of the minced garlic, salt, and red pepper flakes. Toss to coat the shrimp well. 3. In a small ramekin, combine the remaining ¼ cup of olive oil and the remaining minced garlic. 4. Tear off a 12-by-12-inch sheet of aluminum foil. Pour the shrimp into the center of the foil, then fold the sides up and crimp the edges so that it forms an aluminum foil bowl that is open on top. Place this packet into the air fryer basket. 5. Roast the shrimp for 4 minutes, then open the air fryer and place the ramekin with oil and garlic in the basket beside the shrimp packet. Cook for 2 more minutes. 6. Transfer the shrimp on a serving plate or platter with the ramekin of garlic olive oil on the side for dipping. You may also serve with lemon wedges and marinara sauce, if desired.

Per Serving:

calories: 283 | fat: 21g | protein: 23g | carbs: 1g | fiber: 0g | sodium: 427mg

Fried Baby Artichokes with Lemon-Garlic Aioli

Prep time: 5 minutes | Cook time: 50 minutes | Serves 10

Artichokes:	2 cloves garlic, chopped
15 baby artichokes	1 tablespoon fresh lemon juice
½ lemon	½ teaspoon Dijon mustard
3 cups olive oil	½ cup olive oil
Kosher salt, to taste	Kosher salt and ground black pepper, to taste
Aioli:	
1 egg	

1. Make the Artichokes: Wash and drain the artichokes. With a paring knife, strip off the coarse outer leaves around the base and stalk, leaving the softer leaves on. Carefully peel the stalks and trim off all but 2' below the base. Slice off the top ½' of the artichokes. Cut each artichoke in half. Rub the cut surfaces with a lemon half to keep from browning. 2. In a medium saucepan fitted with a deep-fry thermometer over medium heat, warm the oil to about 280°F(138ºC). Working in batches, cook the artichokes in the hot oil until tender, about 15 minutes. Using a slotted spoon, remove and drain on a paper towel–lined plate. Repeat with all the artichoke halves. 3. Increase the heat of the oil to 375°F(190ºC). In batches, cook the precooked baby artichokes until browned at the edges and crisp, about 1 minute. Transfer to a paper towel–lined plate. Season with the salt to taste. Repeat with the remaining artichokes. 4. Make

the aioli: In a blender, pulse together the egg, garlic, lemon juice, and mustard until combined. With the blender running, slowly drizzle in the oil a few drops at a time until the mixture thickens like mayonnaise, about 2 minutes. Transfer to a bowl and season to taste with the salt and pepper. 5. Serve the warm artichokes with the aioli on the side.

Per Serving:

calories: 236 | fat: 17g | protein: 6g | carbs: 21g | fiber: 10g | sodium: 283mg

Asiago Shishito Peppers

Prep time: 5 minutes | Cook time: 10 minutes | Serves 4

Oil, for spraying	½ teaspoon salt
6 ounces (170 g) shishito peppers	½ teaspoon lemon pepper
1 tablespoon olive oil	⅓ cup grated Asiago cheese, divided

1. Line the air fryer basket with parchment and spray lightly with oil. 2. Rinse the shishitos and pat dry with paper towels. 3. In a large bowl, mix together the shishitos, olive oil, salt, and lemon pepper. Place the shishitos in the prepared basket. 4. Roast at 350ºF (177ºC) for 10 minutes, or until blistered but not burned. 5. Sprinkle with half of the cheese and cook for 1 more minute. 6. Transfer to a serving plate. Immediately sprinkle with the remaining cheese and serve.

Per Serving:

calories: 81 | fat: 6g | protein: 3g | carbs: 5g | fiber: 1g | sodium: 443mg

Marinated Olives

Prep time: 5 minutes | Cook time: 5 minutes | Serves 8 to 10

3 tablespoons olive oil	1 cup pitted Kalamata olives
Zest and juice of 1 lemon	1 cup pitted green olives, such as Castelvetrano
½ teaspoon Aleppo pepper or red pepper flakes	2 tablespoons finely chopped fresh parsley
¼ teaspoon ground sumac	

1. In a medium skillet, heat the olive oil over medium heat. Add the lemon zest, Aleppo pepper, and sumac and cook for 1 to 2 minutes, occasionally stirring, until fragrant. Remove from the heat and stir in the olives, lemon juice, and parsley. 2. Transfer the olives to a bowl and serve immediately, or let cool, then transfer to an airtight container and store in the refrigerator for up to 1 week. The flavor will continue to develop and is best after 8 to 12 hours.

Per Serving:

1 cup: calories: 59 | fat: 6g | protein: 0g | carbs: 1g | fiber: 1g | sodium: 115mg

Stuffed Cucumber Cups

Prep time: 5 minutes | Cook time: 0 minutes | Serves 2

1 medium cucumber (about 8 ounces / 227 g, 8 to 9 inches long)
½ cup hummus (any flavor) or white bean dip

4 or 5 cherry tomatoes, sliced in half
2 tablespoons fresh basil, minced

1. Slice the ends off the cucumber (about ½ inch from each side) and slice the cucumber into 1-inch pieces. 2. With a paring knife or a spoon, scoop most of the seeds from the inside of each cucumber piece to make a cup, being careful to not cut all the way through. 3. Fill each cucumber cup with about 1 tablespoon of hummus or bean dip. 4. Top each with a cherry tomato half and a sprinkle of fresh minced basil.

Per Serving:

calories: 135 | fat: 6g | protein: 6g | carbs: 16g | fiber: 5g | sodium: 242mg

Romesco Dip

Prep time: 10 minutes |Cook time:minutes| Serves: 10

1 (12-ounce / 340-g) jar roasted red peppers, drained
1 (14½-ounce / 411-g) can diced tomatoes, undrained
½ cup dry-roasted almonds
2 garlic cloves
2 teaspoons red wine vinegar
1 teaspoon smoked paprika or ½ teaspoon cayenne pepper

¼ teaspoon kosher or sea salt
¼ teaspoon freshly ground black pepper
¼ cup extra-virgin olive oil
⅔ cup torn, day-old bread or toast (about 2 slices)
Assortment of sliced raw vegetables such as carrots, celery, cucumber, green beans, and bell peppers, for serving

1. In a high-powered blender or food processor, combine the roasted peppers, tomatoes and their juices, almonds, garlic, vinegar, smoked paprika, salt, and pepper. 2. Begin puréeing the ingredients on medium speed, and slowly drizzle in the oil with the blender running. Continue to purée until the dip is thoroughly mixed. 3. Add the bread and purée. 4. Serve with raw vegetables for dipping, or store in a jar with a lid for up to one week in the refrigerator.

Per Serving:

calories: 133 | fat: 10g | protein: 3g | carbs: 10g | fiber: 2g | sodium: 515mg

Chapter 9 Vegetables and Sides

Sesame-Ginger Broccoli

Prep time: 10 minutes | Cook time: 15 minutes | Serves 4

3 tablespoons toasted sesame oil
2 teaspoons sesame seeds
1 tablespoon chili-garlic sauce
2 teaspoons minced fresh ginger
½ teaspoon kosher salt
½ teaspoon black pepper
1 (16-ounce / 454-g) package frozen broccoli florets (do not thaw)

1. In a large bowl, combine the sesame oil, sesame seeds, chili-garlic sauce, ginger, salt, and pepper. Stir until well combined. Add the broccoli and toss until well coated. 2. Arrange the broccoli in the air fryer basket. Set the air fryer to 325ºF (163ºC) for 15 minutes, or until the broccoli is crisp, tender, and the edges are lightly browned, gently tossing halfway through the cooking time.

Per Serving:

calories: 143 | fat: 11g | protein: 4g | carbs: 9g | fiber: 4g | sodium: 385mg

Turkish Stuffed Eggplant

Prep time: 10 minutes | Cook time: 2 hours 10 minutes | Serves 6

½ cup extra-virgin olive oil
3 small eggplants
1 teaspoon sea salt
½ teaspoon black pepper
1 large yellow onion, finely chopped
4 garlic cloves, minced
1 (15-ounce / 425-g) can diced tomatoes, with the juice
¼ cup finely chopped fresh flat-leaf parsley
6 (8-inch) round pita breads, quartered and toasted
1 cup plain Greek yogurt

1. Pour ¼ cup of the olive oil into the slow cooker, and generously coat the interior of the crock. 2. Cut each eggplant in half lengthwise. You can leave the stem on. Score the cut side of each half every ¼ inch, being careful not to cut through the skin. 3. Arrange the eggplant halves, skin-side down, in the slow cooker. Sprinkle with 1 teaspoon salt and ½ teaspoon pepper. 4. In a large skillet, heat the remaining ¼ cup olive oil over medium-high heat. Sauté the onion and garlic for 3 minutes, or until the onion begins to soften. 5. Add the tomatoes and parsley to the skillet. Season with salt and pepper. Sauté for another 5 minutes, until the liquid has almost evaporated. 6. Using a large spoon, spoon the tomato mixture over the eggplants, covering each half with some of the mixture. 7. Cover and cook on high for 2 hours or on low for 4 hours. When the dish is finished, the eggplant should feel very tender when you insert the tip of a sharp knife into the thickest part. 8. Uncover the slow cooker, and let the eggplant rest for 10 minutes. Then transfer the eggplant to a serving dish. If there is any juice in the bottom of the cooker, spoon it over the eggplant. Serve hot with toasted pita wedges and yogurt on the side.

Per Serving:

calories: 449 | fat: 22g | protein: 11g | carbs: 59g | fiber: 15g | sodium: 706mg

Garlic Roasted Broccoli

Prep time: 8 minutes | Cook time: 10 to 14 minutes | Serves 6

1 head broccoli, cut into bite-size florets
1 tablespoon avocado oil
2 teaspoons minced garlic
⅛ teaspoon red pepper flakes
Sea salt and freshly ground black pepper, to taste
1 tablespoon freshly squeezed lemon juice
½ teaspoon lemon zest

1. In a large bowl, toss together the broccoli, avocado oil, garlic, red pepper flakes, salt, and pepper. 2. Set the air fryer to 375ºF (191ºC). Arrange the broccoli in a single layer in the air fryer basket, working in batches if necessary. Roast for 10 to 14 minutes, until the broccoli is lightly charred. 3. Place the florets in a medium bowl and toss with the lemon juice and lemon zest. Serve.

Per Serving:

calories: 58 | fat: 3g | protein: 3g | carbs: 7g | fiber: 3g | sodium: 34mg

Crispy Green Beans

Prep time: 5 minutes | Cook time: 8 minutes | Serves 4

2 teaspoons olive oil
½ pound (227 g) fresh green beans, ends trimmed
¼ teaspoon salt
¼ teaspoon ground black pepper

1. In a large bowl, drizzle olive oil over green beans and sprinkle with salt and pepper. 2. Place green beans into ungreased air fryer basket. Adjust the temperature to 350ºF (177ºC) and set the timer for 8 minutes, shaking the basket two times during cooking. Green beans will be dark golden and crispy at the edges when done. Serve warm.

Per Serving:

calories: 33 | fat: 3g | protein: 1g | carbs: 3g | fiber: 1g | sodium: 147mg

Cauliflower Steaks with Creamy Tahini Sauce

Prep time: 10 minutes | Cook time: 45 minutes | Serves 4

¼ cup olive oil
4 garlic cloves, minced
1 teaspoon sea salt
1 teaspoon freshly ground black pepper
2 large heads cauliflower, stem end trimmed (core left intact)
and cut from top to bottom into thick slabs
½ cup tahini
Juice of 1 lemon
¼ cup chopped fresh Italian parsley

1. Preheat the oven to 400°F (205°C). Line a baking sheet with parchment paper. 2. In a small bowl, combine the olive oil, garlic, salt, and pepper. Brush this mixture on both sides of the cauliflower steaks and place them in a single layer on the baking sheet. Drizzle any remaining oil mixture over the cauliflower steaks. Bake for 45 minutes, or until the cauliflower is soft. 3. While the steaks are baking, in a small bowl, stir together the tahini and lemon juice. Season with salt and pepper. 4. Remove the cauliflower steaks from the oven and transfer them to four plates. Drizzle the lemon tahini sauce evenly over the cauliflower and garnish with the parsley. Serve.

Per Serving:

calories: 339 | fat: 30g | protein: 8g | carbs: 15g | fiber: 6g | sodium: 368mg

Sautéed Fava Beans with Olive Oil, Garlic, and Chiles

Prep time: 10 minutes | Cook time: 7 minutes | Serves 4

3½ pounds (1.6 kg) fresh fava beans, shelled (4 cups)
2 tablespoons olive oil
2 cloves garlic, minced
2 teaspoons fresh lemon juice
1 teaspoon finely grated lemon
zest
½ teaspoon crushed red pepper flakes
½ teaspoon salt
¼ teaspoon freshly ground black pepper

1. Bring a medium saucepan of lightly salted water to a boil. Add the shelled favas and cook for 3 to 4 minutes, until tender. Drain the favas and immediately place them in an ice water bath to stop their cooking. When cool, peel the tough outer skin off the beans. 2. Heat the olive oil in a large skillet over medium-high heat. Add the garlic and cook, stirring, until it is aromatic but not browned, about 30 seconds. Add the beans and cook, stirring, until heated through, about 2 minutes. Stir in the lemon juice, lemon zest, red pepper flakes, salt, and pepper and remove from the heat. Serve immediately.

Per Serving:

calories: 576 | fat: 9g | protein: 39g | carbs: 88g | fiber: 38g | sodium: 311mg

Green Veg & Macadamia Smash

Prep time: 25 minutes | Cook time: 15 minutes | Serves 6

⅔ cup macadamia nuts
Enough water to cover and soak the macadamias
7 ounces (198 g) cavolo nero or kale, stalks removed and chopped
1 medium head broccoli, cut into florets, or broccolini
2 cloves garlic, crushed
¼ cup extra-virgin olive oil
2 tablespoons fresh lemon juice
4 medium spring onions, sliced
¼ cup chopped fresh herbs, such as parsley, dill, basil, or mint
Salt and black pepper, to taste

1. Place the macadamias in a small bowl and add enough water to cover them. Soak for about 2 hours, then drain. Discard the water. 2. Fill a large pot with about 1½ cups (360 ml) of water, then insert a steamer colander. Bring to a boil over high heat, then reduce to medium-high. Add the cavolo nero and cook for 6 minutes. Add the broccoli and cook for 8 minutes or until fork-tender. Remove the lid, let the steam escape, and let cool slightly. 3. Place the cooked vegetables in a blender or a food processor. Add the soaked macadamias, garlic, olive oil, lemon juice, spring onions, and fresh herbs (you can reserve some for topping). 4. Process to the desired consistency (smooth or chunky). Season with salt and pepper to taste and serve. To store, let cool completely and store in a sealed container in the fridge for up to 5 days.

Per Serving:

calories: 250 | fat: 22g | protein: 5g | carbs: 12g | fiber: 5g | sodium: 44mg

Puréed Cauliflower Soup

Prep time: 15 minutes | Cook time: 11 minutes | Serves 6

2 tablespoons olive oil
1 medium onion, peeled and chopped
1 stalk celery, chopped
1 medium carrot, peeled and chopped
3 sprigs fresh thyme
4 cups cauliflower florets
2 cups vegetable stock
½ cup half-and-half
¼ cup low-fat plain Greek yogurt
2 tablespoons chopped fresh chives

1. Press the Sauté button on the Instant Pot® and heat oil. Add onion, celery, and carrot. Cook until just tender, about 6 minutes. Add thyme, cauliflower, and stock. Stir well, then press the Cancel button. 2. Close lid, set steam release to Sealing, press the Manual button, and set time to 5 minutes. When the timer beeps, let pressure release naturally, about 15 minutes. 3. Open lid, remove and discard thyme stems, and with an immersion blender, purée soup until smooth. Stir in half-and-half and yogurt. Garnish with chives and serve immediately.

Per Serving:

calories: 113 | fat: 7g | protein: 3g | carbs: 9g | fiber: 2g | sodium: 236mg

Braised Eggplant and Tomatoes

Prep time: 10 minutes | Cook time: 40 minutes |
Serves 4

1 large eggplant, peeled and diced
Pinch sea salt
1 (15-ounce / 425-g) can chopped tomatoes and juices
1 cup chicken broth
2 garlic cloves, smashed
1 tablespoon Italian seasoning
1 bay leaf
Sea salt and freshly ground pepper, to taste

1. Cut the eggplant, and salt both sides to remove bitter juices. Let the eggplant sit for 20 minutes before rinsing and patting dry. 2. Dice eggplant. 3. Put eggplant, tomatoes, chicken broth, garlic, seasoning, and bay leaf in a large saucepot. 4. Bring to a boil and reduce heat to simmer. 5. Cover and simmer for about 30–40 minutes until eggplant is tender. Remove garlic cloves and bay leaf, season to taste, and serve.

Per Serving:

calories: 70 | fat: 1g | protein: 4g | carbs: 14g | fiber: 6g | sodium: 186mg

Baked Tomatoes with Spiced Amaranth Stuffing

Prep time: 10 minutes | Cook time: 50 minutes |
Serves 6

1 tablespoon olive oil
1 small onion, diced
1 clove garlic, minced
1 cup amaranth
1 cup vegetable broth or water
1 cup diced tomatoes, drained
¼ cup chopped fresh parsley
½ teaspoon ground cinnamon
½ cup golden raisins
½ cup toasted pine nuts
¾ teaspoon salt
½ teaspoon freshly ground black pepper
6 large ripe tomatoes

1. Preheat the oven to 375ºF (190ºC). 2. Heat the olive oil over medium heat in a medium saucepan. Add the onion and garlic and cook, stirring frequently, until the onion is softened, about 5 minutes. Stir in the amaranth and then the broth or water and bring to a boil over high heat. Lower the heat to low, cover, and cook, stirring occasionally, for about 20 minutes, until the amaranth is tender and the liquid has been absorbed. 3. Remove the pan from the heat and stir in the diced tomatoes, parsley, cinnamon, raisins, pine nuts, salt, and pepper. 4. Cut a slice off the bottom of each tomato to make a flat bottom for it to sit on. Scoop out the seeds and core of the tomato to make a shell for filling. Arrange the hollowed-out tomatoes in a baking dish. 5. Fill the tomatoes with the amaranth mixture and bake in the preheated oven for about 25 minutes, until the tomatoes have softened, but still hold their shape. Serve hot.

Per Serving:

calories: 306 | fat: 13g | protein: 10g | carbs: 43g | fiber: 7g | sodium: 439mg

Easy Greek Briami (Ratatouille)

Prep time: 15 minutes | Cook time: 40 minutes |
Serves 6

2 russet potatoes, cubed
½ cup Roma tomatoes, cubed
1 eggplant, cubed
1 zucchini, cubed
1 red onion, chopped
1 red bell pepper, chopped
2 garlic cloves, minced
1 teaspoon dried mint
1 teaspoon dried parsley
1 teaspoon dried oregano
½ teaspoon salt
½ teaspoon black pepper
¼ teaspoon red pepper flakes
⅓ cup olive oil
1 (8-ounce / 227-g) can tomato paste
¼ cup vegetable broth
¼ cup water

1. Preheat the air fryer to 320ºF(160ºC). 2. In a large bowl, combine the potatoes, tomatoes, eggplant, zucchini, onion, bell pepper, garlic, mint, parsley, oregano, salt, black pepper, and red pepper flakes. 3. In a small bowl, mix together the olive oil, tomato paste, broth, and water. 4. Pour the oil-and-tomato-paste mixture over the vegetables and toss until everything is coated. 5. Pour the coated vegetables into the air fryer basket in an even layer and roast for 20 minutes. After 20 minutes, stir well and spread out again. Roast for an additional 10 minutes, then repeat the process and cook for another 10 minutes.

Per Serving:

calories: 239 | fat: 13g | protein: 5g | carbs: 31g | fiber: 7g | sodium: 250mg

Toasted Grain and Almond Pilaf

Prep time: 15 minutes | Cook time: 35 minutes |
Serves 2

1 tablespoon olive oil
1 garlic clove, minced
3 scallions, minced
2 ounces (57 g) mushrooms, sliced
¼ cup sliced almonds
½ cup uncooked pearled barley
1½ cups low-sodium chicken stock
½ teaspoon dried thyme
1 tablespoon fresh minced parsley
Salt

1. Heat the oil in a saucepan over medium-high heat. Add the garlic, scallions, mushrooms, and almonds, and sauté for 3 minutes. 2. Add the barley and cook, stirring, for 1 minute to toast it. 3. Add the chicken stock and thyme and bring the mixture to a boil. 4. Cover and reduce the heat to low. Simmer the barley for 30 minutes, or until the liquid is absorbed and the barley is tender. 5. Sprinkle with fresh parsley and season with salt before serving.

Per Serving:

calories: 333 | fat: 14g | protein: 10g | carbs: 46g | fiber: 10g | sodium: 141mg

Greek Bean Soup

Prep time: 10 minutes | Cook time: 45 minutes |

Serves 4

2 tablespoons olive oil
1 large onion, chopped
1 (15-ounce / 425-g) can diced tomatoes
1 (15-ounce / 425-g) can great northern beans, drained and rinsed
2 celery stalks, chopped

2 carrots, cut into long ribbons
⅓ teaspoon chopped fresh thyme
¼ cup chopped fresh Italian parsley
1 bay leaf
Sea salt
Freshly ground black pepper

1. In a Dutch oven, heat the olive oil over medium-high heat. Add the onion and sauté for 4 minutes, or until softened. Add the tomatoes, beans, celery, carrots, thyme, parsley, and bay leaf, then add water to cover by about 2 inches. 2. Bring the soup to a boil, reduce the heat to low, cover, and simmer for 30 minutes, or until the vegetables are tender. 3. Remove the bay leaf, season with salt and pepper, and serve.

Per Serving:

calories: 185 | fat: 7g | protein: 7g | carbs: 25g | fiber: 8g | sodium: 155mg

Wild Mushroom Soup

Prep time: 30 minutes | Cook time: 16 minutes |

Serves 8

3 tablespoons olive oil
1 stalk celery, diced
1 medium carrot, peeled and diced
½ medium yellow onion, peeled and diced
1 clove garlic, peeled and minced
1 (8-ounce / 227-g) container hen of the woods mushrooms, sliced
1 (8-ounce / 227-g) container

porcini or chanterelle mushrooms, sliced
2 cups sliced shiitake mushrooms
2 tablespoons dry sherry
4 cups vegetable broth
2 cups water
1 tablespoon chopped fresh tarragon
½ teaspoon salt
½ teaspoon ground black pepper

1. Press the Sauté button on the Instant Pot® and heat oil. Add celery, carrot, and onion. Cook, stirring often, until softened, about 5 minutes. Add garlic and cook 30 seconds until fragrant, then add mushrooms and cook until beginning to soften, about 5 minutes. 2. Add sherry, broth, water, tarragon, salt, and pepper to pot, and stir well. Press the Cancel button. Close lid, set steam release to Sealing, press the Manual button, and set time to 5 minutes. 3. When the timer beeps, let pressure release naturally, about 15 minutes. Press the Cancel button, open lid, and stir well. Serve hot.

Per Serving:

calories: 98 | fat: 6g | protein: 1g | carbs: 11g | fiber: 2g | sodium: 759mg

Roasted Broccoli with Tahini Yogurt Sauce

Prep time: 15 minutes | Cook time: 30 minutes |

Serves 4

For the Broccoli:
1½ to 2 pounds (680 to 907 g) broccoli, stalk trimmed and cut into slices, head cut into florets
1 lemon, sliced into ¼-inch-thick rounds
3 tablespoons extra-virgin olive oil
½ teaspoon kosher salt

¼ teaspoon freshly ground black pepper
For the Tahini Yogurt Sauce:
½ cup plain Greek yogurt
2 tablespoons tahini
1 tablespoon lemon juice
¼ teaspoon kosher salt
1 teaspoon sesame seeds, for garnish (optional)

Make the Broccoli: 1. Preheat the oven to 425ºF (220ºC). Line a baking sheet with parchment paper or foil. 2. In a large bowl, gently toss the broccoli, lemon slices, olive oil, salt, and black pepper to combine. Arrange the broccoli in a single layer on the prepared baking sheet. Roast 15 minutes, stir, and roast another 15 minutes, until golden brown. Make the Tahini Yogurt Sauce: 3. In a medium bowl, combine the yogurt, tahini, lemon juice, and salt; mix well. 4. Spread the tahini yogurt sauce on a platter or large plate and top with the broccoli and lemon slices. Garnish with the sesame seeds (if desired).

Per Serving:

calories: 245 | fat: 16g | protein: 12g | carbs: 20g | fiber: 7g | sodium: 305mg

Nordic Stone Age Bread

Prep time: 10 minutes | Cook time: 1 hour | Serves 14

½ cup flaxseeds
½ cup chia seeds
½ cup sesame seeds
¼ cup pumpkin seeds
¼ cup sunflower seeds
½ cup whole almonds, chopped
½ cup blanched hazelnuts,

chopped
½ cup pecans or walnuts
1 teaspoon salt, or to taste
1 teaspoon coarse black pepper
4 large eggs
½ cup extra-virgin olive oil or melted ghee

1. Preheat the oven to 285ºF (140ºC) fan assisted or 320ºF (160ºC) conventional. Line a loaf pan with parchment paper. 2. In a mixing bowl, combine all of the dry ingredients. Add the eggs and olive oil and stir through until well combined. Pour the dough into the loaf pan. Transfer to the oven and bake for about 1 hour or until the top is crisp. 3. Remove from the oven and let cool slightly in the pan before transferring to a wire rack to cool completely before slicing. Store at room temperature for up to 3 days loosely covered with a kitchen towel, refrigerate for up to 10 days, or freeze for up to 3 months.

Per Serving:

calories: 251 | fat: 23g | protein: 7g | carbs: 7g | fiber: 5g | sodium: 192mg

Baked Turkey Kibbeh

Prep time: 15 minutes | Cook time: 45 minutes |
Serves 8

Outer Layer:
1½ cups bulgur wheat
1¼ pounds (567 g) ground turkey
1 yellow onion, grated on a box grater
½ cup finely chopped fresh mint
1 teaspoon ground allspice
½ teaspoon ground cinnamon
1 teaspoon kosher salt
¼ teaspoon ground black pepper
Filling:
4 tablespoons olive oil, divided

1 yellow onion, finely chopped
3 cloves garlic, minced
1 pound (454 g) ground turkey
¼ cup finely chopped fresh flat-leaf parsley
½ cup pine nuts, toasted
½ teaspoon ground allspice
½ teaspoon kosher salt
¼ teaspoon ground black pepper
Assembly and Serving:
1 tablespoon olive oil
8 tablespoons low-fat Greek yogurt or labneh
¼ cup thinly sliced fresh mint

1. To make the outer layer: Soak the bulgur overnight in a bowl with enough water to cover by 2'. 2. Drain, squeezing the bulgur until there is no excess moisture. Transfer to a large bowl. 3. With your hands, mix in the turkey, onion, mint, allspice, cinnamon, salt, and pepper until thoroughly combined. 4. To make the filling: In a medium cast-iron skillet over medium heat, warm 2 tablespoons of the oil. Cook the onion and garlic until translucent, about 8 minutes. Add the turkey and cook until no longer pink, about 5 minutes. 5. Stir in the parsley, pine nuts, allspice, salt, and pepper. Drizzle in the remaining 2 tablespoons oil. Transfer to a bowl and wipe out the skillet. 6. To assemble the kibbeh: Preheat an oven to 350°F(180°C). Lightly coat the cast-iron skillet with olive oil. 7. Press half of the outer layer into the bottom of the skillet in an even layer about ¾' thick. Spread the filling evenly over the top. Using wet fingers, use the remaining half of the outer layer to cover the filling. Once the filling is completely covered, smooth with wet hands. 8. Score the surface of the kibbeh into 8 wedges to make it easier to cut and portion after baking. Drizzle the oil over the top and bake until deep brown, about 30 minutes. 9. Serve hot with the yogurt or labneh and a sprinkle of the mint.

Per Serving:

calories: 395 | fat: 21g | protein: 31g | carbs: 24g | fiber: 6g | sodium: 462mg

Five-Spice Roasted Sweet Potatoes

Prep time: 10 minutes | Cook time: 12 minutes |
Serves 4

½ teaspoon ground cinnamon
¼ teaspoon ground cumin
¼ teaspoon paprika
1 teaspoon chile powder
⅛ teaspoon turmeric
½ teaspoon salt (optional)

Freshly ground black pepper, to taste
2 large sweet potatoes, peeled and cut into ¾-inch cubes (about 3 cups)
1 tablespoon olive oil

1. In a large bowl, mix together cinnamon, cumin, paprika, chile

powder, turmeric, salt, and pepper to taste. 2. Add potatoes and stir well. 3. Drizzle the seasoned potatoes with the olive oil and stir until evenly coated. 4. Place seasoned potatoes in a baking pan or an ovenproof dish that fits inside your air fryer basket. 5. Cook for 6 minutes at 390ºF (199ºC), stop, and stir well. 6. Cook for an additional 6 minutes.

Per Serving:

calories: 14 | fat: 3g | protein: 1g | carbs: 14g | fiber: 2g | sodium: 327mg

Dinner Rolls

Prep time: 10 minutes | Cook time: 12 minutes |
Serves 6

1 cup shredded Mozzarella cheese
1 ounce (28 g) full-fat cream cheese
1 cup blanched finely ground

almond flour
¼ cup ground flaxseed
½ teaspoon baking powder
1 large egg

1. Place Mozzarella, cream cheese, and almond flour in a large microwave-safe bowl. Microwave for 1 minute. Mix until smooth. 2. Add flaxseed, baking powder, and egg until fully combined and smooth. Microwave an additional 15 seconds if it becomes too firm. 3. Separate the dough into six pieces and roll into balls. Place the balls into the air fryer basket. 4. Adjust the temperature to 320ºF (160ºC) and air fry for 12 minutes. 5. Allow rolls to cool completely before serving.

Per Serving:

calories: 223 | fat: 17g | protein: 13g | carbs: 7g | fiber: 4g | sodium: 175mg

Curry Roasted Cauliflower

Prep time: 10 minutes | Cook time: 20 minutes |
Serves 4

¼ cup olive oil
2 teaspoons curry powder
½ teaspoon salt
¼ teaspoon freshly ground black pepper

1 head cauliflower, cut into bite-size florets
½ red onion, sliced
2 tablespoons freshly chopped parsley, for garnish (optional)

1. Preheat the air fryer to 400ºF (204ºC). 2. In a large bowl, combine the olive oil, curry powder, salt, and pepper. Add the cauliflower and onion. Toss gently until the vegetables are completely coated with the oil mixture. Transfer the vegetables to the basket of the air fryer. 3. Pausing about halfway through the cooking time to shake the basket, air fry for 20 minutes until the cauliflower is tender and beginning to brown. Top with the parsley, if desired, before serving.

Per Serving:

calories: 141 | fat: 14g | protein: 2g | carbs: 4g | fiber: 2g | sodium: 312mg

Superflax Tortillas

Prep time: 5 minutes | Cook time: 10 minutes | Serves 6

1 packed cup flax meal
⅓ cup coconut flour
¼ cup ground chia seeds
2 tablespoons whole psyllium husks

1 teaspoon salt, or to taste
1 cup lukewarm water
2 tablespoons extra-virgin avocado oil or ghee

1. Place all the dry ingredients in a bowl and mix to combine. (For ground chia seeds, simply place whole seeds into a coffee grinder or food processor and pulse until smooth.) Add the water and mix until well combined. Place the dough in the refrigerator to rest for about 30 minutes. 2. When ready, remove the dough from the fridge and cut it into 4 equal pieces. You will make the remaining 2 tortillas using the excess dough. Place one piece of dough between two pieces of parchment paper and roll it out until very thin. Alternatively, use a silicone roller and a silicone mat. Remove the top piece of parchment paper. Press a large 8-inch (20 cm) lid into the dough (or use a piece of parchment paper cut into a circle of the same size). Press the lid into the dough or trace around it with your knife to cut out the tortilla. 3. Repeat for the remaining pieces of dough. Add the cut-off excess dough to the last piece and create the remaining 2 tortillas from it. If you have any dough left over, simply roll it out and cut it into tortilla-chip shapes. 4. Grease a large pan with the avocado oil and cook 1 tortilla at a time for 2 to 3 minutes on each side over medium heat until lightly browned. Don't overcook: the tortillas should be flexible, not too crispy. 5. Once cool, store the tortillas in a sealed container for up to 1 week and reheat them in a dry pan, if needed.

Per Serving:

calories: 182 | fat: 16g | protein: 4g | carbs: 8g | fiber: 7g | sodium: 396mg

Flatbread

Prep time: 5 minutes | Cook time: 7 minutes | Serves 2

1 cup shredded Mozzarella cheese
¼ cup blanched finely ground

almond flour
1 ounce (28 g) full-fat cream cheese, softened

1. In a large microwave-safe bowl, melt Mozzarella in the microwave for 30 seconds. Stir in almond flour until smooth and then add cream cheese. Continue mixing until dough forms, gently kneading it with wet hands if necessary. 2. Divide the dough into two pieces and roll out to ¼-inch thickness between two pieces of parchment. Cut another piece of parchment to fit your air fryer basket. 3. Place a piece of flatbread onto your parchment and into the air fryer, working in two batches if needed. 4. Adjust the temperature to 320ºF (160ºC) and air fry for 7 minutes. 5. Halfway through the cooking time flip the flatbread. Serve warm.

Per Serving:

calories: 235 | fat: 14g | protein: 23g | carbs: 6g | fiber: 3g | sodium: 475mg

Cauliflower Steaks Gratin

Prep time: 10 minutes | Cook time: 13 minutes | Serves 2

1 head cauliflower
1 tablespoon olive oil
Salt and freshly ground black pepper, to taste
½ teaspoon chopped fresh

thyme leaves
3 tablespoons grated Parmigiano-Reggiano cheese
2 tablespoons panko bread crumbs

1. Preheat the air fryer to 370ºF (188ºC). 2. Cut two steaks out of the center of the cauliflower. To do this, cut the cauliflower in half and then cut one slice about 1-inch thick off each half. The rest of the cauliflower will fall apart into florets, which you can roast on their own or save for another meal. 3. Brush both sides of the cauliflower steaks with olive oil and season with salt, freshly ground black pepper and fresh thyme. Place the cauliflower steaks into the air fryer basket and air fry for 6 minutes. Turn the steaks over and air fry for another 4 minutes. Combine the Parmesan cheese and panko bread crumbs and sprinkle the mixture over the tops of both steaks and air fry for another 3 minutes until the cheese has melted and the bread crumbs have browned. Serve this with some sautéed bitter greens and air-fried blistered tomatoes.

Per Serving:

calories: 192 | fat: 10g | protein: 9g | carbs: 21g | fiber: 6g | sodium: 273mg

Herb Vinaigrette Potato Salad

Prep time: 10 minutes | Cook time: 4 minutes | Serves 10

¼ cup olive oil
3 tablespoons red wine vinegar
¼ cup chopped fresh flat-leaf parsley
2 tablespoons chopped fresh dill
2 tablespoons chopped fresh chives
1 clove garlic, peeled and

minced
½ teaspoon dry mustard powder
¼ teaspoon ground black pepper
2 pounds (907 g) baby Yukon Gold potatoes
1 cup water
1 teaspoon salt

1. Whisk together oil, vinegar, parsley, dill, chives, garlic, mustard, and pepper in a small bowl. Set aside. 2. Place potatoes in a steamer basket. Place the rack in the Instant Pot®, add water and salt, then top with the steamer basket. Close lid, set steam release to Sealing, press the Manual button, and set time to 4 minutes. When the timer beeps, quick-release the pressure until the float valve drops. Press the Cancel button and open lid. 3. Transfer hot potatoes to a serving bowl. Pour dressing over potatoes and gently toss to coat. Serve warm or at room temperature.

Per Serving:

calories: 116 | fat: 6g | protein: 2g | carbs: 16g | fiber: 1g | sodium: 239mg

Coriander-Cumin Roasted Carrots

Prep time: 10 minutes | Cook time: 20 minutes |

Serves 2

½ pound (227 g) rainbow carrots (about 4)

2 tablespoons fresh orange juice

1 tablespoon honey

½ teaspoon coriander

Pinch salt

1. Preheat oven to 400°F(205°C) and set the oven rack to the middle position. 2. Peel the carrots and cut them lengthwise into slices of even thickness. Place them in a large bowl. 3. In a small bowl, mix together the orange juice, honey, coriander, and salt. 4. Pour the orange juice mixture over the carrots and toss well to coat. 5. Spread carrots onto a baking dish in a single layer. 6. Roast for 15 to 20 minutes, or until fork-tender.

Per Serving:

calories: 85 | fat: 0g | protein: 1g | carbs: 21g | fiber: 3g | sodium: 156mg

Brown Rice and Vegetable Pilaf

Prep time: 20 minutes | Cook time: 5 hours | Makes

9 (¾-cup) servings

1 onion, minced

1 cup sliced cremini mushrooms

2 carrots, sliced

2 garlic cloves, minced

1½ cups long-grain brown rice

2½ cups vegetable broth

½ teaspoon salt

½ teaspoon dried marjoram leaves

⅛ teaspoon freshly ground black pepper

⅓ cup grated Parmesan cheese

1. In the slow cooker, combine the onion, mushrooms, carrots, garlic, and rice. 2. Add the broth, salt, marjoram, and pepper, and stir. 3. Cover and cook on low for 5 hours, or until the rice is tender and the liquid is absorbed. 4. Stir in the cheese and serve.

Per Serving:

calories: 68 | fat: 1g | protein: 2g | carbs: 12g | fiber: 1g | sodium: 207mg

Warm Beets with Hazelnuts and Spiced Yogurt

Prep time: 5 minutes | Cook time: 40 minutes |

Serves 4

4 or 5 beets, peeled

¼ cup hazelnuts

½ cup low-fat plain Greek yogurt

1 tablespoon honey

1 tablespoon chopped fresh

mint

1 teaspoon ground cinnamon

¼ teaspoon ground cumin

⅛ teaspoon ground black pepper

1. Place racks in the upper and lower thirds of the oven. Preheat

the oven to 400°F(205°C). 2. Place the beets on a 12' × 12' piece of foil. Fold the foil over the beets, and seal the sides. Bake until the beets are tender enough to be pierced by a fork, about 40 minutes. Remove from the oven, carefully open the packet, and let cool slightly. When cool enough to handle, slice the beets into ¼'-thick rounds. 3. Meanwhile, toast the hazelnuts on a small baking sheet until browned and fragrant, about 5 minutes. Using a paper towel or kitchen towel, rub the skins off. Coarsely chop the nuts and set aside. 4. In a medium bowl, stir together the yogurt, honey, mint, cinnamon, cumin, and pepper. 5. Serve the beets with a dollop of the spiced yogurt and a sprinkle of the nuts.

Per Serving:

calories: 126 | fat: 6g | protein: 5g | carbs: 15g | fiber: 4g | sodium: 74mg

Spicy Creamer Potatoes

Prep time: 10 minutes | Cook time: 8 hours | Makes

7 (1-cup) servings

2 pounds (907 g) creamer potatoes

1 onion, chopped

3 garlic cloves, minced

1 chipotle chile in adobo sauce, minced

2 tablespoons freshly squeezed

lemon juice

2 tablespoons water

1 tablespoon chili powder

½ teaspoon ground cumin

½ teaspoon salt

⅛ teaspoon freshly ground black pepper

1. In the slow cooker, combine all the ingredients and stir. 2. Cover and cook on low for 7 to 8 hours, or until the potatoes are tender, and serve.

Per Serving:

calories: 113 | fat: 0g | protein: 3g | carbs: 25g | fiber: 4g | sodium: 208mg

Lemony Orzo

Prep time: 5 minutes | Cook time: 5 minutes | Yield 2

cups

1 cup dry orzo

1 cup halved grape tomatoes

1 (6-ounce / 170-g) bag baby spinach

2 tablespoons extra-virgin olive

oil

¼ teaspoon salt

Freshly ground black pepper

¾ cup crumbled feta cheese

1 lemon, juiced and zested

1. Bring a medium pot of water to a boil. Stir in the orzo and cook uncovered for 8 minutes. Drain the water, then return the orzo to medium heat. 2. Add in the tomatoes and spinach and cook until the spinach is wilted. Add the oil, salt, and pepper and mix well. Top the dish with feta, lemon juice, and lemon zest, then toss one or two more times and enjoy!

Per Serving:

½ cup: calories: 273 | fat: 13g | protein: 10g | carbs: 32g | fiber: 6g | sodium: 445mg

Garlicky Sautéed Zucchini with Mint

Prep time: 5 minutes | Cook time: 10 minutes |

Serves 4

3 large green zucchini	3 cloves garlic, minced
3 tablespoons extra-virgin olive oil	1 teaspoon salt
	1 teaspoon dried mint
1 large onion, chopped	

1. Cut the zucchini into ½-inch cubes. 2. In a large skillet over medium heat, cook the olive oil, onions, and garlic for 3 minutes, stirring constantly. 3. Add the zucchini and salt to the skillet and toss to combine with the onions and garlic, cooking for 5 minutes. 4. Add the mint to the skillet, tossing to combine. Cook for another 2 minutes. Serve warm.

Per Serving:

calories: 147 | fat: 11g | protein: 4g | carbs: 12g | fiber: 3g | sodium: 607mg

Barley-Stuffed Cabbage Rolls with Pine Nuts and Currants

Prep time: 15 minutes | Cook time: 2 hours | Serves 4

1 large head green cabbage, cored	2 tablespoons chopped fresh flat-leaf parsley
1 tablespoon olive oil	½ teaspoon sea salt
1 large yellow onion, chopped	½ teaspoon black pepper
3 cups cooked pearl barley	½ cup apple juice
3 ounces (85 g) feta cheese, crumbled	1 tablespoon apple cider vinegar
½ cup dried currants	1 (15-ounce / 425-g) can crushed tomatoes, with the juice
2 tablespoons pine nuts, toasted	

1. Steam the cabbage head in a large pot over boiling water for 8 minutes. Remove to a cutting board and let cool slightly. 2. Remove 16 leaves from the cabbage head (reserve the rest of the cabbage for another use). Cut off the raised portion of the center vein of each cabbage leaf (do not cut out the vein). 3. Heat the oil in a large nonstick lidded skillet over medium heat. Add the onion, cover, and cook 6 minutes, or until tender. Remove to a large bowl. 4. Stir the barley, feta cheese, currants, pine nuts, and parsley into the onion mixture. Season with ¼ teaspoon of the salt and ¼ teaspoon of the pepper. 5. Place cabbage leaves on a work surface. On 1 cabbage leaf, spoon about ⅓ cup of the barley mixture into the center. Fold in the edges of the leaf over the barley mixture and roll the cabbage leaf up as if you were making a burrito. Repeat for the remaining 15 cabbage leaves and filling. 6. Arrange the cabbage rolls in the slow cooker. 7. Combine the remaining ¼ teaspoon salt, ¼ teaspoon pepper, the apple juice, apple cider vinegar, and tomatoes. Pour the apple juice mixture evenly over the cabbage rolls. 8. Cover and cook on high 2 hours or on low for 6 to 8 hours. Serve hot.

Per Serving:

calories: 394 | fat: 12g | protein: 12g | carbs: 66g | fiber: 16g | sodium: 560mg

Brussels Sprouts with Pecans and Gorgonzola

Prep time: 10 minutes | Cook time: 25 minutes |

Serves 4

½ cup pecans	Salt and freshly ground black pepper, to taste
1½ pounds (680 g) fresh Brussels sprouts, trimmed and quartered	¼ cup crumbled Gorgonzola cheese
2 tablespoons olive oil	

1. Spread the pecans in a single layer of the air fryer and set the heat to 350ºF (177ºC). Air fry for 3 to 5 minutes until the pecans are lightly browned and fragrant. Transfer the pecans to a plate and continue preheating the air fryer, increasing the heat to 400ºF (204ºC). 2. In a large bowl, toss the Brussels sprouts with the olive oil and season with salt and black pepper to taste. 3. Working in batches if necessary, arrange the Brussels sprouts in a single layer in the air fryer basket. Pausing halfway through the baking time to shake the basket, air fry for 20 to 25 minutes until the sprouts are tender and starting to brown on the edges. 4. Transfer the sprouts to a serving bowl and top with the toasted pecans and Gorgonzola. Serve warm or at room temperature.

Per Serving:

calories: 253 | fat: 18g | protein: 9g | carbs: 17g | fiber: 8g | sodium: 96mg

Lebanese Baba Ghanoush

Prep time: 15 minutes | Cook time: 20 minutes |

Serves 4

1 medium eggplant	1 tablespoon extra-virgin olive oil
2 tablespoons vegetable oil	½ teaspoon smoked paprika
2 tablespoons tahini (sesame paste)	2 tablespoons chopped fresh parsley
2 tablespoons fresh lemon juice	
½ teaspoon kosher salt	

1. Rub the eggplant all over with the vegetable oil. Place the eggplant in the air fryer basket. Set the air fryer to 400ºF (204ºC) for 20 minutes, or until the eggplant skin is blistered and charred. 2. Transfer the eggplant to a resealable plastic bag, seal, and set aside for 15 minutes (the eggplant will finish cooking in the residual heat trapped in the bag). 3. Transfer the eggplant to a large bowl. Peel off and discard the charred skin. Roughly mash the eggplant flesh. Add the tahini, lemon juice, and salt. Stir to combine. 4. Transfer the mixture to a serving bowl. Drizzle with the olive oil. Sprinkle with the paprika and parsley and serve.

Per Serving:

calories: 171 | fat: 15g | protein: 3g | carbs: 10g | fiber: 5g | sodium: 303mg

Roasted Beets with Oranges and Onions

Prep time: 10 minutes | Cook time: 40 minutes |
Serves 6

4 medium beets, trimmed and scrubbed
Juice and zest of 2 oranges
1 red onion, thinly sliced
2 tablespoons olive oil

1 tablespoon red wine vinegar
Juice of 1 lemon
Sea salt and freshly ground pepper, to taste

1. Preheat oven to 400ºF (205ºC). 2. Wrap the beets in a foil pack and close tightly. Place them on a baking sheet and roast 40 minutes until tender enough to be pierced easily with a knife. 3. Cool until easy to handle. 4. Combine the beets with the orange juice and zest, red onion, olive oil, vinegar, and lemon juice. 5. Season with sea salt and freshly ground pepper to taste, and toss lightly. Allow to sit for about 15 minutes for the flavors to meld before serving.

Per Serving:

calories: 86 | fat: 5g | protein: 1g | carbs: 10g | fiber: 2g | sodium: 44mg

Zucchini Fritters with Manchego and Smoked Paprika Yogurt

Prep time: 10 minutes | Cook time: 10 minutes |
Serves 4 to 6

6 small zucchini, grated on the large holes of a box grater
1¼ teaspoons salt, divided
1 cup plain Greek yogurt
2 teaspoons smoked paprika
Juice of ½ lemon
4 ounces (113 g) manchego cheese, grated
¼ cup finely chopped fresh

parsley
4 scallions, thinly sliced
3 eggs, beaten
½ cup all-purpose flour
¼ teaspoon freshly ground black pepper
Neutral-flavored oil (such as grapeseed, safflower, or sunflower seed) for frying

1. Put the grated zucchini in a colander. Sprinkle 1 teaspoon of salt over the top and then toss to combine. Let sit over the sink for at least 20 minutes to drain. Transfer the zucchini to a clean dishtowel and squeeze out as much of the water as you can. 2. Meanwhile, make the yogurt sauce. In a small bowl, stir together the yogurt, smoked paprika, lemon juice, and the remaining ¼ teaspoon of salt. 3. In a large bowl, combine the zucchini, cheese, parsley, scallions, eggs, flour, and pepper and stir to mix. 4. Fill a large saucepan with ½ inch of oil and heat over medium-high heat. When the oil is very hot, drop the batter in by rounded tablespoons, cooking 4 or 5 fritters at a time, flattening each dollop with the back of the spoon. Cook until golden on the bottom, about 2 minutes, then flip and cook on the second side until golden, about 2 minutes more. Transfer the cooked fritters to a plate lined with paper towels to drain and repeat until all of the batter has been cooked.

Per Serving:

calories: 237 | fat: 14g | protein: 11g | carbs: 18g | fiber: 3g | sodium: 655mg

Roasted Acorn Squash

Prep time: 10 minutes | Cook time: 35 minutes |
Serves 6

2 acorn squash, medium to large
2 tablespoons extra-virgin olive oil
1 teaspoon salt, plus more for seasoning

5 tablespoons unsalted butter
¼ cup chopped sage leaves
2 tablespoons fresh thyme leaves
½ teaspoon freshly ground black pepper

1. Preheat the oven to 400°F(205°C). 2. Cut the acorn squash in half lengthwise. Scrape out the seeds with a spoon and cut it horizontally into ¾-inch-thick slices. 3. In a large bowl, drizzle the squash with the olive oil, sprinkle with salt, and toss together to coat. 4. Lay the acorn squash flat on a baking sheet. 5. Put the baking sheet in the oven and bake the squash for 20 minutes. Flip squash over with a spatula and bake for another 15 minutes. 6. Melt the butter in a medium saucepan over medium heat. 7. Add the sage and thyme to the melted butter and let them cook for 30 seconds. 8. Transfer the cooked squash slices to a plate. Spoon the butter/herb mixture over the squash. Season with salt and black pepper. Serve warm.

Per Serving:

calories: 188 | fat: 15g | protein: 1g | carbs: 16g | fiber: 3g | sodium: 393mg

Heirloom Tomato Basil Soup

Prep time: 15 minutes | Cook time: 15 minutes |
Serves 4

1 tablespoon olive oil
1 small onion, peeled and diced
1 stalk celery, sliced
8 medium heirloom tomatoes, seeded and quartered
¼ cup julienned fresh basil

½ teaspoon salt
3 cups low-sodium chicken broth
1 cup heavy cream
1 teaspoon ground black pepper

1. Press the Sauté button on the Instant Pot® and heat oil. Add onion and celery and cook until translucent, about 5 minutes. Add tomatoes and cook for 3 minutes, or until tomatoes are tender and start to break down. Add basil, salt, and broth. Press the Cancel button. 2. Close lid, set steam release to Sealing, press the Manual button, and set time to 7 minutes. When the timer beeps, quick-release the pressure until the float valve drops and then open lid. 3. Add cream and pepper. Purée soup with an immersion blender, or purée in batches in a blender. Ladle into bowls and serve warm.

Per Serving:

calories: 282 | fat: 24g | protein: 4g | carbs: 9g | fiber: 1g | sodium: 466mg

Greek Garlic Dip

Prep time: 10 minutes | Cook time: 30 minutes |

Serves 4

2 potatoes (about 1 pound / 454 g), peeled and quartered	juice
½ cup olive oil	4 garlic cloves, minced
¼ cup freshly squeezed lemon	Sea salt
	Freshly ground black pepper

1. Place the potatoes in a large saucepan and fill the pan three-quarters full with water. Bring the water to a boil over medium-high heat, then reduce the heat to medium and cook the potatoes until fork-tender, 20 to 30 minutes. 2. While the potatoes are boiling, in a medium bowl, stir together the olive oil, lemon juice, and garlic; set aside. 3. Drain the potatoes and return them to the saucepan. Pour in the oil mixture and mash with a potato masher or a fork until well combined and smooth. Taste and season with salt and pepper. Serve.

Per Serving:

calories: 334 | fat: 27g | protein: 3g | carbs: 22g | fiber: 3g | sodium: 47mg

Polenta with Mushroom Bolognese

Prep time: 5 minutes |Cook time: 25 minutes|

Serves: 4

2 (8-ounce / 227-g) packages white button mushrooms	polenta, cut into 8 slices
3 tablespoons extra-virgin olive oil, divided	¼ cup tomato paste
1½ cups finely chopped onion (about ¾ medium onion)	1 tablespoon dried oregano, crushed between your fingers
½ cup finely chopped carrot (about 1 medium carrot)	¼ teaspoon ground nutmeg
4 garlic cloves, minced (about 2 teaspoons)	¼ teaspoon kosher or sea salt
1 (18-ounce / 510-g) tube plain	¼ teaspoon freshly ground black pepper
	½ cup dry red wine
	½ cup whole milk
	½ teaspoon sugar

1. Put half the mushrooms in a food processor bowl and pulse about 15 times until finely chopped but not puréed, similar to the texture of ground meat. Repeat with the remaining mushrooms and set aside. (You can also use the food processor to chop the onion, carrot, and garlic, instead of chopping with a knife.) 2. In a large stockpot over medium-high heat, heat 2 tablespoons of oil. Add the onion and carrot and cook for 5 minutes, stirring occasionally. Add the mushrooms and garlic and cook for 5 minutes, stirring frequently. 3. While the vegetables are cooking, add the remaining 1 tablespoon of oil to a large skillet and heat over medium-high heat. Add 4 slices of polenta to the skillet and cook for 3 to 4 minutes, until golden; flip and cook for 3 to 4 minutes more. Remove the polenta from the skillet, place it on a shallow serving dish, and cover with aluminum foil to keep warm. Repeat with the remaining 4 slices of polenta. 4. To the mushroom mixture in the stockpot, add the tomato paste, oregano, nutmeg, salt, and pepper and stir. Continue cooking for another 2 to 3 minutes, until the vegetables have softened and begun to brown. Add the wine and

cook for 1 to 2 minutes, scraping up any bits from the bottom of the pan while stirring with a wooden spoon. Cook until the wine is nearly all evaporated. Lower the heat to medium. 5. Meanwhile, in a small, microwave-safe bowl, mix the milk and sugar together and microwave on high for 30 to 45 seconds, until very hot. Slowly stir the milk into the mushroom mixture and simmer for 4 more minutes, until the milk is absorbed. To serve, pour the mushroom veggie sauce over the warm polenta slices.

Per Serving:

calories: 313 | fat: 12g | protein: 7g | carbs: 41g | fiber: 4g | sodium: 467mg

Broccoli Tots

Prep time: 15 minutes | Cook time: 10 minutes |

Makes 24 tots

2 cups broccoli florets (about ½ pound / 227 g broccoli crowns)	⅛ teaspoon pepper
1 egg, beaten	2 tablespoons grated Parmesan cheese
⅛ teaspoon onion powder	¼ cup panko bread crumbs
¼ teaspoon salt	Oil for misting

1. Steam broccoli for 2 minutes. Rinse in cold water, drain well, and chop finely. 2. In a large bowl, mix broccoli with all other ingredients except the oil. 3. Scoop out small portions of mixture and shape into 24 tots. Lay them on a cookie sheet or wax paper as you work. 4. Spray tots with oil and place in air fryer basket in single layer. 5. Air fry at 390ºF (199ºC) for 5 minutes. Shake basket and spray with oil again. Cook 5 minutes longer or until browned and crispy.

Per Serving:

2 tots: calories: 21 | fat: 1g | protein: 1g | carbs: 2g | fiber: 0g | sodium: 88mg

Stewed Okra

Prep time: 5 minutes | Cook time: 25 minutes |

Serves 4

¼ cup extra-virgin olive oil	tomato sauce
1 large onion, chopped	2 cups water
4 cloves garlic, finely chopped	½ cup fresh cilantro, finely chopped
1 teaspoon salt	
1 pound (454 g) fresh or frozen okra, cleaned	½ teaspoon freshly ground black pepper
1 (15-ounce / 425-g) can plain	

1. In a large pot over medium heat, stir and cook the olive oil, onion, garlic, and salt for 1 minute. 2. Stir in the okra and cook for 3 minutes. 3. Add the tomato sauce, water, cilantro, and black pepper; stir, cover, and let cook for 15 minutes, stirring occasionally. 4. Serve warm.

Per Serving:

calories: 202 | fat: 14g | protein: 4g | carbs: 19g | fiber: 6g | sodium: 607mg

Eggplant Caponata

Prep time: 20 minutes | Cook time: 5 minutes | Serves 8

¼ cup extra-virgin olive oil
¼ cup white wine
2 tablespoons red wine vinegar
1 teaspoon ground cinnamon
1 large eggplant, peeled and diced
1 medium onion, peeled and diced
1 medium green bell pepper, seeded and diced
1 medium red bell pepper, seeded and diced

2 cloves garlic, peeled and minced
1 (14½-ounce / 411-g) can diced tomatoes
3 stalks celery, diced
½ cup chopped oil-cured olives
½ cup golden raisins
2 tablespoons capers, rinsed and drained
½ teaspoon salt
½ teaspoon ground black pepper

1. Place all ingredients in the Instant Pot®. Stir well to mix. Close lid, set steam release to Sealing, press the Manual button, and set time to 5 minutes. 2. When the timer beeps, quick-release the pressure until the float valve drops. Open the lid and stir well. Serve warm or at room temperature.

Per Serving:

calories: 90 | fat: 1g | protein: 2g | carbs: 17g | fiber: 4g | sodium: 295mg

Garlicky Broccoli Rabe with Artichokes

Prep time: 5 minutes | Cook time: 10 minutes | Serves 4

2 pounds (907 g) fresh broccoli rabe
½ cup extra-virgin olive oil, divided
3 garlic cloves, finely minced
1 teaspoon salt
1 teaspoon red pepper flakes

1 (13¾-ounce / 390-g) can artichoke hearts, drained and quartered
1 tablespoon water
2 tablespoons red wine vinegar
Freshly ground black pepper

1. Trim away any thick lower stems and yellow leaves from the broccoli rabe and discard. Cut into individual florets with a couple inches of thin stem attached. 2. In a large skillet, heat ¼ cup olive oil over medium-high heat. Add the trimmed broccoli, garlic, salt, and red pepper flakes and sauté for 5 minutes, until the broccoli begins to soften. Add the artichoke hearts and sauté for another 2 minutes. 3. Add the water and reduce the heat to low. Cover and simmer until the broccoli stems are tender, 3 to 5 minutes. 4. In a small bowl, whisk together remaining ¼ cup olive oil and the vinegar. Drizzle over the broccoli and artichokes. Season with ground black pepper, if desired.

Per Serving:

calories: 341 | fat: 28g | protein: 11g | carbs: 18g | fiber: 12g | sodium: 750mg

Lemon-Thyme Asparagus

Prep time: 5 minutes | Cook time: 4 to 8 minutes | Serves 4

1 pound (454 g) asparagus, woody ends trimmed off
1 tablespoon avocado oil
½ teaspoon dried thyme or ½ tablespoon chopped fresh thyme
Sea salt and freshly ground

black pepper, to taste
2 ounces (57 g) goat cheese, crumbled
Zest and juice of 1 lemon
Flaky sea salt, for serving (optional)

1. In a medium bowl, toss together the asparagus, avocado oil, and thyme, and season with sea salt and pepper. 2. Place the asparagus in the air fryer basket in a single layer. Set the air fryer to 400ºF (204ºC) and air fry for 4 to 8 minutes, to your desired doneness. 3. Transfer to a serving platter. Top with the goat cheese, lemon zest, and lemon juice. If desired, season with a pinch of flaky salt.

Per Serving:

calories: 121 | fat: 9g | protein: 7g | carbs: 6g | fiber: 3g | sodium: 208mg

Air-Fried Okra

Prep time: 10 minutes | Cook time: 10 minutes | Serves 4

1 egg
½ cup almond milk
½ cup crushed pork rinds
¼ cup grated Parmesan cheese
¼ cup almond flour
1 teaspoon garlic powder

¼ teaspoon freshly ground black pepper
½ pound (227 g) fresh okra, stems removed and chopped into 1-inch slices

1. Preheat the air fryer to 400ºF (204ºC). 2. In a shallow bowl, whisk together the egg and milk. 3. In a second shallow bowl, combine the pork rinds, Parmesan, almond flour, garlic powder, and black pepper. 4. Working with a few slices at a time, dip the okra into the egg mixture followed by the crumb mixture. Press lightly to ensure an even coating. 5. Working in batches if necessary, arrange the okra in a single layer in the air fryer basket and spray lightly with olive oil. Pausing halfway through the cooking time to turn the okra, air fry for 10 minutes until tender and golden brown. Serve warm.

Per Serving:

calories: 200 | fat: 16g | protein: 6g | carbs: 8g | fiber: 2g | sodium: 228mg

Glazed Carrots

Prep time: 10 minutes | Cook time: 8 to 10 minutes | Serves 4

2 teaspoons honey
1 teaspoon orange juice
½ teaspoon grated orange rind
⅛ teaspoon ginger
1 pound (454 g) baby carrots
2 teaspoons olive oil
¼ teaspoon salt

1. Combine honey, orange juice, grated rind, and ginger in a small bowl and set aside. 2. Toss the carrots, oil, and salt together to coat well and pour them into the air fryer basket. 3. Roast at 390ºF (199ºC) for 5 minutes. Shake basket to stir a little and cook for 2 to 4 minutes more, until carrots are barely tender. 4. Pour carrots into a baking pan. 5. Stir the honey mixture to combine well, pour glaze over carrots, and stir to coat. 6. Roast at 360ºF (182ºC) for 1 minute or just until heated through.

Per Serving:

calories: 71 | fat: 2g | protein: 1g | carbs: 12g | fiber: 3g | sodium: 234mg

Green Beans with Potatoes and Basil

Prep time: 20 minutes | Cook time: 10 minutes | Serves 4

2 tablespoons extra-virgin olive oil, plus extra for drizzling
1 onion, chopped fine
2 tablespoons minced fresh oregano or 2 teaspoons dried
2 tablespoons tomato paste
4 garlic cloves, minced
1 (14½-ounce / 411-g) can whole peeled tomatoes, drained with juice reserved, chopped
1 cup water
1 teaspoon table salt
¼ teaspoon pepper
1½ pounds (680 g) green beans, trimmed and cut into 2-inch lengths
1 pound (454 g) Yukon Gold potatoes, peeled and cut into 1-inch pieces
3 tablespoons chopped fresh basil or parsley
2 tablespoons toasted pine nuts
Shaved Parmesan cheese

1. Using highest sauté function, heat oil in Instant Pot until shimmering. Add onion and cook until softened, about 5 minutes. Stir in oregano, tomato paste, and garlic and cook until fragrant, about 30 seconds. Stir in tomatoes and their juice, water, salt, and pepper, then stir in green beans and potatoes. Lock lid in place and close pressure release valve. Select high pressure cook function and cook for 5 minutes. 2. Turn off Instant Pot and quick-release pressure. Carefully remove lid, allowing steam to escape away from you. Season with salt and pepper to taste. Sprinkle individual portions with basil, pine nuts, and Parmesan and drizzle with extra oil. Serve.

Per Serving:

calories: 280 | fat: 10g | protein: 7g | carbs: 42g | fiber: 8g | sodium: 880mg

Honey and Spice Glazed Carrots

Prep time: 5 minutes | Cook time: 5 minutes | Serves 4

4 large carrots, peeled and sliced on the diagonal into ½-inch-thick rounds
1 teaspoon ground cinnamon
1 teaspoon ground ginger
3 tablespoons olive oil
½ cup honey
1 tablespoon red wine vinegar
1 tablespoon chopped flat-leaf parsley
1 tablespoon chopped cilantro
2 tablespoons toasted pine nuts

1. Bring a large saucepan of lightly salted water to a boil and add the carrots. Cover and cook for about 5 minutes, until the carrots are just tender. Drain in a colander, then transfer to a medium bowl. 2. Add the cinnamon, ginger, olive oil, honey, and vinegar and toss to combine well. Add the parsley and cilantro and toss again to incorporate. Garnish with the pine nuts. Serve immediately or let cool to room temperature.

Per Serving:

calories: 281 | fat: 14g | protein: 1g | carbs: 43g | fiber: 2g | sodium: 48mg

Puff Pastry Turnover with Roasted Vegetables

Prep time: 10 minutes | Cook time: 35 minutes | Serves 4 to 6

Nonstick cooking spray
1 zucchini, cut in ¼-inch-thick slices
½ bunch asparagus, cut into quarters
1 package (6-inch) whole-grain pastry discs, in the freezer section (Goya brand preferred), at room temperature
1 large egg, beaten

1. Preheat the oven to 350°F(180°C). 2. Spray a baking sheet with cooking spray and arrange the zucchini and asparagus on it in a single layer. Roast for 15 to 20 minutes, until tender. Set aside to cool. 3. Allow the pastry dough to warm to room temperature. Place the discs on a floured surface. 4. Place a roasted zucchini slice on one half of each disc, then top with asparagus. Fold the empty side over the full side and pinch the turnover closed with a fork. 5. Once all discs are full and closed, brush the turnovers with the beaten egg and put them onto a baking sheet. Bake for 10 to 15 minutes, until golden brown. Let cool completely before eating.

Per Serving:

calories: 334 | fat: 15g | protein: 9g | carbs: 42g | fiber: 4g | sodium: 741mg

Rosemary New Potatoes

Prep time: 10 minutes | Cook time: 5 to 6 minutes | Serves 4

3 large red potatoes (enough to make 3 cups sliced)
¼ teaspoon ground rosemary
¼ teaspoon ground thyme

⅛ teaspoon salt
⅛ teaspoon ground black pepper
2 teaspoons extra-light olive oil

1. Preheat the air fryer to 330°F (166°C). 2. Place potatoes in large bowl and sprinkle with rosemary, thyme, salt, and pepper. 3. Stir with a spoon to distribute seasonings evenly. 4. Add oil to potatoes and stir again to coat well. 5. Air fry at 330°F (166°C) for 4 minutes. Stir and break apart any that have stuck together. 6. Cook an additional 1 to 2 minutes or until fork-tender.

Per Serving:

calories: 214 | fat: 3g | protein: 5g | carbs: 44g | fiber: 5g | sodium: 127mg

Chapter 10 Vegetarian Mains

Stuffed Portobellos

Prep time: 10 minutes | Cook time: 8 minutes | Serves 4

3 ounces (85 g) cream cheese, softened
½ medium zucchini, trimmed and chopped
¼ cup seeded and chopped red bell pepper
1½ cups chopped fresh spinach

leaves
4 large portobello mushrooms, stems removed
2 tablespoons coconut oil, melted
½ teaspoon salt

1. In a medium bowl, mix cream cheese, zucchini, pepper, and spinach. 2. Drizzle mushrooms with coconut oil and sprinkle with salt. Scoop ¼ zucchini mixture into each mushroom. 3. Place mushrooms into ungreased air fryer basket. Adjust the temperature to 400ºF (204ºC) and air fry for 8 minutes. Portobellos will be tender and tops will be browned when done. Serve warm.

Per Serving:

calories: 151 | fat: 13g | protein: 4g | carbs: 6g | fiber: 2g | sodium: 427mg

Greek Frittata with Tomato-Olive Salad

Prep time: 10 minutes | Cook time: 25 minutes | Serves 4 to 6

Frittata:
2 tablespoons olive oil
6 scallions, thinly sliced
4 cups (about 5 ounces / 142 g) baby spinach leaves
8 eggs
¼ cup whole-wheat breadcrumbs, divided
1 cup (about 3 ounces / 85 g) crumbled feta cheese
¾ teaspoon salt
¼ teaspoon freshly ground black pepper

Tomato-Olive Salad:
2 tablespoons olive oil
1 tablespoon lemon juice
¼ teaspoon dried oregano
½ teaspoon salt
¼ teaspoon freshly ground black pepper
1 pint cherry, grape, or other small tomatoes, halved
3 pepperoncini, stemmed and chopped
½ cup coarsely chopped pitted Kalamata olives

1. Preheat the oven to 450°F(235ºC). 2. Heat the olive oil in an oven-safe skillet set over medium-high heat. Add the scallions and spinach and cook, stirring frequently, for about 4 minutes, until the spinach wilts. 3. In a medium bowl, whisk together the eggs, 2 tablespoons breadcrumbs, cheese, ¾ cup water, salt, and pepper. Pour the egg mixture into the skillet with the spinach and onions and stir to mix. Sprinkle the remaining 2 tablespoons of breadcrumbs evenly over the top. Bake the frittata in the preheated oven for about 20 minutes, until the egg is set and the top is lightly browned. 4. While the frittata is cooking, make the salad. In a medium bowl, whisk together the olive oil, lemon juice, oregano, salt, and pepper. Add the tomatoes, pepperoncini, and olives and toss to mix well. 5. Invert the frittata onto a serving platter and slice it into wedges. Serve warm or at room temperature with the tomato-olive salad.

Per Serving:

calories: 246 | fat: 19g | protein: 11g | carbs: 8g | fiber: 1g | sodium: 832mg

Roasted Portobello Mushrooms with Kale and Red Onion

Prep time: 15 minutes | Cook time: 30 minutes | Serves 4

¼ cup white wine vinegar
3 tablespoons extra-virgin olive oil, divided
½ teaspoon honey
¾ teaspoon kosher salt, divided
¼ teaspoon freshly ground black pepper
4 large (4 to 5 ounces / 113 to 142 g each) portobello

mushrooms, stems removed
1 red onion, julienned
2 garlic cloves, minced
1 (8-ounce / 227-g) bunch kale, stemmed and chopped small
¼ teaspoon red pepper flakes
¼ cup grated Parmesan or Romano cheese

1. Line a baking sheet with parchment paper or foil. In a medium bowl, whisk together the vinegar, 1½ tablespoons of the olive oil, honey, ¼ teaspoon of the salt, and the black pepper. Arrange the mushrooms on the baking sheet and pour the marinade over them. Marinate for 15 to 30 minutes. 2. Meanwhile, preheat the oven to 400ºF (205ºC). 3. Bake the mushrooms for 20 minutes, turning over halfway through. 4. Heat the remaining 1½ tablespoons olive oil in a large skillet or ovenproof sauté pan over medium-high heat. Add the onion and the remaining ½ teaspoon salt and sauté until golden brown, 5 to 6 minutes. Add the garlic and sauté for 30 seconds. Add the kale and red pepper flakes and sauté until the kale cooks down, about 5 minutes. 5. Remove the mushrooms from the oven and increase the temperature to broil. 6. Carefully pour the liquid from the baking sheet into the pan with the kale mixture; mix well. 7. Turn the mushrooms over so that the stem side is facing up. Spoon some of the kale mixture on top of each mushroom. Sprinkle 1 tablespoon Parmesan cheese on top of each. 8. Broil until golden brown, 3 to 4 minutes.

Per Serving:

calories: 200 | fat: 13g | protein: 8g | carbs: 16g | fiber: 4g | sodium: 365mg

Provençal Ratatouille with Herbed Breadcrumbs and Goat Cheese

Prep time: 10 minutes | Cook time: 1 hour 5 minutes | Serves 4

6 tablespoons olive oil, divided
2 medium onions, diced
2 cloves garlic, minced
2 medium eggplants, halved lengthwise and cut into ¾-inch thick half rounds
3 medium zucchini, halved lengthwise and cut into ¾-inch thick half rounds
2 red bell peppers, seeded and cut into 1½-inch pieces
1 green bell pepper, seeded and cut into 1½-inch pieces
1 (14-ounce / 397-g) can diced tomatoes, drained
1 teaspoon salt
½ teaspoon freshly ground black pepper
8 ounces (227 g) fresh breadcrumbs
1 tablespoon chopped fresh parsley
1 tablespoon chopped fresh basil
1 tablespoon chopped fresh chives
6 ounces (170 g) soft, fresh goat cheese

1. Preheat the oven to 375°F(190°C). 2. Heat 5 tablespoons of the olive oil in a large skillet over medium heat. Add the onions and garlic and cook, stirring frequently, until the onions are soft and beginning to turn golden, about 8 minutes. Add the eggplant, zucchini, and bell peppers and cook, turning the vegetables occasionally, for another 10 minutes. Stir in the tomatoes, salt, and pepper and let simmer for 15 minutes. 3. While the vegetables are simmering, stir together the breadcrumbs, the remaining tablespoon of olive oil, the parsley, basil, and chives. 4. Transfer the vegetable mixture to a large baking dish, spreading it out into an even layer. Crumble the goat cheese over the top, then sprinkle the breadcrumb mixture evenly over the top. Bake in the preheated oven for about 30 minutes, until the topping is golden brown and crisp. Serve hot.

Per Serving:

calories: 644 | fat: 37g | protein: 21g | carbs: 63g | fiber: 16g | sodium: 861mg

Fava Bean Purée with Chicory

Prep time: 5 minutes | Cook time: 2 hours 10 minutes | Serves 4

½ pound (227 g) dried fava beans, soaked in water overnight and drained
1 pound (454 g) chicory leaves
¼ cup olive oil
1 small onion, chopped
1 clove garlic, minced
Salt

1. In a saucepan, cover the fava beans by at least an inch of water and bring to a boil over medium-high heat. Reduce the heat to low, cover, and simmer until very tender, about 2 hours. Check the pot from time to time to make sure there is enough water and add more as needed. 2. Drain off any excess water and then mash the beans with a potato masher. 3. While the beans are cooking, bring a large pot of salted water to a boil. Add the chicory and cook for about 3 minutes, until tender. Drain. 4. In a medium skillet, heat the olive oil over medium-high heat. Add the onion and a pinch of salt and cook, stirring frequently, until softened and beginning to brown, about 5 minutes. Add the garlic and cook, stirring, for another minute. Transfer half of the onion mixture, along with the oil, to the bowl with the mashed beans and stir to mix. Taste and add salt as needed. 5. Serve the purée topped with some of the remaining onions and oil, with the chicory leaves on the side.

Per Serving:

calories: 336 | fat: 14g | protein: 17g | carbs: 40g | fiber: 19g | sodium: 59mg

Pesto Vegetable Skewers

Prep time: 30 minutes | Cook time: 8 minutes | Makes 8 skewers

1 medium zucchini, trimmed and cut into ½-inch slices
½ medium yellow onion, peeled and cut into 1-inch squares
1 medium red bell pepper, seeded and cut into 1-inch squares
16 whole cremini mushrooms
⅓ cup basil pesto
½ teaspoon salt
¼ teaspoon ground black pepper

1. Divide zucchini slices, onion, and bell pepper into eight even portions. Place on 6-inch skewers for a total of eight kebabs. Add 2 mushrooms to each skewer and brush kebabs generously with pesto. 2. Sprinkle each kebab with salt and black pepper on all sides, then place into ungreased air fryer basket. Adjust the temperature to 375ºF (191ºC) and air fry for 8 minutes, turning kebabs halfway through cooking. Vegetables will be browned at the edges and tender-crisp when done. Serve warm.

Per Serving:

calories: 75 | fat: 6g | protein: 3g | carbs: 4g | fiber: 1g | sodium: 243mg

Freekeh, Chickpea, and Herb Salad

Prep time: 15 minutes | Cook time: 10 minutes | Serves 4 to 6

1 (15-ounce / 425-g) can chickpeas, rinsed and drained
1 cup cooked freekeh
1 cup thinly sliced celery
1 bunch scallions, both white and green parts, finely chopped
½ cup chopped fresh flat-leaf parsley
¼ cup chopped fresh mint
3 tablespoons chopped celery leaves
½ teaspoon kosher salt
⅓ cup extra-virgin olive oil
¼ cup freshly squeezed lemon juice
¼ teaspoon cumin seeds
1 teaspoon garlic powder

1. In a large bowl, combine the chickpeas, freekeh, celery, scallions, parsley, mint, celery leaves, and salt and toss lightly. 2. In a small bowl, whisk together the olive oil, lemon juice, cumin seeds, and garlic powder. Once combined, add to freekeh salad.

Per Serving:

calories: 350 | fat: 19g | protein: 9g | carbs: 38g | fiber: 9g | sodium: 329mg

Tortellini in Red Pepper Sauce

Prep time: 15 minutes | Cook time: 10 minutes | Serves 4

1 (16-ounce / 454-g) container fresh cheese tortellini (usually green and white pasta)
1 (16-ounce / 454-g) jar roasted red peppers, drained
1 teaspoon garlic powder
¼ cup tahini
1 tablespoon red pepper oil (optional)

1. Bring a large pot of water to a boil and cook the tortellini according to package directions. 2. In a blender, combine the red peppers with the garlic powder and process until smooth. Once blended, add the tahini until the sauce is thickened. If the sauce gets too thick, add up to 1 tablespoon red pepper oil (if using). 3. Once tortellini are cooked, drain and leave pasta in colander. Add the sauce to the bottom of the empty pot and heat for 2 minutes. Then, add the tortellini back into the pot and cook for 2 more minutes. Serve and enjoy!

Per Serving:

calories: 350 | fat: 11g | protein: 12g | carbs: 46g | fiber: 4g | sodium: 192mg

Moroccan Vegetable Tagine

Prep time: 20 minutes | Cook time: 1 hour | Serves 6

½ cup extra-virgin olive oil
2 medium yellow onions, sliced
6 celery stalks, sliced into ¼-inch crescents
6 garlic cloves, minced
1 teaspoon ground cumin
1 teaspoon ginger powder
1 teaspoon salt
½ teaspoon paprika
½ teaspoon ground cinnamon
¼ teaspoon freshly ground black pepper
2 cups vegetable stock
1 medium eggplant, cut into 1-inch cubes
2 medium zucchini, cut into ½-inch-thick semicircles
2 cups cauliflower florets
1 (13¾-ounce / 390-g) can artichoke hearts, drained and quartered
1 cup halved and pitted green olives
½ cup chopped fresh flat-leaf parsley, for garnish
½ cup chopped fresh cilantro leaves, for garnish
Greek yogurt, for garnish (optional)

1. In a large, thick soup pot or Dutch oven, heat the olive oil over medium-high heat. Add the onion and celery and sauté until softened, 6 to 8 minutes. Add the garlic, cumin, ginger, salt, paprika, cinnamon, and pepper and sauté for another 2 minutes. 2. Add the stock and bring to a boil. Reduce the heat to low and add the eggplant, zucchini, and cauliflower. Simmer on low heat, covered, until the vegetables are tender, 30 to 35 minutes. Add the artichoke hearts and olives, cover, and simmer for another 15 minutes. 3. Serve garnished with parsley, cilantro, and Greek yogurt (if using).

Per Serving:

calories: 265 | fat: 21g | protein: 5g | carbs: 19g | fiber: 9g | sodium: 858mg

Balsamic Marinated Tofu with Basil and Oregano

Prep time: 10 minutes | Cook time: 30 minutes | Serves 4

¼ cup extra-virgin olive oil
¼ cup balsamic vinegar
2 tablespoons low-sodium soy sauce or gluten-free tamari
3 garlic cloves, grated
2 teaspoons pure maple syrup
Zest of 1 lemon
1 teaspoon dried basil
1 teaspoon dried oregano
½ teaspoon dried thyme
½ teaspoon dried sage
¼ teaspoon kosher salt
¼ teaspoon freshly ground black pepper
¼ teaspoon red pepper flakes (optional)
1 (16-ounce / 454-g) block extra firm tofu, drained and patted dry, cut into ½-inch or 1-inch cubes

1. In a bowl or gallon zip-top bag, mix together the olive oil, vinegar, soy sauce, garlic, maple syrup, lemon zest, basil, oregano, thyme, sage, salt, black pepper, and red pepper flakes, if desired. Add the tofu and mix gently. Put in the refrigerator and marinate for 30 minutes, or up to overnight if you desire. 2. Preheat the oven to 425ºF (220ºC). Line a baking sheet with parchment paper or foil. Arrange the marinated tofu in a single layer on the prepared baking sheet. Bake for 20 to 30 minutes, turning over halfway through, until slightly crispy on the outside and tender on the inside.

Per Serving:

calories: 225 | fat: 16g | protein: 13g | carbs: 9g | fiber: 2g | sodium: 265mg

Mediterranean Baked Chickpeas

Prep time: 15 minutes | Cook time: 15 minutes | Serves 4

1 tablespoon extra-virgin olive oil
½ medium onion, chopped
3 garlic cloves, chopped
2 teaspoons smoked paprika
¼ teaspoon ground cumin
4 cups halved cherry tomatoes
2 (15-ounce / 425-g) cans chickpeas, drained and rinsed
½ cup plain, unsweetened, full-fat Greek yogurt, for serving
1 cup crumbled feta, for serving

1. Preheat the oven to 425ºF (220ºC). 2. In an oven-safe sauté pan or skillet, heat the oil over medium heat and sauté the onion and garlic. Cook for about 5 minutes, until softened and fragrant. Stir in the paprika and cumin and cook for 2 minutes. Stir in the tomatoes and chickpeas. 3. Bring to a simmer for 5 to 10 minutes before placing in the oven. 4. Roast in oven for 25 to 30 minutes, until bubbling and thickened. To serve, top with Greek yogurt and feta.

Per Serving:

calories: 412 | fat: 15g | protein: 20g | carbs: 51g | fiber: 13g | sodium: 444mg

Root Vegetable Soup with Garlic Aioli

Prep time: 10 minutes | Cook time 25 minutes |

Serves 4

For the Soup:
8 cups vegetable broth
½ teaspoon salt
1 medium leek, cut into thick rounds
1 pound (454 g) carrots, peeled and diced
1 pound (454 g) potatoes, peeled and diced

1 pound (454 g) turnips, peeled and cut into 1-inch cubes
1 red bell pepper, cut into strips
2 tablespoons fresh oregano
For the Aioli:
5 garlic cloves, minced
¼ teaspoon salt
⅔ cup olive oil
1 drop lemon juice

1. Bring the broth and salt to a boil and add the vegetables one at a time, letting the water return to a boil after each addition. Add the carrots first, then the leeks, potatoes, turnips, and finally the red bell peppers. Let the vegetables cook for about 3 minutes after adding the green beans and bringing to a boil. The process will take about 20 minutes in total. 2. Meanwhile, make the aioli. In a mortar and pestle, grind the garlic to a paste with the salt. Using a whisk and whisking constantly, add the olive oil in a thin stream. Continue whisking until the mixture thickens to the consistency of mayonnaise. Add the lemon juice. 3. Serve the vegetables in the broth, dolloped with the aioli and garnished with the fresh oregano.

Per Serving:

calories: 538 | fat: 37g | protein: 5g | carbs: 50g | fiber: 9g | sodium: 773mg

Quinoa Lentil "Meatballs" with Quick Tomato Sauce

Prep time: 25 minutes | Cook time: 45 minutes |

Serves 4

For the Meatballs:
Olive oil cooking spray
2 large eggs, beaten
1 tablespoon no-salt-added tomato paste
½ teaspoon kosher salt
½ cup grated Parmesan cheese
½ onion, roughly chopped
¼ cup fresh parsley
1 garlic clove, peeled
1½ cups cooked lentils
1 cup cooked quinoa

For the Tomato Sauce:
1 tablespoon extra-virgin olive oil
1 onion, minced
½ teaspoon dried oregano
½ teaspoon kosher salt
2 garlic cloves, minced
1 (28-ounce / 794-g) can no-salt-added crushed tomatoes
½ teaspoon honey
¼ cup fresh basil, chopped

Make the Meatballs: 1. Preheat the oven to 400ºF (205ºC). Lightly grease a 12-cup muffin pan with olive oil cooking spray. 2. In a large bowl, whisk together the eggs, tomato paste, and salt until fully combined. Mix in the Parmesan cheese. 3. In a food processor, add the onion, parsley, and garlic. Process until minced. Add to the egg mixture and stir together. Add the lentils to the food processor and process until puréed into a thick paste. Add to the large bowl and mix together. Add the quinoa and mix well. 4. Form balls, slightly larger than a golf ball, with ¼ cup of the quinoa mixture. Place each ball in a muffin pan cup. Note: The mixture will be somewhat soft but should hold together. 5. Bake 25 to 30 minutes, until golden brown. Make the Tomato Sauce: 6. Heat the olive oil in a large saucepan over medium heat. Add the onion, oregano, and salt and sauté until light golden brown, about 5 minutes. Add the garlic and cook for 30 seconds. 7. Stir in the tomatoes and honey. Increase the heat to high and cook, stirring often, until simmering, then decrease the heat to medium-low and cook for 10 minutes. Remove from the heat and stir in the basil. Serve with the meatballs.

Per Serving:

3 meatballs: calories: 360 | fat: 10g | protein: 20g | carbs: 48g | fiber: 14g | sodium: 520mg

Roasted Ratatouille Pasta

Prep time: 10 minutes | Cook time: 20 minutes |

Serves 2

1 small eggplant (about 8 ounces / 227 g)
1 small zucchini
1 portobello mushroom
1 Roma tomato, halved
½ medium sweet red pepper, seeded
½ teaspoon salt, plus additional for the pasta water

1 teaspoon Italian herb seasoning
1 tablespoon olive oil
2 cups farfalle pasta (about 8 ounces / 227 g)
2 tablespoons minced sun-dried tomatoes in olive oil with herbs
2 tablespoons prepared pesto

1. Slice the ends off the eggplant and zucchini. Cut them lengthwise into ½-inch slices. 2. Place the eggplant, zucchini, mushroom, tomato, and red pepper in a large bowl and sprinkle with ½ teaspoon of salt. Using your hands, toss the vegetables well so that they're covered evenly with the salt. Let them rest for about 10 minutes. 3. While the vegetables are resting, preheat the oven to 400°F (205ºC) and set the rack to the bottom position. Line a baking sheet with parchment paper. 4. When the oven is hot, drain off any liquid from the vegetables and pat them dry with a paper towel. Add the Italian herb seasoning and olive oil to the vegetables and toss well to coat both sides. 5. Lay the vegetables out in a single layer on the baking sheet. Roast them for 15 to 20 minutes, flipping them over after about 10 minutes or once they start to brown on the underside. When the vegetables are charred in spots, remove them from the oven. 6. While the vegetables are roasting, fill a large saucepan with water. Add salt and cook the pasta according to package directions. Drain the pasta, reserving ½ cup of the pasta water. 7. When cool enough to handle, cut the vegetables into large chunks (about 2 inches) and add them to the hot pasta. 8. Stir in the sun-dried tomatoes and pesto and toss everything well.

Per Serving:

calories: 612 | fat: 16g | protein: 23g | carbs: 110g | fiber: 23g | sodium: 776mg

Rustic Vegetable and Brown Rice Bowl

Prep time: 15 minutes | Cook time: 20 minutes |

Serves 4

Nonstick cooking spray
2 cups broccoli florets
2 cups cauliflower florets
1 (15-ounce / 425-g) can chickpeas, drained and rinsed
1 cup carrots sliced 1 inch thick
2 to 3 tablespoons extra-virgin olive oil, divided
Salt
Freshly ground black pepper
2 to 3 tablespoons sesame seeds, for garnish
2 cups cooked brown rice
For the Dressing:
3 to 4 tablespoons tahini
2 tablespoons honey
1 lemon, juiced
1 garlic clove, minced
Salt
Freshly ground black pepper

1. Preheat the oven to 400ºF (205ºC). Spray two baking sheets with cooking spray. 2. Cover the first baking sheet with the broccoli and cauliflower and the second with the chickpeas and carrots. Toss each sheet with half of the oil and season with salt and pepper before placing in oven. 3. Cook the carrots and chickpeas for 10 minutes, leaving the carrots still just crisp, and the broccoli and cauliflower for 20 minutes, until tender. Stir each halfway through cooking. 4. To make the dressing, in a small bowl, mix the tahini, honey, lemon juice, and garlic. Season with salt and pepper and set aside. 5. Divide the rice into individual bowls, then layer with vegetables and drizzle dressing over the dish.

Per Serving:

calories: 454 | fat: 18g | protein: 12g | carbs: 62g | fiber: 11g | sodium: 61mg

Mozzarella and Sun-Dried Portobello Mushroom Pizza

Prep time: 10 minutes | Cook time: 10 minutes |

Serves 4

4 large portobello mushroom caps
3 tablespoons extra-virgin olive oil
Salt
Freshly ground black pepper
4 sun-dried tomatoes
1 cup mozzarella cheese, divided
½ to ¾ cup low-sodium tomato sauce

1. Preheat the broiler on high. 2. On a baking sheet, drizzle the mushroom caps with the olive oil and season with salt and pepper. Broil the portobello mushrooms for 5 minutes on each side, flipping once, until tender. 3. Fill each mushroom cap with 1 sun-dried tomato, 2 tablespoons of cheese, and 2 to 3 tablespoons of sauce. Top each with 2 tablespoons of cheese. Place the caps back under the broiler for a final 2 to 3 minutes, then quarter the mushrooms and serve.

Per Serving:

calories: 218| fat: 16g | protein: 11g | carbs: 12g | fiber: 2g | sodium: 244mg

Ricotta, Basil, and Pistachio-Stuffed Zucchini

Prep time: 15 minutes | Cook time: 25 minutes |

Serves 4

2 medium zucchini, halved lengthwise
1 tablespoon extra-virgin olive oil
1 onion, diced
1 teaspoon kosher salt
2 garlic cloves, minced
¾ cup ricotta cheese
¼ cup unsalted pistachios, shelled and chopped
¼ cup fresh basil, chopped
1 large egg, beaten
¼ teaspoon freshly ground black pepper

1. Preheat the oven to 425ºF (220ºC). Line a baking sheet with parchment paper or foil. 2. Scoop out the seeds/pulp from the zucchini, leaving ¼-inch flesh around the edges. Transfer the pulp to a cutting board and chop the pulp. 3. Heat the olive oil in a large skillet or sauté pan over medium heat. Add the onion, pulp, and salt and sauté about 5 minutes. Add the garlic and sauté 30 seconds. 4. In a medium bowl, combine the ricotta cheese, pistachios, basil, egg, and black pepper. Add the onion mixture and mix together well. 5. Place the 4 zucchini halves on the prepared baking sheet. Fill the zucchini halves with the ricotta mixture. Bake for 20 minutes, or until golden brown.

Per Serving:

calories: 200 | fat: 12g | protein: 11g | carbs: 14g | fiber: 3g | sodium: 360mg

Stuffed Pepper Stew

Prep time: 20 minutes | Cook time: 50 minutes |

Serves 2

2 tablespoons olive oil
2 sweet peppers, diced (about 2 cups)
½ large onion, minced
1 garlic clove, minced
1 teaspoon oregano
1 tablespoon gluten-free
vegetarian Worcestershire sauce
1 cup low-sodium vegetable stock
1 cup low-sodium tomato juice
¼ cup brown lentils
¼ cup brown rice
Salt

1. Heat olive oil in a Dutch oven over medium-high heat. Add the sweet peppers and onion and sauté for 10 minutes, or until the peppers are wilted and the onion starts to turn golden. 2. Add the garlic, oregano, and Worcestershire sauce, and cook for another 30 seconds. Add the vegetable stock, tomato juice, lentils, and rice. 3. Bring the mixture to a boil. Cover, and reduce the heat to medium-low. Simmer for 45 minutes, or until the rice is cooked and the lentils are softened. Season with salt.

Per Serving:

calories: 379 | fat: 16g | protein: 11g | carbs: 53g | fiber: 7g | sodium: 392mg

Sheet Pan Roasted Chickpeas and Vegetables with Harissa Yogurt

Prep time: 10 minutes | Cook time: 30 minutes | Serves 2

4 cups cauliflower florets (about ½ small head)
2 medium carrots, peeled, halved, and then sliced into quarters lengthwise
2 tablespoons olive oil, divided
½ teaspoon garlic powder, divided

½ teaspoon salt, divided
2 teaspoons za'atar spice mix, divided
1 (15-ounce / 425-g) can chickpeas, drained, rinsed, and patted dry
¾ cup plain Greek yogurt
1 teaspoon harissa spice paste

1. Preheat the oven to 400ºF (205ºC) and set the rack to the middle position. Line a sheet pan with foil or parchment paper. 2. Place the cauliflower and carrots in a large bowl. Drizzle with 1 tablespoon olive oil and sprinkle with ¼ teaspoon of garlic powder, ¼ teaspoon of salt, and 1 teaspoon of za'atar. Toss well to combine. 3. Spread the vegetables onto one half of the sheet pan in a single layer. 4. Place the chickpeas in the same bowl and season with the remaining 1 tablespoon of oil, ¼ teaspoon of garlic powder, and ¼ teaspoon of salt, and the remaining za'atar. Toss well to combine. 5. Spread the chickpeas onto the other half of the sheet pan. 6. Roast for 30 minutes, or until the vegetables are tender and the chickpeas start to turn golden. Flip the vegetables halfway through the cooking time, and give the chickpeas a stir so they cook evenly. 7. The chickpeas may need an extra few minutes if you like them crispy. If so, remove the vegetables and leave the chickpeas in until they're cooked to desired crispiness. 8. While the vegetables are roasting, combine the yogurt and harissa in a small bowl. Taste, and add additional harissa as desired.

Per Serving:

calories: 467 | fat: 23g | protein: 18g | carbs: 54g | fiber: 15g | sodium: 632mg

Roasted Veggie Bowl

Prep time: 10 minutes | Cook time: 15 minutes | Serves 2

1 cup broccoli florets
1 cup quartered Brussels sprouts
½ cup cauliflower florets
¼ medium white onion, peeled and sliced ¼ inch thick

½ medium green bell pepper, seeded and sliced ¼ inch thick
1 tablespoon coconut oil
2 teaspoons chili powder
½ teaspoon garlic powder
½ teaspoon cumin

1. Toss all ingredients together in a large bowl until vegetables are fully coated with oil and seasoning. 2. Pour vegetables into the air fryer basket. 3. Adjust the temperature to 360ºF (182ºC) and roast for 15 minutes. 4. Shake two or three times during cooking. Serve warm.

Per Serving:

calories: 112 | fat: 7.68g | protein: 3.64g | carbs: 10.67g | sugars: 3.08g | fiber: 4.6g | sodium: 106mg

Kate's Warm Mediterranean Farro Bowl

Prep time: 15 minutes | Cook time: 10 minutes | Serves 4 to 6

⅓ cup extra-virgin olive oil
½ cup chopped red bell pepper
⅓ cup chopped red onions
2 garlic cloves, minced
1 cup zucchini, cut in ½-inch slices
½ cup canned chickpeas, drained and rinsed
½ cup coarsely chopped artichokes
3 cups cooked farro

Salt
Freshly ground black pepper
¼ cup sliced olives, for serving (optional)
½ cup crumbled feta cheese, for serving (optional)
2 tablespoons fresh basil, chiffonade, for serving (optional)
3 tablespoons balsamic reduction, for serving (optional)

1. In a large sauté pan or skillet, heat the oil over medium heat and sauté the pepper, onions, and garlic for about 5 minutes, until tender. 2. Add the zucchini, chickpeas, and artichokes, then stir and continue to sauté vegetables, approximately 5 more minutes, until just soft. 3. Stir in the cooked farro, tossing to combine and cooking enough to heat through. Season with salt and pepper and remove from the heat. 4. Transfer the contents of the pan into the serving vessels or bowls. 5. Top with olives, feta, and basil (if using). Drizzle with balsamic reduction (if using) to finish.

Per Serving:

calories: 367 | fat: 20g | protein: 9g | carbs: 51g | fiber: 9g | sodium: 87mg

Herbed Ricotta–Stuffed Mushrooms

Prep time: 10 minutes | Cook time: 30 minutes | Serves 4

6 tablespoons extra-virgin olive oil, divided
4 portobello mushroom caps, cleaned and gills removed
1 cup whole-milk ricotta cheese
⅓ cup chopped fresh herbs

(such as basil, parsley, rosemary, oregano, or thyme)
2 garlic cloves, finely minced
½ teaspoon salt
¼ teaspoon freshly ground black pepper

1. Preheat the oven to 400ºF (205ºC). 2. Line a baking sheet with parchment or foil and drizzle with 2 tablespoons olive oil, spreading evenly. Place the mushroom caps on the baking sheet, gill-side up. 3. In a medium bowl, mix together the ricotta, herbs, 2 tablespoons olive oil, garlic, salt, and pepper. Stuff each mushroom cap with one-quarter of the cheese mixture, pressing down if needed. Drizzle with remaining 2 tablespoons olive oil and bake until golden brown and the mushrooms are soft, 30 to 35 minutes, depending on the size of the mushrooms.

Per Serving:

calories: 308 | fat: 29g | protein: 9g | carbs: 6g | fiber: 1g | sodium: 351mg

Turkish Red Lentil and Bulgur Kofte

Prep time: 10 minutes | Cook time: 45 minutes |

Serves 4

⅓ cup olive oil, plus 2 tablespoons, divided, plus more for brushing
1 cup red lentils
½ cup bulgur
1 teaspoon salt
1 medium onion, finely diced

2 tablespoons tomato paste
1 teaspoon ground cumin
¼ cup finely chopped flat-leaf parsley
3 scallions, thinly sliced
Juice of ½ lemon

1. Preheat the oven to 400°F(205°C). 2. Brush a large, rimmed baking sheet with olive oil. 3. In a medium saucepan, combine the lentils with 2 cups water and bring to a boil. Reduce the heat to low and cook, stirring occasionally, for about 15 minutes, until the lentils are tender and have soaked up most of the liquid. Remove from the heat, stir in the bulgur and salt, cover, and let sit for 15 minutes or so, until the bulgur is tender. 4. Meanwhile, heat ⅓ cup olive oil in a medium skillet over medium-high heat. Add the onion and cook, stirring frequently, until softened, about 5 minutes. Stir in the tomato paste and cook for 2 minutes more. Remove from the heat and stir in the cumin. 5. Add the cooked onion mixture to the lentil-bulgur mixture and stir to combine. Add the parsley, scallions, and lemon juice and stir to mix well. 6. Shape the mixture into walnut-sized balls and place them on the prepared baking sheet. Brush the balls with the remaining 2 tablespoons of olive oil and bake for 15 to 20 minutes, until golden brown. Serve hot.

Per Serving:

calories: 460 | fat: 25g | protein: 16g | carbs: 48g | fiber: 19g | sodium: 604mg

Pesto Spinach Flatbread

Prep time: 10 minutes | Cook time: 8 minutes |

Serves 4

1 cup blanched finely ground almond flour
2 ounces (57 g) cream cheese
2 cups shredded Mozzarella

cheese
1 cup chopped fresh spinach leaves
2 tablespoons basil pesto

1. Place flour, cream cheese, and Mozzarella in a large microwave-safe bowl and microwave on high 45 seconds, then stir. 2. Fold in spinach and microwave an additional 15 seconds. Stir until a soft dough ball forms. 3. Cut two pieces of parchment paper to fit air fryer basket. Separate dough into two sections and press each out on ungreased parchment to create 6-inch rounds. 4. Spread 1 tablespoon pesto over each flatbread and place rounds on parchment into ungreased air fryer basket. Adjust the temperature to 350°F (177°C) and air fry for 8 minutes, turning crusts halfway through cooking. Flatbread will be golden when done. 5. Let cool 5 minutes before slicing and serving.

Per Serving:

calories: 387 | fat: 28g | protein: 28g | carbs: 10g | fiber: 5g | sodium: 556mg

Cauliflower Steak with Gremolata

Prep time: 15 minutes | Cook time: 25 minutes |

Serves 4

2 tablespoons olive oil
1 tablespoon Italian seasoning
1 large head cauliflower, outer leaves removed and sliced lengthwise through the core into thick "steaks"
Salt and freshly ground black pepper, to taste
¼ cup Parmesan cheese

Gremolata:
1 bunch Italian parsley (about 1 cup packed)
2 cloves garlic
Zest of 1 small lemon, plus 1 to 2 teaspoons lemon juice
½ cup olive oil
Salt and pepper, to taste

1. Preheat the air fryer to 400°F (204°C). 2. In a small bowl, combine the olive oil and Italian seasoning. Brush both sides of each cauliflower "steak" generously with the oil. Season to taste with salt and black pepper. 3. Working in batches if necessary, arrange the cauliflower in a single layer in the air fryer basket. Pausing halfway through the cooking time to turn the "steaks," air fry for 15 to 20 minutes until the cauliflower is tender and the edges begin to brown. Sprinkle with the Parmesan and air fry for 5 minutes longer. 4. To make the gremolata: In a food processor fitted with a metal blade, combine the parsley, garlic, and lemon zest and juice. With the motor running, add the olive oil in a steady stream until the mixture forms a bright green sauce. Season to taste with salt and black pepper. Serve the cauliflower steaks with the gremolata spooned over the top.

Per Serving:

calories: 336 | fat: 30g | protein: 7g | carbs: 15g | fiber: 5g | sodium: 340mg

Parmesan Artichokes

Prep time: 10 minutes | Cook time: 10 minutes |

Serves 4

2 medium artichokes, trimmed and quartered, center removed
2 tablespoons coconut oil
1 large egg, beaten
½ cup grated vegetarian

Parmesan cheese
¼ cup blanched finely ground almond flour
½ teaspoon crushed red pepper flakes

1. In a large bowl, toss artichokes in coconut oil and then dip each piece into the egg. 2. Mix the Parmesan and almond flour in a large bowl. Add artichoke pieces and toss to cover as completely as possible, sprinkle with pepper flakes. Place into the air fryer basket. 3. Adjust the temperature to 400°F (204°C) and air fry for 10 minutes. 4. Toss the basket two times during cooking. Serve warm.

Per Serving:

calories: 207 | fat: 13g | protein: 10g | carbs: 15g | fiber: 5g | sodium: 211mg

Caprese Eggplant Stacks

Prep time: 5 minutes | Cook time: 12 minutes | Serves 4

1 medium eggplant, cut into ¼-inch slices
2 large tomatoes, cut into ¼-inch slices
4 ounces (113 g) fresh

Mozzarella, cut into ½-ounce / 14-g slices
2 tablespoons olive oil
¼ cup fresh basil, sliced

1. In a baking dish, place four slices of eggplant on the bottom. Place a slice of tomato on top of each eggplant round, then Mozzarella, then eggplant. Repeat as necessary. 2. Drizzle with olive oil. Cover dish with foil and place dish into the air fryer basket. 3. Adjust the temperature to 350ºF (177ºC) and bake for 12 minutes. 4. When done, eggplant will be tender. Garnish with fresh basil to serve.

Per Serving:

calories: 97 | fat: 7g | protein: 2g | carbs: 8g | fiber: 4g | sodium: 11mg

Zucchini Lasagna

Prep time: 15 minutes | Cook time: 1 hour | Serves 8

½ cup extra-virgin olive oil, divided
4 to 5 medium zucchini squash
1 teaspoon salt
8 ounces (227 g) frozen spinach, thawed and well drained (about 1 cup)
2 cups whole-milk ricotta cheese
¼ cup chopped fresh basil or 2 teaspoons dried basil

1 teaspoon garlic powder
½ teaspoon freshly ground black pepper
2 cups shredded fresh whole-milk mozzarella cheese
1¾ cups shredded Parmesan cheese
½ (24-ounce / 680-g) jar low-sugar marinara sauce (less than 5 grams sugar)

1. Preheat the oven to 425ºF (220ºC). 2. Line two baking sheets with parchment paper or aluminum foil and drizzle each with 2 tablespoons olive oil, spreading evenly. 3. Slice the zucchini lengthwise into ¼-inch-thick long slices and place on the prepared baking sheet in a single layer. Sprinkle with ½ teaspoon salt per sheet. Bake until softened, but not mushy, 15 to 18 minutes. Remove from the oven and allow to cool slightly before assembling the lasagna. 4. Reduce the oven temperature to 375ºF (190ºC). 5. While the zucchini cooks, prep the filling. In a large bowl, combine the spinach, ricotta, basil, garlic powder, and pepper. In a small bowl, mix together the mozzarella and Parmesan cheeses. In a medium bowl, combine the marinara sauce and remaining ¼ cup olive oil and stir to fully incorporate the oil into sauce. 6. To assemble the lasagna, spoon a third of the marinara sauce mixture into the bottom of a 9-by-13-inch glass baking dish and spread evenly. Place 1 layer of softened zucchini slices to fully cover the sauce, then add a third of the ricotta-spinach mixture and spread evenly on top of the zucchini. Sprinkle a third of the mozzarella-Parmesan mixture on top of the ricotta. Repeat with 2 more cycles of these layers: marinara, zucchini, ricotta-spinach, then cheese blend. 7. Bake until the cheese is bubbly and melted, 30 to 35

minutes. Turn the broiler to low and broil until the top is golden brown, about 5 minutes. Remove from the oven and allow to cool slightly before slicing.

Per Serving:

calories: 473 | fat: 36g | protein: 23g | carbs: 17g | fiber: 3g | sodium: 868mg

Pistachio Mint Pesto Pasta

Prep time: 10 minutes | Cook time: 10 minutes | Serves 4

8 ounces (227 g) whole-wheat pasta
1 cup fresh mint
½ cup fresh basil
⅓ cup unsalted pistachios,

shelled
1 garlic clove, peeled
½ teaspoon kosher salt
Juice of ½ lime
⅓ cup extra-virgin olive oil

1. Cook the pasta according to the package directions. Drain, reserving ½ cup of the pasta water, and set aside. 2. In a food processor, add the mint, basil, pistachios, garlic, salt, and lime juice. Process until the pistachios are coarsely ground. Add the olive oil in a slow, steady stream and process until incorporated. 3. In a large bowl, mix the pasta with the pistachio pesto; toss well to incorporate. If a thinner, more saucy consistency is desired, add some of the reserved pasta water and toss well.

Per Serving:

calories: 420 | fat: 3g | protein: 11g | carbs: 48g | fiber: 2g | sodium: 150mg

Cheesy Cauliflower Pizza Crust

Prep time: 15 minutes | Cook time: 11 minutes | Serves 2

1 (12-ounce / 340-g) steamer bag cauliflower
½ cup shredded sharp Cheddar cheese
1 large egg

2 tablespoons blanched finely ground almond flour
1 teaspoon Italian blend seasoning

1. Cook cauliflower according to package instructions. Remove from bag and place into cheesecloth or paper towel to remove excess water. Place cauliflower into a large bowl. 2. Add cheese, egg, almond flour, and Italian seasoning to the bowl and mix well. 3. Cut a piece of parchment to fit your air fryer basket. Press cauliflower into 6-inch round circle. Place into the air fryer basket. 4. Adjust the temperature to 360ºF (182ºC) and air fry for 11 minutes. 5. After 7 minutes, flip the pizza crust. 6. Add preferred toppings to pizza. Place back into air fryer basket and cook an additional 4 minutes or until fully cooked and golden. Serve immediately.

Per Serving:

calories: 251 | fat: 17g | protein: 15g | carbs: 12g | fiber: 5g | sodium: 375mg

Quinoa with Almonds and Cranberries

Prep time: 15 minutes | Cook time: 0 minutes |

Serves 4

2 cups cooked quinoa
⅓ teaspoon cranberries or currants
¼ cup sliced almonds
2 garlic cloves, minced
1¼ teaspoons salt
½ teaspoon ground cumin
½ teaspoon turmeric
¼ teaspoon ground cinnamon
¼ teaspoon freshly ground black pepper

1. In a large bowl, toss the quinoa, cranberries, almonds, garlic, salt, cumin, turmeric, cinnamon, and pepper and stir to combine. Enjoy alone or with roasted cauliflower.

Per Serving:

calories: 194 | fat: 6g | protein: 7g | carbs: 31g | fiber: 4g | sodium: 727mg

Crustless Spinach Cheese Pie

Prep time: 10 minutes | Cook time: 20 minutes |

Serves 4

6 large eggs
¼ cup heavy whipping cream
1 cup frozen chopped spinach, drained
1 cup shredded sharp Cheddar cheese
¼ cup diced yellow onion

1. In a medium bowl, whisk eggs and add cream. Add remaining ingredients to bowl. 2. Pour into a round baking dish. Place into the air fryer basket. 3. Adjust the temperature to 320ºF (160ºC) and bake for 20 minutes. 4. Eggs will be firm and slightly browned when cooked. Serve immediately.

Per Serving:

calories: 263 | fat: 20g | protein: 18g | carbs: 4g | fiber: 1g | sodium: 321mg

Baked Tofu with Sun-Dried Tomatoes and Artichokes

Prep time: 15 minutes | Cook time: 30 minutes |

Serves 4

1 (16-ounce / 454-g) package extra-firm tofu, drained and patted dry, cut into 1-inch cubes
2 tablespoons extra-virgin olive oil, divided
2 tablespoons lemon juice, divided
1 tablespoon low-sodium soy sauce or gluten-free tamari
1 onion, diced
½ teaspoon kosher salt
2 garlic cloves, minced
1 (14-ounce / 397-g) can artichoke hearts, drained
8 sun-dried tomato halves packed in oil, drained and chopped
¼ teaspoon freshly ground black pepper
1 tablespoon white wine vinegar
Zest of 1 lemon
¼ cup fresh parsley, chopped

1. Preheat the oven to 400ºF (205ºC). Line a baking sheet with foil or parchment paper. 2. In a bowl, combine the tofu, 1 tablespoon of the olive oil, 1 tablespoon of the lemon juice, and the soy sauce. Allow to sit and marinate for 15 to 30 minutes. Arrange the tofu in a single layer on the prepared baking sheet and bake for 20 minutes, turning once, until light golden brown. 3. Heat the remaining 1 tablespoon olive oil in a large skillet or sauté pan over medium heat. Add the onion and salt; sauté until translucent, 5 to 6 minutes. Add the garlic and sauté for 30 seconds. Add the artichoke hearts, sun-dried tomatoes, and black pepper and sauté for 5 minutes. Add the white wine vinegar and the remaining 1 tablespoon lemon juice and deglaze the pan, scraping up any brown bits. Remove the pan from the heat and stir in the lemon zest and parsley. Gently mix in the baked tofu.

Per Serving:

calories: 230 | fat: 14g | protein: 14g | carbs: 13g | fiber: 5g | sodium: 500mg

Mushroom Ragù with Parmesan Polenta

Prep time: 20 minutes | Cook time: 30 minutes |

Serves 2

½ ounce (14 g) dried porcini mushrooms (optional but recommended)
2 tablespoons olive oil
1 pound (454 g) baby bella (cremini) mushrooms, quartered
1 large shallot, minced (about ⅓ cup)
1 garlic clove, minced
1 tablespoon flour
2 teaspoons tomato paste
½ cup red wine
1 cup mushroom stock (or reserved liquid from soaking the porcini mushrooms, if using)
½ teaspoon dried thyme
1 fresh rosemary sprig
1½ cups water
½ teaspoon salt
⅓ cup instant polenta
2 tablespoons grated Parmesan cheese

1. If using the dried porcini mushrooms, soak them in 1 cup of hot water for about 15 minutes to soften them. When they're softened, scoop them out of the water, reserving the soaking liquid. (I strain it through a coffee filter to remove any possible grit.) Mince the porcini mushrooms. 2. Heat the olive oil in a large sauté pan over medium-high heat. Add the mushrooms, shallot, and garlic, and sauté for 10 minutes, or until the vegetables are wilted and starting to caramelize. 3. Add the flour and tomato paste, and cook for another 30 seconds. Add the red wine, mushroom stock or porcini soaking liquid, thyme, and rosemary. Bring the mixture to a boil, stirring constantly until it thickens. Reduce the heat and let it simmer for 10 minutes. 4. While the mushrooms are simmering, bring the water to a boil in a saucepan and add salt. 5. Add the instant polenta and stir quickly while it thickens. Stir in the Parmesan cheese. Taste and add additional salt if needed.

Per Serving:

calories: 451 | fat: 16g | protein: 14g | carbs: 58g | fiber: 5g | sodium: 165mg

Eggs Poached in Moroccan Tomato Sauce

Prep time: 10 minutes | Cook time: 35 minutes |

Serves 4

1 tablespoon olive oil	1 teaspoon salt
1 medium yellow onion, diced	¼ cup tomato paste
2 red bell peppers, seeded and diced	1 (28-ounce / 794-g) can diced tomatoes, drained
1¾ teaspoons sweet paprika	8 eggs
1 teaspoon ras al hanout	¼ cup chopped cilantro
½ teaspoon cayenne pepper	

1. Heat the olive oil in a skillet over medium-high heat. Add the onion and bell peppers and cook, stirring frequently, until softened, about 5 minutes. Stir in the paprika, ras al hanout, cayenne, salt, and tomato paste and cook, stirring occasionally, for 5 minutes. 2. Stir in the diced tomatoes, reduce the heat to medium-low, and simmer for about 15 minutes, until the tomatoes break down and the sauce thickens. 3. Make 8 wells in the sauce and drop one egg into each. Cover the pan and cook for about 10 minutes, until the whites are fully set, but the yolks are still runny. 4. Spoon the sauce and eggs into serving bowls and serve hot, garnished with cilantro.

Per Serving:

calories: 238 | fat: 13g | protein: 15g | carbs: 18g | fiber: 5g | sodium: 735mg

Eggplants Stuffed with Walnuts and Feta

Prep time: 10 minutes | Cook time: 55 minutes |

Serves 6

3 medium eggplants, halved lengthwise	pieces
2 teaspoons salt, divided	2¼ teaspoons ground cinnamon
¼ cup olive oil, plus 2 tablespoons, divided	1½ teaspoons dried oregano
2 medium onions, diced	½ teaspoon freshly ground black pepper
1½ pints cherry or grape tomatoes, halved	¼ cup whole-wheat breadcrumbs
¾ cup roughly chopped walnut	⅔ cup (about 3 ounces / 85 g) crumbled feta cheese

1. Scoop out the flesh of the eggplants, leaving a ½-inch thick border of flesh in the skins. Dice the flesh that you removed and place it in a colander set over the sink. Sprinkle 1½ teaspoons of salt over the diced eggplant and inside the eggplant shells and let stand for 30 minutes. Rinse the shells and the pieces and pat dry with paper towels. 2. Heat ¼ cup of olive oil in a large skillet over medium heat. Add the eggplant shells, skin-side down, and cook for about 4 minutes, until browned and softened. Turn over and cook on the cut side until golden brown and soft, about 4 minutes more. Transfer to a plate lined with paper towel to drain. 3. Drain off all but about 1 to 2 tablespoons of the oil in the skillet and heat over medium-high heat. Add the onions and cook, stirring, until beginning to soften, about 3 minutes. Add the diced eggplant,

tomatoes, walnuts, cinnamon, oregano, ¼ cup water, the remaining ½ teaspoon of salt, and the pepper. Cook, stirring occasionally, until the vegetables are golden brown and softened, about 8 minutes. 4. Preheat the broiler to high. 5. In a small bowl, toss together the breadcrumbs and 1 tablespoon olive oil. 6. Arrange the eggplant shells cut-side up on a large, rimmed baking sheet. Brush each shell with about ½ teaspoon of olive oil. Cook under the broiler until tender and just starting to turn golden brown, about 5 minutes. Remove the eggplants from the broiler and reduce the heat of the oven to 375°F (190°C). 7. Spoon the sautéed vegetable mixture into the eggplant shells, dividing equally. Sprinkle the breadcrumbs over the tops of the filled eggplants, dividing equally. Sprinkle the cheese on top, again dividing equally. Bake in the oven until the filling and shells are heated through and the topping is nicely browned and crisp, about 35 minutes.

Per Serving:

calories: 274 | fat: 15g | protein: 7g | carbs: 34g | fiber: 13g | sodium: 973mg

Beet and Carrot Fritters with Yogurt Sauce

Prep time: 15 minutes | Cook time: 15 minutes |

Serves 2

For the Yogurt Sauce:	1 scallion, minced
⅓ cup plain Greek yogurt	2 tablespoons fresh minced parsley
1 tablespoon freshly squeezed lemon juice	¼ cup brown rice flour or unseasoned bread crumbs
Zest of ½ lemon	¼ teaspoon garlic powder
¼ teaspoon garlic powder	¼ teaspoon salt
¼ teaspoon salt	1 large egg, beaten
For the Fritters:	¼ cup feta cheese, crumbled
1 large carrot, peeled	2 tablespoons olive oil (more if needed)
1 small potato, peeled	
1 medium golden or red beet, peeled	

Make the Yogurt Sauce: In a small bowl, mix together the yogurt, lemon juice and zest, garlic powder, and salt. Set aside. Make the Fritters: 1. Shred the carrot, potato, and beet in a food processor with the shredding blade. You can also use a mandoline with a julienne shredding blade or a vegetable peeler. Squeeze out any moisture from the vegetables and place them in a large bowl. 2. Add the scallion, parsley, rice flour, garlic powder, salt, and egg. Stir the mixture well to combine. Add the feta cheese and stir briefly, leaving chunks of feta cheese throughout. 3. Heat a large nonstick sauté pan over medium-high heat and add 1 tablespoon of the olive oil. 4. Make the fritters by scooping about 3 tablespoons of the vegetable mixture into your hands and flattening it into a firm disc about 3 inches in diameter. 5. Place 2 fritters at a time in the pan and let them cook for about two minutes. Check to see if the underside is golden, and then flip and repeat on the other side. Remove from the heat, add the rest of the olive oil to the pan, and repeat with the remaining vegetable mixture. 6. To serve, spoon about 1 tablespoon of the yogurt sauce on top of each fritter.

Per Serving:

calories: 295 | fat: 14g | protein: 6g | carbs: 44g | fiber: 5g | sodium: 482mg

Baked Falafel Sliders

Prep time: 10 minutes | Cook time: 30 minutes | Makes 6 sliders

Olive oil cooking spray
1 (15-ounce / 425-g) can no-salt-added or low-sodium chickpeas, drained and rinsed
1 onion, roughly chopped
2 garlic cloves, peeled
2 tablespoons fresh parsley, chopped

2 tablespoons whole-wheat flour
½ teaspoon ground coriander
½ teaspoon ground cumin
½ teaspoon baking powder
½ teaspoon kosher salt
¼ teaspoon freshly ground black pepper

1. Preheat the oven to 350ºF (180ºC). Line a baking sheet with parchment paper or foil and lightly spray with olive oil cooking spray. 2. In a food processor, add the chickpeas, onion, garlic, parsley, flour, coriander, cumin, baking powder, salt, and black pepper. Process until smooth, stopping to scrape down the sides of the bowl. 3. Make 6 slider patties, each with a heaping ¼ cup of mixture, and arrange on the prepared baking sheet. Bake for 30 minutes, turning over halfway through.

Per Serving:

1 slider: calories: 90 | fat: 1g | protein: 4g | carbs:17 g | fiber: 3g | sodium: 110mg

Cauliflower Rice-Stuffed Peppers

Prep time: 10 minutes | Cook time: 15 minutes | Serves 4

2 cups uncooked cauliflower rice
¾ cup drained canned petite diced tomatoes
2 tablespoons olive oil
1 cup shredded Mozzarella cheese

¼ teaspoon salt
¼ teaspoon ground black pepper
4 medium green bell peppers, tops removed, seeded

1. In a large bowl, mix all ingredients except bell peppers. Scoop mixture evenly into peppers. 2. Place peppers into ungreased air fryer basket. Adjust the temperature to 350ºF (177ºC) and air fry for 15 minutes. Peppers will be tender and cheese will be melted when done. Serve warm.

Per Serving:

calories: 144 | fat: 7g | protein: 11g | carbs: 11g | fiber: 5g | sodium: 380mg

Crispy Eggplant Rounds

Prep time: 15 minutes | Cook time: 10 minutes | Serves 4

1 large eggplant, ends trimmed, cut into ½-inch slices
½ teaspoon salt
2 ounces (57 g) Parmesan 100% cheese crisps, finely ground

½ teaspoon paprika
¼ teaspoon garlic powder
1 large egg

1. Sprinkle eggplant rounds with salt. Place rounds on a kitchen towel for 30 minutes to draw out excess water. Pat rounds dry. 2. In a medium bowl, mix cheese crisps, paprika, and garlic powder. In a separate medium bowl, whisk egg. Dip each eggplant round in egg, then gently press into cheese crisps to coat both sides. 3. Place eggplant rounds into ungreased air fryer basket. Adjust the temperature to 400ºF (204ºC) and air fry for 10 minutes, turning rounds halfway through cooking. Eggplant will be golden and crispy when done. Serve warm.

Per Serving:

calories: 113 | fat: 5g | protein: 7g | carbs: 10g | fiber: 4g | sodium: 567mg

Chapter 11 Desserts

Strawberry Panna Cotta

Prep time: 10 minutes | Cook time: 10 minutes |

Serves 4

2 tablespoons warm water
2 teaspoons gelatin powder
2 cups heavy cream
1 cup sliced strawberries, plus more for garnish
1 to 2 tablespoons sugar-free

sweetener of choice (optional)
1½ teaspoons pure vanilla extract
4 to 6 fresh mint leaves, for garnish (optional)

1. Pour the warm water into a small bowl. Sprinkle the gelatin over the water and stir well to dissolve. Allow the mixture to sit for 10 minutes. 2. In a blender or a large bowl, if using an immersion blender, combine the cream, strawberries, sweetener (if using), and vanilla. Blend until the mixture is smooth and the strawberries are well puréed. 3. Transfer the mixture to a saucepan and heat over medium-low heat until just below a simmer. Remove from the heat and cool for 5 minutes. 4. Whisking constantly, add in the gelatin mixture until smooth. Divide the custard between ramekins or small glass bowls, cover and refrigerate until set, 4 to 6 hours. 5. Serve chilled, garnishing with additional sliced strawberries or mint leaves (if using).

Per Serving:

calories: 229 | fat: 22g | protein: 3g | carbs: 5g | fiber: 1g | sodium: 26mg

Grilled Stone Fruit with Whipped Ricotta

Prep time: 10 minutes |Cook time: 10 minutes|

Serves: 4

Nonstick cooking spray
4 peaches or nectarines (or 8 apricots or plums), halved and pitted
2 teaspoons extra-virgin olive oil
¾ cup whole-milk ricotta

cheese
1 tablespoon honey
¼ teaspoon freshly grated nutmeg
4 sprigs mint, for garnish (optional)

1. Spray the cold grill or a grill pan with nonstick cooking spray. Heat the grill or grill pan to medium heat. 2. Place a large, empty bowl in the refrigerator to chill. 3. Brush the fruit all over with the oil. Place the fruit cut-side down on the grill or pan and cook for 3 to 5 minutes, or until grill marks appear. (If you're using a grill pan, cook in two batches.) Using tongs, turn the fruit over. Cover the grill (or the grill pan with aluminum foil) and cook for 4 to

6 minutes, until the fruit is easily pierced with a sharp knife. Set aside to cool. 4. Remove the bowl from the refrigerator and add the ricotta. Using an electric beater, beat the ricotta on high for 2 minutes. Add the honey and nutmeg and beat for 1 more minute. Divide the warm (or room temperature) fruit among 4 serving bowls, top with the ricotta mixture, and a sprig of mint (if using) and serve.

Per Serving:

calories: 180 | fat: 9g | protein: 7g | carbs: 21g | fiber: 3g | sodium: 39mg

Greek Yogurt with Honey and Pomegranates

Prep time: 5 minutes | Cook time: 0 minutes | Serves 4

4 cups plain full-fat Greek yogurt
½ cup pomegranate seeds

¼ cup honey
Sugar, for topping (optional)

1. Evenly divide the yogurt among four bowls. Evenly divide the pomegranate seeds among the bowls and drizzle each with the honey. 2. Sprinkle each bowl with a pinch of sugar, if desired, and serve.

Per Serving:

calories: 232 | fat: 8g | protein: 9g | carbs: 33g | fiber: 1g | sodium: 114mg

Slow-Cooked Fruit Medley

Prep time: 10 minutes | Cook time: 3 to 5 hours |

Serves 4 to 6

Nonstick cooking spray
1 pound (454 g) fresh or frozen fruit of your choice, stemmed and chopped as needed

⅓ cup almond milk or low-sugar fruit juice of your choice
½ cup honey

1. Generously coat a slow cooker with cooking spray, or line the bottom and sides with parchment paper or aluminum foil. 2. In a slow cooker, combine the fruit and milk. Gently stir to mix. 3. Drizzle the fruit with the honey. 4. Cover the cooker and cook for 3 to 5 hours on Low heat.

Per Serving:

calories: 192 | fat: 0g | protein: 1g | carbs: 50g | fiber: 3g | sodium: 27mg

Cocoa and Coconut Banana Slices

Prep time: 10 minutes | Cook time: 0 minutes |

Serves 1

1 banana, peeled and sliced
2 tablespoons unsweetened, shredded coconut

1 tablespoon unsweetened cocoa powder
1 teaspoon honey

1. Lay the banana slices on a parchment-lined baking sheet in a single layer. Put in the freezer for about 10 minutes, until firm but not frozen solid. Mix the coconut with the cocoa powder in a small bowl. 2. Roll the banana slices in honey, followed by the coconut mixture. 3. You can either eat immediately or put back in the freezer for a frozen, sweet treat.

Per Serving:

calories: 187 | fat: 4g | protein: 3g | carbs: 41g | fiber: 6g | sodium: 33mg

Crispy Apple Phyllo Tart

Prep time: 15 minutes | Cook time: 30 minutes |

Serves 4

5 teaspoons extra virgin olive oil
2 teaspoons fresh lemon juice
¼ teaspoon ground cinnamon
1½ teaspoons granulated sugar, divided

1 large apple (any variety), peeled and cut into ⅛-inch thick slices
5 phyllo sheets, defrosted
1 teaspoon all-purpose flour
1½ teaspoons apricot jam

1. Preheat the oven to 350°F (180°C). Line a baking sheet with parchment paper, and pour the olive oil into a small dish. Set aside. 2. In a separate small bowl, combine the lemon juice, cinnamon, 1 teaspoon of the sugar, and the apple slices. Mix well to ensure the apple slices are coated in the seasonings. Set aside. 3. On a clean working surface, stack the phyllo sheets one on top of the other. Place a large bowl with an approximate diameter of 15 inches on top of the sheets, then draw a sharp knife around the edge of the bowl to cut out a circle through all 5 sheets. Discard the remaining phyllo. 4. Working quickly, place the first sheet on the lined baking sheet and then brush with the olive oil. Repeat the process by placing a second sheet on top of the first sheet, then brushing the second sheet with olive oil. Repeat until all the phyllo sheets are in a single stack. 5. Sprinkle the flour and remaining sugar over the top of the sheets. Arrange the apples in overlapping circles 4 inches from the edge of the phyllo. 6. Fold the edges of the phyllo in and then twist them all around the apple filling to form a crust edge. Brush the edge with the remaining olive oil. Bake for 30 minutes or until the crust is golden and the apples are browned on the edges. 7. While the tart is baking, heat the apricot jam in a small sauce pan over low heat until it's melted. 8. When the tart is done baking, brush the apples with the jam sauce. Slice the tart into 4 equal servings and serve warm. Store at room temperature, covered in plastic wrap, for up to 2 days.

Per Serving:

calories: 165 | fat: 7g | protein: 2g | carbs: 24g | fiber: 2g | sodium: 116mg

Grilled Fruit Kebabs with Honey Labneh

Prep time: 15 minutes | Cook time: 10 minutes |

Serves 2

⅔ cup prepared labneh, or, if making your own, ⅔ cup full-fat plain Greek yogurt
2 tablespoons honey
1 teaspoon vanilla extract

Pinch salt
3 cups fresh fruit cut into 2-inch chunks (pineapple, cantaloupe, nectarines, strawberries, plums, or mango)

1. If making your own labneh, place a colander over a bowl and line it with cheesecloth. Place the Greek yogurt in the cheesecloth and wrap it up. Put the bowl in the refrigerator and let sit for at least 12 to 24 hours, until it's thick like soft cheese. 2. Mix honey, vanilla, and salt into labneh. Stir well to combine and set it aside. 3. Heat the grill to medium (about 300°F/ 150ºC) and oil the grill grate. Alternatively, you can cook these on the stovetop in a heavy grill pan (cast iron works well). 4. Thread the fruit onto skewers and grill for 4 minutes on each side, or until fruit is softened and has grill marks on each side. 5. Serve the fruit with labneh to dip.

Per Serving:

calories: 292 | fat: 6g | protein: 5g | carbs: 60g | fiber: 4g | sodium: 131mg

Mediterranean Orange Yogurt Cake

Prep time: 10 minutes | Cook time: 3 to 5 hours |

Serves 4 to 6

Nonstick cooking spray
¾ cup all-purpose flour
¾ cup whole-wheat flour
2 teaspoons baking powder
¼ teaspoon salt
1 cup coconut palm sugar
½ cup plain Greek yogurt

½ cup mild-flavored, extra-virgin olive oil
3 large eggs
2 teaspoons vanilla extract
Grated zest of 1 orange
Juice of 1 orange

1. Generously coat a slow cooker with cooking spray, or line the bottom and sides with parchment paper or aluminum foil. 2. In a large bowl, whisk together the all-purpose and whole-wheat flours, baking powder, and salt. 3. In another large bowl, whisk together the sugar, yogurt, olive oil, eggs, vanilla, orange zest, and orange juice until smooth. 4. Add the dry ingredients to the wet ingredients and mix together until well-blended. Pour the batter into the prepared slow cooker. 5. Cover the cooker and cook for 3 to 5 hours on Low heat, or until the middle has set and a knife inserted into it comes out clean.

Per Serving:

calories: 544 | fat: 33g | protein: 11g | carbs: 53g | fiber: 4g | sodium: 482mg

Cranberry-Orange Cheesecake Pears

Prep time: 10 minutes | Cook time: 30 minutes |

Serves 5

5 firm pears	½ cup low-fat cream cheese,
1 cup unsweetened cranberry	softened
juice	¼ teaspoon ground ginger
1 cup freshly squeezed orange	¼ teaspoon almond extract
juice	¼ cup dried, unsweetened
1 tablespoon pure vanilla	cranberries
extract	¼ cup sliced almonds, toasted
½ teaspoon ground cinnamon	

1. Peel the pears and slice off the bottoms so they sit upright. Remove the inside cores, and put the pears in a wide saucepan. 2. Add the cranberry and orange juice, as well as the vanilla and cinnamon extract. 3. Bring to a boil, and reduce to a simmer. 4. Cover and simmer on low heat for 25–30 minutes, until pears are soft but not falling apart. 5. Beat the cream cheese with the ginger and almond extract. 6. Stir the cranberries and almonds into the cream cheese mixture. 7. Once the pears have cooled, spoon the cream cheese into them. 8. Boil the remaining juices down to a syrup, and drizzle over the top of the filled pears.

Per Serving:

calories: 187 | fat: 6g | protein: 4g | carbs: 29g | fiber: 6g | sodium: 88mg

Karithopita (Greek Juicy Walnut Cake)

Prep time: 10 minutes | Cook time: 30 minutes |

Serves 8

¼ cup extra virgin olive oil plus	¼ cup whole-wheat flour
1 teaspoon for brushing	¼ teaspoon baking powder
½ cup walnut halves	¼ teaspoon baking soda
¼ cup granulated sugar	¼ teaspoon ground cinnamon
¼ cup brown sugar	Syrup:
1 egg	⅓ cup water
1 tablespoon pure vanilla	¼ cup granulated sugar
extract	1 cinnamon stick
¼ cup orange juice, strained	1 tablespoon orange juice
½ cup all-purpose flour	

1. Preheat the oven to 350°F (180°C). Brush an 8 × 4-inch loaf pan with 1 teaspoon of the olive oil, and then line the pan with parchment paper. 2. Prepare the syrup by combining the water, sugar, and cinnamon stick in a small pan placed over medium heat. Bring to a boil and then boil for 2 minutes, then remove the pan from the heat. Remove the cinnamon stick, add the orange juice, then stir and set aside to cool. 3. Pulse the walnuts in a food processor until you achieve a cornmeal-like consistency. (Do not over-grind.) 4. In a large bowl, combine ¼ cup of the olive oil, the granulated sugar, and the brown sugar. Stir until the sugar is dissolved, then add the egg. Add the vanilla extract and orange juice. Mix well. 5. In a small bowl, combine the all-purpose flour and whole-wheat flour with the baking powder, baking soda, and cinnamon. 6. Add the flour mixture to the olive oil mixture and mix

just until the flour has been incorporated. Add ¼ cup of the ground walnuts and mix until they are distributed throughout the batter. 7. Pour the batter into the prepared pan. Bake for 25–30 minutes or until a toothpick inserted into the cake comes out clean. 8. Use a toothpick to poke 8 holes across the top of the cake and then pour the syrup over the entire surface of the cake. Sprinkle the remaining ground walnuts over the top, and then set the cake aside to rest for 30 minutes before cutting it in equal-sized 1-inch slices. Store in an airtight container in the refrigerator for up to 5 days.

Per Serving:

calories: 240 | fat: 12g | protein: 3g | carbs: 30g | fiber: 1g | sodium: 52mg

Mascarpone and Fig Crostini

Prep time: 10 minutes | Cook time: 10 minutes |

Serves 6 to 8

1 long French baguette	1 (8-ounce / 227-g) tub
4 tablespoons (½ stick) salted	mascarpone cheese
butter, melted	1 (12-ounce / 340-g) jar fig jam

1. Preheat the oven to 350°F(180°C). 2. Slice the bread into ¼-inch-thick slices. 3. Arrange the sliced bread on a baking sheet and brush each slice with the melted butter. 4. Put the baking sheet in the oven and toast the bread for 5 to 7 minutes, just until golden brown. 5. Let the bread cool slightly. Spread about a teaspoon or so of the mascarpone cheese on each piece of bread. 6. Top with a teaspoon or so of the jam. Serve immediately.

Per Serving:

calories: 445 | fat: 24g | protein: 3g | carbs: 48g | fiber: 5g | sodium: 314mg

Creamy Spiced Almond Milk

Prep time: 5 minutes | Cook time: 1 minute | Serves 6

1 cup raw almonds	1 teaspoon vanilla bean paste
5 cups filtered water, divided	½ teaspoon pumpkin pie spice

1. Add almonds and 1 cup water to the Instant Pot®. Close lid, set steam release to Sealing, press the Manual button, and set time to 1 minute. 2. When the timer beeps, quick-release the pressure until the float valve drops. Press the Cancel button and open lid. Strain almonds and rinse under cool water. Transfer to a high-powered blender with remaining 3.cups water. Purée for 2 minutes on high speed. 4. Pour mixture into a nut milk bag set over a large bowl. Squeeze bag to extract all liquid. Stir in vanilla and pumpkin pie spice. Transfer to a Mason jar or sealed jug and refrigerate for 8 hours. Stir or shake gently before serving.

Per Serving:

calories: 86 | fat: 8g | protein: 3g | carbs: 3g | fiber: 2g | sodium: 0mg

Crunchy Sesame Cookies

Prep time: 10 minutes | Cook time: 15 minutes |
Yield 14 to 16

1 cup sesame seeds, hulled
1 cup sugar
8 tablespoons (1 stick) salted

butter, softened
2 large eggs
1¼ cups flour

1. Preheat the oven to 350°F(180°C). Toast the sesame seeds on a baking sheet for 3 minutes. Set aside and let cool. 2. Using a mixer, cream together the sugar and butter. 3. Add the eggs one at a time until well-blended. 4. Add the flour and toasted sesame seeds and mix until well-blended. 5. Drop spoonfuls of cookie dough onto a baking sheet and form them into round balls, about 1-inch in diameter, similar to a walnut. 6. Put in the oven and bake for 5 to 7 minutes or until golden brown. 7. Let the cookies cool and enjoy.

Per Serving:

calories: 218 | fat: 12g | protein: 4g | carbs: 25g | fiber: 2g | sodium: 58mg

Lemon Berry Cream Pops

Prep time: 10 minutes | Cook time: 5 minutes |
Makes 8 ice pops

Cream Pops:
2 cups coconut cream
1 tablespoon unsweetened
vanilla extract
Optional: low-carb sweetener,
to taste
2 cups raspberries, fresh or
frozen and defrosted

Coating:
1⅓ cups coconut butter
¼ cup virgin coconut oil
Zest from 2 lemons, about 2
tablespoons
1 teaspoon unsweetened vanilla
extract

1. To make the cream pops: In a bowl, whisk the coconut cream with the vanilla and optional sweetener until smooth and creamy. In another bowl, crush the raspberries using a fork, then add them to the bowl with the coconut cream and mix to combine. 2. Divide the mixture among eight ⅓-cup ice pop molds. Freeze until solid for 3 hours, or until set. 3. To easily remove the ice pops from the molds, fill a pot as tall as the ice pops with warm (not hot) water and dip the ice pop molds in for 15 to 20 seconds. Remove the ice pops from the molds and then freeze again. 4. Meanwhile, prepare the coating: Place the coconut butter and coconut oil in a small saucepan over low heat. Stir until smooth, remove from the heat, and add the lemon zest and vanilla. Let cool to room temperature. 5. Remove the ice pops from the freezer, two at a time, and, holding the ice pops over the saucepan, use a spoon to drizzle the coating all over. Return to the freezer until fully set, about 10 minutes. Store in the freezer in a resealable bag for up to 3 months.

Per Serving:

calories: 549 | fat: 8g | protein: 3g | carbs: 58g | fiber: 3g | sodium: 7mg

Tortilla Fried Pies

Prep time: 10 minutes | Cook time: 5 minutes per
batch | Makes 12 pies

12 small flour tortillas (4-inch
diameter)
½ cup fig preserves
¼ cup sliced almonds

2 tablespoons shredded,
unsweetened coconut
Oil for misting or cooking spray

1. Wrap refrigerated tortillas in damp paper towels and heat in microwave 30 seconds to warm. 2. Working with one tortilla at a time, place 2 teaspoons fig preserves, 1 teaspoon sliced almonds, and ½ teaspoon coconut in the center of each. 3. Moisten outer edges of tortilla all around. 4. Fold one side of tortilla over filling to make a half-moon shape and press down lightly on center. Using the tines of a fork, press down firmly on edges of tortilla to seal in filling. 5. Mist both sides with oil or cooking spray. 6. Place hand pies in air fryer basket close but not overlapping. It's fine to lean some against the sides and corners of the basket. You may need to cook in 2 batches. 7. Air fry at 390ºF (199ºC) for 5 minutes or until lightly browned. Serve hot. 8. Refrigerate any leftover pies in a closed container. To serve later, toss them back in the air fryer basket and cook for 2 or 3 minutes to reheat.

Per Serving:

1 pie: calories: 137 | fat: 4g | protein: 4g | carbs: 22g | fiber: 2g | sodium: 279mg

Poached Pears with Greek Yogurt and Pistachio

Prep time: 10 minutes | Cook time: 3 minutes |
Serves 8

2 cups water
1¾ cups apple cider
¼ cup lemon juice
1 cinnamon stick
1 teaspoon vanilla bean paste

4 large Bartlett pears, peeled
1 cup low-fat plain Greek
yogurt
½ cup unsalted roasted
pistachio meats

1. Add water, apple cider, lemon juice, cinnamon, vanilla, and pears to the Instant Pot®. Close lid, set steam release to Sealing, press the Manual button, and set time to 3 minutes. 2. When the timer beeps, quick-release the pressure until the float valve drops. Press the Cancel button and open lid. With a slotted spoon remove pears to a plate and allow to cool to room temperature. 3. To serve, carefully slice pears in half with a sharp paring knife and scoop out core with a melon baller. Lay pear halves on dessert plates or in shallow bowls. Top with yogurt and garnish with pistachios. Serve immediately.

Per Serving:

calories: 181 | fat: 7g | protein: 7g | carbs: 23g | fiber: 4g | sodium: 11mg

Strawberry-Pomegranate Molasses Sauce

Prep time: 10 minutes | Cook time: 5 minutes |

Serves 6

3 tablespoons olive oil
¼ cup honey
2 pints strawberries, hulled and halved
1 to 2 tablespoons pomegranate
molasses
2 tablespoons chopped fresh mint
Greek yogurt, for serving

1. In a medium saucepan, heat the olive oil over medium heat. Add the strawberries; cook until their juices are released. Stir in the honey and cook for 1 to 2 minutes. Stir in the molasses and mint. Serve warm over Greek yogurt.

Per Serving:

calories: 189 | fat: 7g | protein: 4g | carbs: 24g | fiber: 3g | sodium: 12mg

Koulourakia (Olive Oil Cinnamon Cookies)

Prep time: 25 minutes | Cook time: 25 to 30 minutes

| Serves 15

¼ cup extra virgin olive oil
¼ cup granulated sugar
¼ cup orange juice, strained
1¼ cups all-purpose flour plus extra if needed
¼ teaspoon baking powder
¼ teaspoon baking soda
¼ teaspoon ground cinnamon
Cinnamon-Sugar Coating:
1½ tablespoons granulated sugar
¾ teaspoon ground cinnamon

1. Preheat the oven to 350°F (180°C). Line a large baking sheet with parchment paper. 2. In a large bowl, combine the olive oil, sugar, and orange juice. Mix with a rubber spatula until the sugar has completely dissolved. 3. In a small bowl, combine the flour, baking powder, baking soda, and cinnamon. Stir to combine. 4. Gradually add the flour mixture to the olive oil mixture while gently mixing and folding with the spatula until a smooth, shiny, pliable dough that does not stick to your hands is formed. Pick up the dough with your hands and fold it once or twice to make sure it has the proper consistency. If the dough is still sticky, add more flour in small amounts. (Be careful not to add more flour than needed.) Cover the dough with plastic wrap and set it aside to rest for 5 minutes at room temperature. 5. While the dough is resting, make the cinnamon-sugar coating by combining the sugar and cinnamon in a small bowl and mixing well. 6. When the dough is rested, coat your fingers with a few drops of olive oil and begin shaping the cookies by taking about 1 teaspoon of the dough and rolling it out into a thin cord about 6 inches long, then set it aside. Continue the process until you have 10–12 cords, then dip each cord in the cinnamon-sugar mixture and fold it in half and twist it into a braid, or shape it into a ring or spiral. Place the cookies on the prepared baking sheet, and bake for 12–15 minutes or until golden brown. 7. While the first batch is baking, begin shaping the next batch. Once the first batch is done baking, remove the pan from the oven and let them sit for 5 minutes before transferring them to a wire rack to cool completely. Repeat the process with the remaining dough. Store in an airtight container for up to 3 weeks.

Per Serving:

calories: 90 | fat: 4g | protein: 1g | carbs: 13g | fiber: 0g | sodium: 22mg

Red-Wine Poached Pears

Prep time: 10 minutes | Cook time: 20 minutes |

Serves 2

2 cups red wine, such as Merlot or Zinfandel, more if necessary
2 firm pears, peeled
2 to3 cardamom pods, split
1 cinnamon stick
2 peppercorns
1 bay leaf

1. Put all ingredients in a large pot and bring to a boil. Make sure the pears are submerged in the wine. 2. Reduce heat and simmer for 15–20 minutes until the pears are tender when poked with a fork. 3. Remove the pears from the wine, and allow to cool. 4. Bring the wine to a boil, and cook until it reduces to a syrup. 5. Strain and drizzle the pears with the warmed syrup before serving.

Per Serving:

calories: 268 | fat: 0g | protein: 1g | carbs: 22g | fiber: 6g | sodium: 0mg

Fruit Compote

Prep time: 15 minutes | Cook time: 11 minutes |

Serves 6

1 cup apple juice
1 cup dry white wine
2 tablespoons honey
1 cinnamon stick
¼ teaspoon ground nutmeg
1 tablespoon grated lemon zest
1½ tablespoons grated orange
zest
3 large apples, peeled, cored, and chopped
3 large pears, peeled, cored, and chopped
½ cup dried cherries

1. Place all ingredients in the Instant Pot® and stir well. Close lid, set steam release to Sealing, press the Manual button, and set time to 1 minute. When the timer beeps, quick-release the pressure until the float valve drops. Press the Cancel button and open lid. 2. Use a slotted spoon to transfer fruit to a serving bowl. Remove and discard cinnamon stick. Press the Sauté button and bring juice in the pot to a boil. Cook, stirring constantly, until reduced to a syrup that will coat the back of a spoon, about 10 minutes. 3. Stir syrup into fruit mixture. Allow to cool slightly, then cover with plastic wrap and refrigerate overnight.

Per Serving:

calories: 211 | fat: 1g | protein: 2g | carbs: 44g | fiber: 5g | sodium: 7mg

Date and Honey Almond Milk Ice Cream

Prep time: 10 minutes | Cook time: 5 minutes | Serves 4

¾ cup (about 4 ounces/ 113 g) pitted dates
¼ cup honey
½ cup water

2 cups cold unsweetened almond milk
2 teaspoons vanilla extract

1. Combine the dates and water in a small saucepan and bring to a boil over high heat. Remove the pan from the heat, cover, and let stand for 15 minutes. 2. In a blender, combine the almond milk, dates, the date soaking water, honey, and the vanilla and process until very smooth. 3. Cover the blender jar and refrigerate the mixture until cold, at least 1 hour. 4. Transfer the mixture to an electric ice cream maker and freeze according to the manufacturer's instructions. 5. Serve immediately or transfer to a freezer-safe storage container and freeze for 4 hours (or longer). Serve frozen.

Per Serving:

calories: 106 | fat: 2g | protein: 1g | carbs: 23g | fiber: 3g | sodium: 92mg

Apricot and Mint No-Bake Parfait

Prep time: 10 minutes | Cook time: 0 minutes | Serves 6

4 ounces (113 g) Neufchâtel or other light cream cheese
1 (7-ounce / 198-g) container 2% Greek yogurt
½ cup plus 2 tablespoons sugar
2 teaspoons vanilla extract
1 tablespoon fresh lemon juice

1 pound (454 g) apricots, rinsed, pitted, and cut into bite-size pieces
2 tablespoons finely chopped fresh mint, plus whole leaves for garnish if desired

1. In the bowl of a stand mixer fitted with the paddle attachment, beat the Neufchâtel cheese and yogurt on low speed until well combined, about 2 minutes, scraping down the bowl as needed. Add ½ cup of the sugar, the vanilla, and the lemon juice. Mix until smooth and free of lumps, 2 to 3 minutes; set aside. 2. In a medium bowl, combine the apricots, mint, and remaining 2 tablespoons sugar. Stir occasionally, waiting to serve until after the apricots have released their juices and have softened. 3. Line up six 6-to 8-ounce (170-to 227-g) glasses. Using an ice cream scoop, spoon 3 to 4 tablespoons of the cheesecake mixture evenly into the bottom of each glass. (Alternatively, transfer the cheesecake mixture to a piping bag or a small zip-top bag with one corner snipped and pipe the mixture into the glasses.) Add a layer of the same amount of apricots to each glass. Repeat so you have two layers of cheesecake mixture and two layers of the apricots, ending with the apricots.) Garnish with the mint, if desired, and serve.

Per Serving:

calories: 132 | fat: 2g | protein: 5g | carbs: 23g | fiber: 2g | sodium: 35mg

Honey-Vanilla Apple Pie with Olive Oil Crust

Prep time: 10 minutes | Cook time: 45 minutes | Serves 8

For the crust:
¼ cup olive oil
1½ cups whole-wheat flour
½ teaspoon sea salt
2 tablespoons ice water
For the filling:
4 large apples of your choice,

peeled, cored, and sliced
Juice of 1 lemon
1 tablespoon pure vanilla extract
1 tablespoon honey
½ teaspoon sea salt
Olive oil

Make the crust: 1. Put the olive oil, flour, and sea salt in a food processor and process until dough forms. 2. Slowly add the water and pulse until you have a stiff dough. 3. Form the dough into 2 equal-sized balls, wrap in plastic wrap, and put in the refrigerator while you make the filling. Make the filling: 1. Combine the apples, lemon juice, vanilla, honey, and sea salt in a large bowl. 2. Stir and allow to sit for at least 10 minutes. Preheat oven to 400°F (205°C). 3. Roll 1 crust out on a lightly floured surface. Transfer to a 9-inch pie plate and top with filling. 4. Roll the other ball of dough out and put on top of the pie. Cut a few slices in the top to vent the pie, and lightly brush the top of the pie with olive oil. 5. Bake for 45 minutes, or until top is browned and apples are bubbly. 6. Allow to cool completely before slicing and serving with your favorite frozen yogurt.

Per Serving:

calories: 208 | fat: 8g | protein: 3g | carbs: 34g | fiber: 5g | sodium: 293mg

Peaches Poached in Rose Water

Prep time: 15 minutes | Cook time: 1 minute | Serves 6

1 cup water
1 cup rose water
¼ cup wildflower honey
8 green cardamom pods, lightly crushed

1 teaspoon vanilla bean paste
6 large yellow peaches, pitted and quartered
½ cup chopped unsalted roasted pistachio meats

1. Add water, rose water, honey, cardamom, and vanilla to the Instant Pot®. Whisk well, then add peaches. Close lid, set steam release to Sealing, press the Manual button, and set time to 1 minute. 2. When the timer beeps, quick-release the pressure until the float valve drops. Press the Cancel button and open lid. Allow peaches to stand for 10 minutes. Carefully remove peaches from poaching liquid with a slotted spoon. 3. Slip skins from peach slices. Arrange slices on a plate and garnish with pistachios. Serve warm or at room temperature.

Per Serving:

calories: 145 | fat: 3g | protein: 2g | carbs: 28g | fiber: 2g | sodium: 8mg

Grilled Pineapple Dessert

Prep time: 5 minutes | Cook time: 12 minutes |

Serves 4

Oil for misting or cooking spray
4½-inch-thick slices fresh
pineapple, core removed
1 tablespoon honey
¼ teaspoon brandy

2 tablespoons slivered almonds,
toasted
Vanilla frozen yogurt or
coconut sorbet

1. Spray both sides of pineapple slices with oil or cooking spray. Place into air fryer basket. 2. Air fry at 390°F (199°C) for 6 minutes. Turn slices over and cook for an additional 6 minutes. 3. Mix together the honey and brandy. 4. Remove cooked pineapple slices from air fryer, sprinkle with toasted almonds, and drizzle with honey mixture. 5. Serve with a scoop of frozen yogurt or sorbet on the side.

Per Serving:

calories: 65 | fat: 2g | protein: 1g | carbs: 11g | fiber: 1g | sodium: 1mg

Lemon Fool

Prep time: 25minutes |Cook time: 5 minutes|

Serves: 4

1 cup 2% plain Greek yogurt
1 medium lemon
¼ cup cold water
1½ teaspoons cornstarch

3½ tablespoons honey, divided
⅔ cup heavy (whipping) cream
Fresh fruit and mint leaves, for
serving (optional)

1. Place a large glass bowl and the metal beaters from your electric mixer in the refrigerator to chill. Add the yogurt to a medium glass bowl, and place that bowl in the refrigerator to chill as well. 2. Using a Microplane or citrus zester, zest the lemon into a medium, microwave-safe bowl. Halve the lemon, and squeeze 1 tablespoon of lemon juice into the bowl. Add the water and cornstarch, and stir well. Whisk in 3 tablespoons of honey. Microwave the lemon mixture on high for 1 minute; stir and microwave for an additional 10 to 30 seconds, until the mixture is thick and bubbling. 3. Remove the bowl of yogurt from the refrigerator, and whisk in the warm lemon mixture. Place the yogurt back in the refrigerator. 4. Remove the large chilled bowl and the beaters from the refrigerator. Assemble your electric mixer with the chilled beaters. Pour the cream into the chilled bowl, and beat until soft peaks form—1 to 3 minutes, depending on the freshness of your cream. 5. Take the chilled yogurt mixture out of the refrigerator. Gently fold it into the whipped cream using a rubber scraper; lift and turn the mixture to prevent the cream from deflating. Chill until serving, at least 15 minutes but no longer than 1 hour. 6. To serve, spoon the lemon fool into four glasses or dessert dishes and drizzle with the remaining ½ tablespoon of honey. Top with fresh fruit and mint, if desired.

Per Serving:

calories: 172 | fat: 8g | protein: 4g | carbs: 22g | fiber: 1g | sodium: 52mg

Pears Poached in Pomegranate and Wine

Prep time: 5 minutes | Cook time: 60 minutes |

Serves 4

4 ripe, firm Bosc pears, peeled,
left whole, and stems left intact
1½ cups pomegranate juice
1 cup sweet, white dessert wine,

such as vin santo
½ cup pomegranate seeds (seeds
from about ½ whole fruit)

1. Slice off a bit of the bottom of each pear to create a flat surface so that the pears can stand upright. If desired, use an apple corer to remove the cores of the fruit, working from the bottom. 2. Lay the pears in a large saucepan on their sides and pour the juice and wine over the top. Set over medium-high heat and bring to a simmer. Cover the pan, reduce the heat, and let the pears simmer, turning twice, for about 40 minutes, until the pears are tender. Transfer the pears to a shallow bowl, leaving the cooking liquid in the saucepan. 3. Turn the heat under the saucepan to high and bring the poaching liquid to a boil. Cook, stirring frequently, for about 15 to 20 minutes, until the liquid becomes thick and syrupy and is reduced to about ½ cup. 4. Spoon a bit of the syrup onto each of 4 serving plates and top each with a pear, sitting it upright. Drizzle a bit more of the sauce over the pears and garnish with the pomegranate seeds. Serve immediately.

Per Serving:

calories: 208 | fat: 0g | protein: 1g | carbs: 46g | fiber: 7g | sodium: 7mg

Ricotta-Lemon Cheesecake

Prep time: 5 minutes | Cook time: 1 hour | Serves 8 to 10

2 (8-ounce / 227-g) packages
full-fat cream cheese
1 (16-ounce / 454-g) container
full-fat ricotta cheese

1½ cups granulated sugar
1 tablespoon lemon zest
5 large eggs
Nonstick cooking spray

1. Preheat the oven to 350°F (180°C) . 2. Using a mixer, blend together the cream cheese and ricotta cheese. 3. Blend in the sugar and lemon zest. 4. Blend in the eggs; drop in 1 egg at a time, blend for 10 seconds, and repeat. 5. Line a 9-inch springform pan with parchment paper and nonstick spray. Wrap the bottom of the pan with foil. Pour the cheesecake batter into the pan. 6. To make a water bath, get a baking or roasting pan larger than the cheesecake pan. Fill the roasting pan about ⅓ of the way up with warm water. Put the cheesecake pan into the water bath. Put the whole thing in the oven and let the cheesecake bake for 1 hour. 7. After baking is complete, remove the cheesecake pan from the water bath and remove the foil. Let the cheesecake cool for 1 hour on the countertop. Then put it in the fridge to cool for at least 3 hours before serving.

Per Serving:

calories: 489 | fat: 31g | protein: 15g | carbs: 42g | fiber: 0g | sodium: 264mg

Dried Fruit Compote

Prep time: 15 minutes | Cook time: 8 minutes |
Serves 6

8 ounces (227 g) dried apricots, quartered	1 cup golden raisins
8 ounces (227 g) dried peaches, quartered	1½ cups orange juice
	1 cinnamon stick
	4 whole cloves

1. Place all ingredients in the Instant Pot®. Stir to combine. Close lid, set steam release to Sealing, press the Manual button, and set time to 3 minutes. When the timer beeps, let pressure release naturally, about 20 minutes. Press the Cancel button and open lid. 2. Remove and discard cinnamon stick and cloves. Press the Sauté button and simmer for 5–6 minutes. Serve warm or allow to cool, and then cover and refrigerate for up to a week.

Per Serving:

calories: 258 | fat: 0g | protein: 4g | carbs: 63g | fiber: 5g | sodium: 7mg

Honeyed Roasted Apples with Walnuts

Prep time: 5 minutes | Cook time: 12 to 15 minutes |
Serves 4

2 Granny Smith apples	½ teaspoon ground cinnamon
¼ cup certified gluten-free rolled oats	2 tablespoons chopped walnuts
2 tablespoons honey	Pinch salt
	1 tablespoon olive oil

1. Preheat the air fryer to 380°F(193ºC). 2. Core the apples and slice them in half. 3. In a medium bowl, mix together the oats, honey, cinnamon, walnuts, salt, and olive oil. 4. Scoop a quarter of the oat mixture onto the top of each half apple. 5. Place the apples in the air fryer basket, and roast for 12 to 15 minutes, or until the apples are fork-tender.

Per Serving:

calories: 144 | fat: 6g | protein: 1g | carbs: 22g | fiber: 3g | sodium: 2mg

Olive Oil Ice Cream

Prep time: 5 minutes | Cook time: 25 minutes |
Serves 8

4 large egg yolks	cup whole milk
⅓ cup powdered sugar-free sweetener (such as stevia or monk fruit extract)	1 teaspoon vanilla extract
	⅛ teaspoon salt
2 cups half-and-half or 1 cup heavy whipping cream and 1	¼ cup light fruity extra-virgin olive oil

1. Freeze the bowl of an ice cream maker for at least 12 hours or overnight. 2. In a large bowl, whisk together the egg yolks and

sugar-free sweetener. 3. In a small saucepan, heat the half-and-half over medium heat until just below a boil. Remove from the heat and allow to cool slightly. 4. Slowly pour the warm half-and-half into the egg mixture, whisking constantly to avoid cooking the eggs. Return the eggs and cream to the saucepan over low heat. 5. Whisking constantly, cook over low heat until thickened, 15 to 20 minutes. Remove from the heat and stir in the vanilla extract and salt. Whisk in the olive oil and transfer to a glass bowl. Allow to cool, cover, and refrigerate for at least 6 hours. 6. Freeze custard in an ice cream maker according to manufacturer's directions.

Per Serving:

calories: 168 | fat: 15g | protein: 2g | carbs: 8g | fiber: 0g | sodium: 49mg

Greek Yogurt Ricotta Mousse

Prep time: 1 hour 5 minutes | Cook time: 0 minutes |
Serves 4

9 ounces (255 g) full-fat ricotta cheese	3 teaspoons fresh lemon juice
4½ ounces (128 g) 2% Greek yogurt	½ teaspoon pure vanilla extract
	2 tablespoons granulated sugar

1. Combine all of the ingredients in a food processor. Blend until smooth, about 1 minute. 2. Divide the mousse between 4 serving glasses. Cover and transfer to the refrigerator to chill for 1 hour before serving. Store covered in the refrigerator for up to 4 days.

Per Serving:

calories: 156 | fat: 8g | protein: 10g | carbs: 10g | fiber: 0g | sodium: 65mg

Halva Protein Slices

Prep time: 5 minutes | Cook time: 0 minutes | Serves
16

¾ cup tahini	vanilla extract
⅓ cup coconut butter	½ teaspoon cinnamon
¼ cup virgin coconut oil	⅛ teaspoon salt
1 cup collagen powder	Optional: low-carb sweetener,
½ teaspoon vanilla powder or	to taste
1½ teaspoons unsweetened	

1. To soften the tahini and the coconut butter, place them in a small saucepan over low heat with the coconut oil. Remove from the heat and set aside to cool for a few minutes. 2. Add the remaining ingredients and optional sweetener. Stir to combine, then pour the mixture into an 8 × 8-inch (20 × 20 cm) parchment-lined pan or a silicone pan, or any pan or container lined with parchment paper. Place in the fridge for at least 1 hour or until fully set. 3. Cut into 16 pieces and serve. To store, keep refrigerated for up to 2 weeks or freeze to up to 3 months.

Per Serving:

calories: 131 | fat: 13g | protein: 2g | carbs: 3g | fiber: 1g | sodium: 33mg

Individual Apple Pockets

Prep time: 5 minutes | Cook time: 15 minutes | Serves 6

1 organic puff pastry, rolled out, at room temperature
1 Gala apple, peeled and sliced
¼ cup brown sugar
⅛ teaspoon ground cinnamon
⅛ teaspoon ground cardamom
Nonstick cooking spray
Honey, for topping

1. Preheat the oven to 350°F(180°C). 2. Cut the pastry dough into 4 even discs. Peel and slice the apple. In a small bowl, toss the slices with brown sugar, cinnamon, and cardamom. 3. Spray a muffin tin very well with nonstick cooking spray. Be sure to spray only the muffin holders you plan to use. 4. Once sprayed, line the bottom of the muffin tin with the dough and place 1 or 2 broken apple slices on top. Fold the remaining dough over the apple and drizzle with honey. 5. Bake for 15 minutes or until brown and bubbly.

Per Serving:
calories: 250 | fat: 15g | protein: 3g | carbs: 30g | fiber: 1g | sodium: 98mg

Honey Ricotta with Espresso and Chocolate Chips

Prep time: 5 minutes | Cook time: 0 minutes | Serves 2

8 ounces (227 g) ricotta cheese
2 tablespoons honey
2 tablespoons espresso, chilled
or room temperature
1 teaspoon dark chocolate chips or chocolate shavings

1. In a medium bowl, whip together the ricotta cheese and honey until light and smooth, 4 to 5 minutes. 2. Spoon the ricotta cheese-honey mixture evenly into 2 dessert bowls. Drizzle 1 tablespoon espresso into each dish and sprinkle with chocolate chips or shavings.

Per Serving:
calories: 235 | fat: 10g | protein: 13g | carbs: 25g | fiber: 0g | sodium: 115mg

Red Grapefruit Granita

Prep time: 5 minutes | Cook time: 0 minutes | Serves 4 to 6

3 cups red grapefruit sections
1 cup freshly squeezed red grapefruit juice
¼ cup honey
1 tablespoon freshly squeezed lime juice
Fresh basil leaves for garnish

1. Remove as much pith (white part) and membrane as possible from the grapefruit segments. 2. Combine all ingredients except the basil in a blender or food processor and pulse just until smooth. 3. Pour the mixture into a shallow glass baking dish and place in the freezer for 1 hour. Stir with a fork and freeze for another 30 minutes, then repeat. To serve, scoop into small dessert glasses and garnish with fresh basil leaves.

Per Serving:
calories: 94 | fat: 0g | protein: 1g | carbs: 24g | fiber: 1g | sodium: 1mg

Poached Apricots and Pistachios with Greek Yogurt

Prep time: 2 minutes | Cook time: 18 minutes | Serves 4

½ cup orange juice
2 tablespoons brandy
2 tablespoons honey
¾ cup water
1 cinnamon stick
12 dried apricots
⅓ cup 2% Greek yogurt
2 tablespoons mascarpone cheese
2 tablespoons shelled pistachios

1. Place a saucepan over medium heat and add the orange juice, brandy, honey, and water. Stir to combine, then add the cinnamon stick. 2. Once the honey has dissolved, add the apricots. Bring the mixture to a boil, then cover, reduce the heat to low, and simmer for 15 minutes. 3. While the apricots are simmering, combine the Greek yogurt and mascarpone cheese in a small serving bowl. Stir until smooth, then set aside. 4. When the cooking time for the apricots is complete, uncover, add the pistachios, and continue simmering for 3 more minutes. Remove the pan from the heat. 5. To serve, divide the Greek yogurt–mascarpone cheese mixture into 4 serving bowls and top each serving with 3 apricots, a few pistachios, and 1 teaspoon of the syrup. The apricots and syrup can be stored in a jar at room temperature for up to 1 month.

Per Serving:
calories: 146 | fat: 3g | protein: 4g | carbs: 28g | fiber: 4g | sodium: 62mg

Strawberry Ricotta Parfaits

Prep time: 10 minutes | Cook time: 0 minutes | Serves 4

2 cups ricotta cheese
¼ cup honey
2 cups sliced strawberries
1 teaspoon sugar
Toppings such as sliced almonds, fresh mint, and lemon zest (optional)

1. In a medium bowl, whisk together the ricotta and honey until well blended. Place the bowl in the refrigerator for a few minutes to firm up the mixture. 2. In a medium bowl, toss together the strawberries and sugar. 3. In each of four small glasses, layer 1 tablespoon of the ricotta mixture, then top with a layer of the strawberries and finally another layer of the ricotta. 4. Finish with your preferred toppings, if desired, then serve.

Per Serving:
calories: 311 | fat: 16g | protein: 14g | carbs: 29g | fiber: 2g | sodium: 106mg

Greek Island Almond Cocoa Bites

Prep time: 5 minutes | Cook time: 0 minutes | Serves 6

½ cup roasted, unsalted whole almonds (with skins)
3 tablespoons granulated sugar, divided
1½ teaspoons unsweetened cocoa powder

1¼ tablespoons unseasoned breadcrumbs
¾ teaspoon pure vanilla extract
1½ teaspoons orange juice

1. Place the almonds in a food processor and process until you have a coarse ground texture. 2. In a medium bowl, combine the ground almonds, 2 tablespoons sugar, the cocoa powder, and the breadcrumbs. Mix well. 3. In a small bowl, combine the vanilla extract and orange juice. Stir and then add the mixture to the almond mixture. Mix well. 4. Measure out a teaspoon of the mixture. Squeeze the mixture with your hand to make the dough stick together, then mold the dough into a small ball. 5. Add the remaining tablespoon of the sugar to a shallow bowl. Roll the balls in the sugar until covered, then transfer the bites to an airtight container. Store covered at room temperature for up to 1 week.

Per Serving:

calories: 102 | fat: 6g | protein: 3g | carbs: 10g | fiber: 2g | sodium: 11mg

Chocolate Turtle Hummus

Prep time: 15 minutes | Cook time: 0 minutes | Serves 2

For the Caramel:
2 tablespoons coconut oil
1 tablespoon maple syrup
1 tablespoon almond butter
Pinch salt
For the Hummus:

½ cup chickpeas, drained and rinsed
2 tablespoons unsweetened cocoa powder
1 tablespoon maple syrup, plus more to taste
2 tablespoons almond milk, or more as needed, to thin
Pinch salt
2 tablespoons pecans

Make the caramel 1. put the coconut oil in a small microwave-safe bowl. If it's solid, microwave it for about 15 seconds to melt it. 2. Stir in the maple syrup, almond butter, and salt. 3. Place the caramel in the refrigerator for 5 to 10 minutes to thicken. Make the hummus 1. In a food processor, combine the chickpeas, cocoa powder, maple syrup, almond milk, and pinch of salt, and process until smooth. Scrape down the sides to make sure everything is incorporated. 2. If the hummus seems too thick, add another tablespoon of almond milk. 3. Add the pecans and pulse 6 times to roughly chop them. 4. Transfer the hummus to a serving bowl and when the caramel is thickened, swirl it into the hummus. Gently fold it in, but don't mix it in completely. 5. Serve with fresh fruit or pretzels.

Per Serving:

calories: 321 | fat: 22g | protein: 7g | carbs: 30g | fiber: 6g | sodium: 100mg

Chapter 12 Salads

Greek Black-Eyed Pea Salad

Prep time: 10 minutes | Cook time: 0 minutes |
Serves 4

2 tablespoons olive oil
Juice of 1 lemon (about 2 tablespoons)
1 garlic clove, minced
1 teaspoon ground cumin
1 (15½-ounce / 439-g) can no-salt-added black-eyed peas, drained and rinsed
1 red bell pepper, seeded and chopped

1 shallot, finely chopped
2 scallions (green onions), chopped
2 tablespoons chopped fresh dill
¼ cup chopped fresh parsley
½ cup pitted Kalamata olives, sliced
½ cup crumbled feta cheese (optional)

1. In a large bowl, whisk together the olive oil, lemon juice, garlic, and cumin. 2. Add the black-eyed peas, bell pepper, shallot, scallions, dill, parsley, olives, and feta (if using) and toss to combine. Serve.

Per Serving:
calories: 213 | fat: 14g | protein: 7g | carbs: 16g | fiber: 5g | sodium: 426mg

Roasted Cauliflower "Steak" Salad

Prep time: 10 minutes | Cook time: 50 minutes |
Serves 4

2 tablespoons olive oil, divided
2 large heads cauliflower (about 3 pounds / 1.4 kg each), trimmed of outer leaves
2 teaspoons za'atar
1½ teaspoons kosher salt, divided
1¼ teaspoons ground black pepper, divided
1 teaspoon ground cumin

2 large carrots
8 ounces (227 g) dandelion greens, tough stems removed
½ cup low-fat plain Greek yogurt
2 tablespoons tahini
2 tablespoons fresh lemon juice
1 tablespoon water
1 clove garlic, minced

1. Preheat the oven to 450°F(235°C). Brush a large baking sheet with some of the oil. 2. Place the cauliflower on a cutting board, stem side down. Cut down the middle, through the core and stem, and then cut two 1'-thick "steaks" from the middle. Repeat with the other cauliflower head. Set aside the remaining cauliflower for another use. Brush both sides of the steaks with the remaining oil and set on the baking sheet. 3. Combine the za'atar, 1 teaspoon of the salt, 1 teaspoon of the pepper, and the cumin. Sprinkle on the cauliflower steaks. Bake until the bottom is deeply golden, about 30 minutes. Flip and bake until tender, 10 to 15 minutes. 4. Meanwhile, set the carrots on a cutting board and use a vegetable peeler to peel them into ribbons. Add to a large bowl with the dandelion greens. 5. In a small bowl, combine the yogurt, tahini, lemon juice, water, garlic, the remaining ½ teaspoon salt, and the remaining ¼ teaspoon pepper. 6. Dab 3 tablespoons of the dressing onto the carrot-dandelion mix. With a spoon or your hands, massage the dressing into the mix for 5 minutes. 7. Remove the steaks from the oven and transfer to individual plates. Drizzle each with 2 tablespoons of the dressing and top with 1 cup of the salad.

Per Serving:
calories: 214 | fat: 12g | protein: 9g | carbs: 21g | fiber: 7g | sodium: 849mg

Spinach Salad with Pomegranate, Lentils, and Pistachios

Prep time: 10 minutes | Cook time: 30 minutes |
Serves 4

1 tablespoon extra-virgin olive oil
1 shallot, finely chopped
1 small red chile pepper, such as a Fresno, finely chopped (wear plastic gloves when handling)
½ teaspoon ground cumin
¼ teaspoon ground coriander seeds
¼ teaspoon ground cinnamon
Pinch of kosher salt
1 cup French green lentils,

rinsed
3 cups water
6 cups baby spinach
½ cup pomegranate seeds
¼ cup chopped fresh cilantro
¼ cup chopped fresh flat-leaf parsley
¼ cup chopped pistachi os
2 tablespoons fresh lemon juice
1 teaspoon finely grated lemon peel
Ground black pepper, to taste

1. In a medium saucepan over medium heat, warm the oil until shimmering. Cook the shallot and chile pepper, stirring, until the shallot is translucent, about 8 minutes. Stir in the cumin, coriander, cinnamon, and salt until fragrant, about 1 minute. Add the lentils and water and bring to a boil. Cover and reduce the heat to a simmer. Cook, stirring occasionally, until the lentils are completely tender and the liquid has been absorbed, about 30 minutes. 2. In a large bowl, toss the lentils with the spinach, pomegranate seeds, cilantro, parsley, pistachios, lemon juice, lemon peel, and pepper to taste.

Per Serving:
calories: 279 | fat: 7g | protein: 15g | carbs: 39g | fiber: 10g | sodium: 198mg

Taverna-Style Greek Salad

Prep time: 20 minutes | Cook time: 0 minutes | Serves 4

4 to 5 medium tomatoes, roughly chopped
1 large cucumber, peeled and roughly chopped
1 medium green bell pepper, sliced
1 small red onion, sliced
16 pitted Kalamata olives
¼ cup capers, or more olives

1 teaspoon dried oregano or fresh herbs of your choice, such as parsley, cilantro, chives, or basil, divided
½ cup extra-virgin olive oil, divided
1 pack feta cheese
Optional: salt, pepper, and fresh oregano, for garnish

1. Place the vegetables in a large serving bowl. Add the olives, capers, feta, half of the dried oregano and half of the olive oil. Mix to combine. Place the whole piece of feta cheese on top, sprinkle with the remaining dried oregano, and drizzle with the remaining olive oil. Season to taste and serve immediately, or store in the fridge for up to 1 day.

Per Serving:

calories: 320 | fat: 31g | protein: 3g | carbs: 11g | fiber: 4g | sodium: 445mg

Italian Summer Vegetable Barley Salad

Prep time: 1 minutes | Cook time: 25 to 45 minutes | Serves 4

1 cup uncooked barley (hulled or pearl)
3 cups water
¾ teaspoon fine sea salt, divided
1 teaspoon plus 3 tablespoons extra virgin olive oil, divided
3 tablespoons fresh lemon juice
2 medium zucchini, washed and

chopped
15 Kalamata olives, pitted and sliced or chopped
¼ cup chopped fresh parsley
¼ cup chopped fresh basil
1 cup cherry tomatoes, halved
½ teaspoon freshly ground black pepper

1. Place the barley in a medium pot and add 3 cups of water and ¼ teaspoon of the sea salt. Bring to a boil over high heat, then reduce the heat to low. Simmer for 25–40 minutes, depending on the type of barley you're using, adding small amounts of hot water if the barley appears to be drying out. Cook until the barley is soft but still chewy, then transfer to a mesh strainer and rinse with cold water. 2. Empty the rinsed barley into a large bowl, drizzle 1 teaspoon of the olive oil over the top, fluff with a fork, and then set aside. 3. In a small bowl, combine the remaining 3 tablespoons of olive oil and the lemon juice. Whisk until the dressing thickens. 4. In a large bowl, combine the barley, zucchini, olives, parsley, and basil. Toss and then add the cherry tomatoes, remaining ½ teaspoon of sea salt, and black pepper. Toss gently, drizzle the dressing over the top, and continue tossing until the ingredients are coated with the dressing. Serve promptly. Store covered in the refrigerator for up to 3 days.

Per Serving:

calories: 308 | fat: 13g | protein: 7g | carbs: 45g | fiber: 10g | sodium: 614mg

Tossed Green Mediterranean Salad

Prep time: 15 minutes | Cook time: 0 minutes | Serves 4

1 medium head romaine lettuce, washed, dried, and chopped into bite-sized pieces
2 medium cucumbers, peeled and sliced
3 spring onions (white parts only), sliced

½ cup finely chopped fresh dill
⅓ cup extra virgin olive oil
2 tablespoons fresh lemon juice
¼ teaspoon fine sea salt
4 ounces (113 g) crumbled feta
7 Kalamata olives, pitted

1. Add the lettuce, cucumber, spring onions, and dill to a large bowl. Toss to combine. 2. In a small bowl, whisk together the olive oil and lemon juice. Pour the dressing over the salad, toss, then sprinkle the sea salt over the top. 3. Sprinkle the feta and olives over the top and then gently toss the salad one more time. Serve promptly. (This recipe is best served fresh.)

Per Serving:

calories: 284 | fat: 25g | protein: 7g | carbs: 10g | fiber: 5g | sodium: 496mg

Panzanella (Tuscan Bread and Tomatoes Salad)

Prep time: 10 minutes | Cook time: 20 minutes | Serves 6

4 ounces (113 g) sourdough bread, cut into 1' slices
3 tablespoons extra-virgin olive oil, divided
2 tablespoons red wine vinegar
2 cloves garlic, mashed to a paste
1 teaspoon finely chopped fresh oregano or ½ teaspoon dried
1 teaspoon fresh thyme leaves
½ teaspoon Dijon mustard
Pinch of kosher salt

Few grinds of ground black pepper
2 pounds (907 g) ripe tomatoes (mixed colors)
6 ounces (170 g) fresh mozzarella pearls
1 cucumber, cut into ½'-thick half-moons
1 small red onion, thinly sliced
1 cup baby arugula
½ cup torn fresh basil

1. Coat a grill rack or grill pan with olive oil and prepare to medium-high heat. 2. Brush 1 tablespoon of the oil all over the bread slices. Grill the bread on both sides until grill marks appear, about 2 minutes per side. Cut the bread into 1' cubes. 3. In a large bowl, whisk together the vinegar, garlic, oregano, thyme, mustard, salt, pepper, and the remaining 2 tablespoons oil until emulsified. 4. Add the bread, tomatoes, mozzarella, cucumber, onion, arugula, and basil. Toss to combine and let sit for 10 minutes to soak up the flavors.

Per Serving:

calories: 219 | fat: 12g | protein: 10g | carbs: 19g | fiber: 3g | sodium: 222mg

Zucchini and Ricotta Salad

Prep time: 5 minutes | Cook time: 2 minutes | Serves 1

2 teaspoons raw pine nuts
5 ounces (142 g) whole-milk ricotta cheese
1 tablespoon chopped fresh mint
1 teaspoon chopped fresh basil
1 tablespoon chopped fresh parsley
Pinch of fine sea salt
1 medium zucchini, very thinly sliced horizontally with a

mandoline slicer
Pinch of freshly ground black pepper
For the Dressing:
1½ tablespoons extra virgin olive oil
1 tablespoon fresh lemon juice
Pinch of fine sea salt
Pinch of freshly ground black pepper

1. Add the pine nuts to a small pan placed over medium heat. Toast the nuts, turning them frequently, for 2 minutes or until golden. Set aside. 2. In a food processor, combine the ricotta, mint, basil, parsley, and a pinch of sea salt. Process until smooth and then set aside. 3. Make the dressing by combining the olive oil and lemon juice in a small bowl. Use a fork to stir rapidly until the mixture thickens, then add a pinch of sea salt and a pinch of black pepper. Stir again. 4. Place the sliced zucchini in a medium bowl. Add half of the dressing, and toss to coat the zucchini. 5. To serve, place half of the ricotta mixture in the center of a serving plate, then layer the zucchini in a circle, covering the cheese. Add the rest of the cheese in the center and on top of the zucchini, then sprinkle the toasted pine nuts over the top. Drizzle the remaining dressing over the top, and finish with a pinch of black pepper. Store covered in the refrigerator for up to 1 day.

Per Serving:

calories: 504 | fat: 43g | protein: 19g | carbs: 13g | fiber: 3g | sodium: 136mg

Yellow and White Hearts of Palm Salad

Prep time: 10 minutes | Cook time: 0 minutes |
Serves 4

2 (14-ounce / 397-g) cans hearts of palm, drained and cut into ½-inch-thick slices
1 avocado, cut into ½-inch pieces
1 cup halved yellow cherry tomatoes
½ small shallot, thinly sliced
¼ cup coarsely chopped flat-

leaf parsley
2 tablespoons low-fat mayonnaise
2 tablespoons extra-virgin olive oil
¼ teaspoon salt
⅛ teaspoon freshly ground black pepper

1. In a large bowl, toss the hearts of palm, avocado, tomatoes, shallot, and parsley. 2. In a small bowl, whisk the mayonnaise, olive oil, salt, and pepper, then mix into the large bowl.

Per Serving:

calories: 192 | fat: 15g | protein: 5g | carbs: 14g | fiber: 7g | sodium: 841mg

Roasted Cauliflower and Arugula Salad with Pomegranate and Pine Nuts

Prep time: 20 minutes | Cook time: 20 minutes |
Serves 4

1 head cauliflower, trimmed and cut into 1-inch florets
2 tablespoons extra-virgin olive oil, plus more for drizzling (optional)
1 teaspoon ground cumin

½ teaspoon kosher salt
¼ teaspoon freshly ground black pepper
5 ounces (142 g) arugula
⅓ cup pomegranate seeds
¼ cup pine nuts, toasted

1. Preheat the oven to 425ºF (220ºC). Line a baking sheet with parchment paper or foil. 2. In a large bowl, combine the cauliflower, olive oil, cumin, salt, and black pepper. Spread in a single layer on the prepared baking sheet and roast for 20 minutes, tossing halfway through. 3. Divide the arugula among 4 plates. Top with the cauliflower, pomegranate seeds, and pine nuts. 4. Serve with a simple drizzle of olive oil.

Per Serving:

calories: 190 | fat: 14g | protein: 6g | carbs: 16g | fiber: 6g | sodium: 210mg

Melon Caprese Salad

Prep time: 20 minutes |Cook time: 0 minutes|
Serves: 6

1 cantaloupe, quartered and seeded
½ small seedless watermelon
1 cup grape tomatoes
2 cups fresh mozzarella balls (about 8 ounces / 227 g)
⅓ cup fresh basil or mint

leaves, torn into small pieces
2 tablespoons extra-virgin olive oil
1 tablespoon balsamic vinegar
¼ teaspoon freshly ground black pepper
¼ teaspoon kosher or sea salt

1. Using a melon baller or a metal, teaspoon-size measuring spoon, scoop balls out of the cantaloupe. You should get about 2½ to 3 cups from one cantaloupe. (If you prefer, cut the melon into bite-size pieces instead of making balls.) Put them in a large colander over a large serving bowl. 2. Using the same method, ball or cut the watermelon into bite-size pieces; you should get about 2 cups. Put the watermelon balls in the colander with the cantaloupe. 3. Let the fruit drain for 10 minutes. Pour the juice from the bowl into a container to refrigerate and save for drinking or adding to smoothies. Wipe the bowl dry, and put in the cut fruit. 4. Add the tomatoes, mozzarella, basil, oil, vinegar, pepper, and salt to the fruit mixture. Gently mix until everything is incorporated and serve.

Per Serving:

calories: 297 | fat: 12g | protein: 14g | carbs: 39g | fiber: 3g | sodium: 123mg

Roasted Golden Beet, Avocado, and Watercress Salad

Prep time: 15 minutes | Cook time: 1 hour | Serves 4

1 bunch (about 1½ pounds / 680 g) golden beets
1 tablespoon extra-virgin olive oil
1 tablespoon white wine vinegar
½ teaspoon kosher salt
¼ teaspoon freshly ground black pepper
1 bunch (about 4 ounces / 113 g) watercress
1 avocado, peeled, pitted, and diced
¼ cup crumbled feta cheese
¼ cup walnuts, toasted
1 tablespoon fresh chives, chopped

1. Preheat the oven to 425ºF (220ºC). Wash and trim the beets (cut an inch above the beet root, leaving the long tail if desired), then wrap each beet individually in foil. Place the beets on a baking sheet and roast until fully cooked, 45 to 60 minutes depending on the size of each beet. Start checking at 45 minutes; if easily pierced with a fork, the beets are cooked. 2. Remove the beets from the oven and allow them to cool. Under cold running water, slough off the skin. Cut the beets into bite-size cubes or wedges. 3. In a large bowl, whisk together the olive oil, vinegar, salt, and black pepper. Add the watercress and beets and toss well. Add the avocado, feta, walnuts, and chives and mix gently.

Per Serving:

calories: 235 | fat: 16g | protein: 6g | carbs: 21g | fiber: 8g | sodium: 365mg

Marinated Greek Salad with Oregano and Goat Cheese

Prep time: 10 minutes | Cook time: 0 minutes | Serves 4

½ cup white wine vinegar
1 small garlic clove, minced
1 teaspoon crumbled dried Greek oregano
½ teaspoon salt
¼ teaspoon freshly ground black pepper
2 Persian cucumbers, sliced thinly
4 to 6 long, skinny red or yellow banana peppers or other mild peppers
1 medium red onion, cut into rings
1 pint mixed small heirloom tomatoes, halved
2 ounces (57 g) crumbled goat cheese or feta

1. In a large, nonreactive (glass, ceramic, or plastic) bowl, whisk together the vinegar, garlic, oregano, salt, and pepper. Add the cucumbers, peppers, and onion and toss to mix. Cover and refrigerate for at least 1 hour. 2. Add the tomatoes to the bowl and toss to coat. Serve topped with the cheese.

Per Serving:

calories: 98 | fat: 4g | protein: 4g | carbs: 13g | fiber: 3g | sodium: 460mg

Toasted Pita Bread Salad

Prep time: 10 minutes | Cook time: 0 minutes | Serves 4

For the Dressing:
½ cup lemon juice
½ cup olive oil
1 small clove garlic, minced
1 teaspoon salt
½ teaspoon ground sumac
¼ teaspoon freshly ground black pepper
For the Salad:
2 cups shredded romaine lettuce
1 large or 2 small cucumbers, seeded and diced
2 medium tomatoes, diced
½ cup chopped fresh flat-leaf parsley leaves
¼ cup chopped fresh mint leaves
1 small green bell pepper, diced
1 bunch scallions, thinly sliced
2 whole-wheat pita bread rounds, toasted and broken into quarter-sized pieces
Ground sumac for garnish

1. To make the dressing, whisk together the lemon juice, olive oil, garlic, salt, sumac, and pepper in a small bowl. 2. To make the salad, in a large bowl, combine the lettuce, cucumber, tomatoes, parsley, mint, bell pepper, scallions, and pita bread. Toss to combine. Add the dressing and toss again to coat well. 3. Serve immediately sprinkled with sumac.

Per Serving:

calories: 359 | fat: 27g | protein: 6g | carbs: 29g | fiber: 6g | sodium: 777mg

Mediterranean Potato Salad

Prep time: 10 minutes |Cook time: 20 minutes| Serves: 6

2 pounds (907 g) Yukon Gold baby potatoes, cut into 1-inch cubes
3 tablespoons freshly squeezed lemon juice (from about 1 medium lemon)
3 tablespoons extra-virgin olive oil
1 tablespoon olive brine
¼ teaspoon kosher or sea salt
1 (2¼-ounce / 35-g) can sliced olives (about ½ cup)
1 cup sliced celery (about 2 stalks) or fennel
2 tablespoons chopped fresh oregano
2 tablespoons torn fresh mint

1. In a medium saucepan, cover the potatoes with cold water until the waterline is one inch above the potatoes. Set over high heat, bring the potatoes to a boil, then turn down the heat to medium-low. Simmer for 12 to 15 minutes, until the potatoes are just fork tender. 2. While the potatoes are cooking, in a small bowl, whisk together the lemon juice, oil, olive brine, and salt. 3. Drain the potatoes in a colander and transfer to a serving bowl. Immediately pour about 3 tablespoons of the dressing over the potatoes. Gently mix in the olives and celery. 4. Before serving, gently mix in the oregano, mint, and the remaining dressing.

Per Serving:

calories: 192 | fat: 8g | protein: 3g | carbs: 28g | fiber: 4g | sodium: 195mg

Simple Insalata Mista (Mixed Salad) with Honey Balsamic Dressing

Prep time: 15 minutes | Cook time: 0 minutes | Serves 2

For the Dressing:
¼ cup balsamic vinegar
¼ cup olive oil
1 tablespoon honey
1 teaspoon Dijon mustard
¼ teaspoon salt, plus more to taste
¼ teaspoon garlic powder
Pinch freshly ground black pepper
For the Salad:

4 cups chopped red leaf lettuce
½ cup cherry or grape tomatoes, halved
½ English cucumber, sliced in quarters lengthwise and then cut into bite-size pieces
Any combination fresh, torn herbs (parsley, oregano, basil, chives, etc.)
1 tablespoon roasted sunflower seeds

Make the Dressing: Combine the vinegar, olive oil, honey, mustard, salt, garlic powder, and pepper in a jar with a lid. Shake well. Make the Salad: 1. In a large bowl, combine the lettuce, tomatoes, cucumber, and herbs. 2. Toss well to combine. 3. Pour all or as much dressing as desired over the tossed salad and toss again to coat the salad with dressing. 4. Top with the sunflower seeds.

Per Serving:
calories: 339 | fat: 26g | protein: 4g | carbs: 24g | fiber: 3g | sodium: 171mg

Arugula Spinach Salad with Shaved Parmesan

Prep time: 10 minutes | Cook time: 2 minutes | Serves 3

3 tablespoons raw pine nuts
3 cups arugula
3 cups baby leaf spinach
5 dried figs, pitted and chopped
2½ ounces (71 g) shaved Parmesan cheese

For the Dressing:
4 teaspoons balsamic vinegar
1 teaspoon Dijon mustard
1 teaspoon honey
5 tablespoons extra virgin olive oil

1. In a small pan over low heat, toast the pine nuts for 2 minutes or until they begin to brown. Promptly remove them from the heat and transfer to a small bowl. 2. Make the dressing by combining the balsamic vinegar, Dijon mustard, and honey in a small bowl. Using a fork to whisk, gradually add the olive oil while continuously mixing. 3. In a large bowl, toss the arugula and baby spinach and then top with the figs, Parmesan cheese, and toasted pine nuts. Drizzle the dressing over the top and toss until the ingredients are thoroughly coated with the dressing. Serve promptly. (This salad is best served fresh.)

Per Serving:
calories: 416 | fat: 35g | protein: 10g | carbs: 18g | fiber: 3g | sodium: 478mg

Easy Greek Salad

Prep time: 10 minutes | Cook time: 0 minutes | Serves 4 to 6

1 head iceberg lettuce
1 pint (2 cups) cherry tomatoes
1 large cucumber
1 medium onion
½ cup extra-virgin olive oil
¼ cup lemon juice

1 teaspoon salt
1 clove garlic, minced
1 cup Kalamata olives, pitted
1 (6-ounce / 170-g) package feta cheese, crumbled

1. Cut the lettuce into 1-inch pieces and put them in a large salad bowl. 2. Cut the tomatoes in half and add them to the salad bowl. 3. Slice the cucumber into bite-size pieces and add them to the salad bowl. 4. Thinly slice the onion and add it to the salad bowl. 5. In another small bowl, whisk together the olive oil, lemon juice, salt, and garlic. Pour the dressing over the salad and gently toss to evenly coat. 6. Top the salad with the Kalamata olives and feta cheese and serve.

Per Serving:
calories: 297 | fat: 27g | protein: 6g | carbs: 11g | fiber: 3g | sodium: 661mg

Red Pepper, Pomegranate, and Walnut Salad

Prep time: 5 minutes | Cook time: 40 minutes | Serves 4

2 red bell peppers, halved and seeded
1 teaspoon plus 2 tablespoons olive oil
4 teaspoons pomegranate molasses, divided
2 teaspoons fresh lemon juice
¼ teaspoon kosher salt

⅛ teaspoon ground black pepper
4 plum tomatoes, halved, seeded, and chopped
¼ cup walnut halves, chopped
¼ cup chopped fresh flat-leaf parsley

1. Preheat the oven to 450°F(235°C). 2. Brush the bell peppers all over with 1 teaspoon of the oil and place cut side up on a large rimmed baking sheet. Drizzle 2 teaspoons of the pomegranate molasses in the cavities of the bell peppers. Roast the bell peppers until they have softened and the skins have charred, turning once during cooking, 30 to 40 minutes. Remove from the oven and cool to room temperature. Remove the skins and chop the peppers coarsely. 3. In a large bowl, whisk together the lemon juice, salt, black pepper, the remaining 2 tablespoons oil, and the remaining 2 teaspoons pomegranate molasses. Add the bell peppers, tomatoes, walnuts, and parsley and toss gently to combine. Serve at room temperature.

Per Serving:
calories: 166 | fat: 13g | protein: 2g | carbs: 11g | fiber: 3g | sodium: 153mg

Raw Zucchini Salad

Prep time: 15 minutes | Cook time: 0 minutes |

Serves 2

1 medium zucchini, shredded or sliced paper thin	Sea salt and freshly ground pepper, to taste
6 cherry tomatoes, halved	3–4 basil leaves, thinly sliced
3 tablespoons olive oil	2 tablespoons freshly grated,
Juice of 1 lemon	low-fat Parmesan cheese

1. Layer the zucchini slices on 2 plates in even layers. Top with the tomatoes. 2. Drizzle with the olive oil and lemon juice. Season to taste. 3. Top with the basil and sprinkle with cheese before serving.

Per Serving:

calories: 256 | fat: 21g | protein: 2g | carbs: 19g | fiber: 3g | sodium: 3mg

Four-Bean Salad

Prep time: 20 minutes | Cook time: 0 minutes |

Serves 4

½ cup white beans, cooked	chopped
½ cup black-eyed peas, cooked	2 tablespoons olive oil
½ cup fava beans, cooked	1 teaspoon ground cumin
½ cup lima beans, cooked	Juice of 1 lemon
1 red bell pepper, diced	Sea salt and freshly ground
1 small bunch flat-leaf parsley,	pepper, to taste

1. You can cook the beans a day or two in advance to speed up the preparation of this dish. 2. Combine all ingredients in a large bowl and mix well. Season to taste. 3. Allow to sit for 30 minutes, so the flavors can come together before serving.

Per Serving:

calories: 189 | fat: 7g | protein: 8g | carbs: 24g | fiber: 7g | sodium: 14mg

Moroccan Tomato and Roasted Chile Salad

Prep time: 15 minutes | Cook time: 0 minutes |

Serves 6

2 large green bell peppers	1 small bunch flat-leaf parsley,
1 hot red chili Fresno or jalapeño pepper	chopped
4 large tomatoes, peeled, seeded, and diced	4 tablespoons olive oil
	1 teaspoon ground cumin
1 large cucumber, peeled and diced	Juice of 1 lemon
	Sea salt and freshly ground pepper, to taste

1. Preheat broiler on high. Broil all of the peppers and chilies until the skin blackens and blisters. 2. Place the peppers and chilies in a paper bag. Seal and set aside to cool. Combine the rest of the ingredients in a medium bowl and mix well. 3. Take peppers and chilies out from the bag and remove the skins. Seed and chop the peppers and add them to the salad. 4. Season with sea salt and freshly ground pepper. 5. Toss to combine and let sit for 15–20 minutes before serving.

Per Serving:

calories: 128 | fat: 10g | protein: 2g | carbs: 10g | fiber: 3g | sodium: 16mg

Mediterranean No-Mayo Potato Salad

Prep time: 5 minutes | Cook time: 15 minutes |

Serves 4

2 pounds (907 g) potatoes (white or Yukon Gold varieties), peeled and cut into 1½-inch chunks	3 tablespoons red wine vinegar
	½ medium red onion, chopped
	2 tablespoons dried oregano
¼ cup extra virgin olive oil	½ teaspoon fine sea salt

1. Fill a medium pot with water and place it over high heat. When the water comes to a boil, carefully place the potatoes in the water, reduce the heat to medium, and simmer for 12–15 minutes or until the potatoes can be pierced with a fork but are not falling apart. Use a slotted spoon to transfer the potatoes to a colander, rinse briefly with cold water, then set aside to drain. 2. In a small bowl, whisk the olive oil and red wine vinegar. 3. Transfer the potatoes to a large bowl. Add the olive oil and vinegar mixture to the potatoes and toss gently and then add the onions. Rub the oregano between your fingers to release the aroma, then sprinkle it over the potatoes and toss again. Add the sea salt and toss once more. Store in an airtight container in the refrigerator for up to 3 days.

Per Serving:

calories: 347 | fat: 14g | protein: 5g | carbs: 50g | fiber: 6g | sodium: 309mg

Watermelon Burrata Salad

Prep time: 10 minutes | Cook time: 0 minutes |

Serves 4

2 cups cubes or chunks watermelon	4 fresh basil leaves, sliced chiffonade-style (roll up leaves of basil, and slice into thin strips)
1½ cups small burrata cheese balls, cut into medium chunks	
1 small red onion or 2 shallots, thinly sliced into half-moons	1 tablespoon lemon zest
	Salt and freshly ground black pepper, to taste
¼ cup olive oil	
¼ cup balsamic vinegar	

1. In a large bowl, mix all the ingredients. Refrigerate until chilled before serving.

Per Serving:

1 cup: calories: 224 | fat: 14g | protein: 14g | carbs: 12g | fiber: 1g | sodium: 560mg

Mediterranean Salad with Bulgur

Prep time: 27 minutes | Cook time: 12 minutes |

Serves 4

1 cup water
½ cup dried bulgur
1 (9-ounce / 255-g) bag chopped romaine lettuce
1 English cucumber, cut into ¼-inch-thick slices
1 red bell pepper, chopped
½ cup raw hulled pumpkin seeds

20 kalamata olives, pitted and halved lengthwise
¼ cup extra-virgin olive oil
Juice of 1 small orange
Juice of 1 small lemon
¼ teaspoon dried oregano
Sea salt
Freshly ground black pepper

1. In a medium saucepan, combine the water and bulgur and bring to a boil over medium heat. Reduce the heat to low, cover, and cook until the bulgur is tender, about 12 minutes. Drain off any excess liquid, fluff the bulgur with a fork, and set aside. 2. In a medium bowl, toss together the lettuce, cucumber, bell pepper, bulgur, pumpkin seeds, and olives and set aside. 3. In a small bowl, stir together the olive oil, orange juice, lemon juice, and oregano. Season with salt and black pepper. 4. Add 3 tablespoons of the dressing to the salad and toss to coat. Taste, add more dressing and season with additional salt and/or black pepper if needed, then serve.

Per Serving:

calories: 322 | fat: 23g | protein: 8g | carbs: 24g | fiber: 6g | sodium: 262mg

French Lentil Salad with Parsley and Mint

Prep time: 20 minutes | Cook time:25 minutes |

Serves 6

For the Lentils:
1 cup French lentils
1 garlic clove, smashed
1 dried bay leaf
For the Salad:
2 tablespoons extra-virgin olive oil
2 tablespoons red wine vinegar
½ teaspoon ground cumin

½ teaspoon kosher salt
¼ teaspoon freshly ground black pepper
2 celery stalks, diced small
1 bell pepper, diced small
½ red onion, diced small
¼ cup fresh parsley, chopped
¼ cup fresh mint, chopped

Make the Lentils: 1. Put the lentils, garlic, and bay leaf in a large saucepan. Cover with water by about 3 inches and bring to a boil. Reduce the heat, cover, and simmer until tender, 20 to 30 minutes. 2. Drain the lentils to remove any remaining water after cooking. Remove the garlic and bay leaf. Make the Salad: 3. In a large bowl, whisk together the olive oil, vinegar, cumin, salt, and black pepper. Add the celery, bell pepper, onion, parsley, and mint and toss to combine. 4. Add the lentils and mix well.

Per Serving:

calories: 200 | fat: 8g | protein: 10g | carbs: 26g | fiber: 10g | sodium: 165mg

Roasted Broccoli Panzanella Salad

Prep time: 10 minutes |Cook time: 20 minutes|

Serves: 4

1 pound (454 g) broccoli (about 3 medium stalks), trimmed, cut into 1-inch florets and ½-inch stem slices
3 tablespoons extra-virgin olive oil, divided
1 pint cherry or grape tomatoes (about 1½ cups)
1½ teaspoons honey, divided
3 cups cubed whole-grain

crusty bread
1 tablespoon balsamic vinegar
½ teaspoon freshly ground black pepper
¼ teaspoon kosher or sea salt
Grated Parmesan cheese (or other hard cheese) and chopped fresh oregano leaves, for serving (optional)

1. Place a large, rimmed baking sheet in the oven. Preheat the oven to 450°F(235ºC) with the pan inside. 2. Put the broccoli in a large bowl, and drizzle with 1 tablespoon of the oil. Toss to coat. 3. Carefully remove the hot baking sheet from the oven and spoon the broccoli onto it, leaving some oil in the bottom of the bowl. Add the tomatoes to the same bowl, and toss to coat with the leftover oil (don't add any more oil). Toss the tomatoes with 1 teaspoon of honey, and scrape them onto the baking sheet with the broccoli. 4. Roast for 15 minutes, stirring halfway through. Remove the sheet from the oven, and add the bread cubes. Roast for 3 more minutes. The broccoli is ready when it appears slightly charred on the tips and is tender-crisp when poked with a fork. 5. Spoon the vegetable mixture onto a serving plate or into a large, flat bowl. 6. In a small bowl, whisk the remaining 2 tablespoons of oil together with the vinegar, the remaining ½ teaspoon of honey, and the pepper and salt. Pour over the salad, and toss gently. Sprinkle with cheese and oregano, if desired, and serve.

Per Serving:

calories: 197 | fat: 12g | protein: 7g | carbs: 19g | fiber: 5g | sodium: 296mg

Asparagus Salad

Prep time: 10 minutes | Cook time: 0 minutes |

Serves 4

1 pound (454 g) asparagus
Sea salt and freshly ground pepper, to taste

4 tablespoons olive oil
1 tablespoon balsamic vinegar
1 tablespoon lemon zest

1. Either roast the asparagus or, with a vegetable peeler, shave it into thin strips. 2. Season to taste. 3. Toss with the olive oil and vinegar, garnish with a sprinkle of lemon zest, and serve.

Per Serving:

calories: 146 | fat: 14g | protein: 3g | carbs: 5g | fiber: 3g | sodium: 4mg

Spinach-Arugula Salad with Nectarines and Lemon Dressing

Prep time: 15 minutes | Cook time: 0 minutes | Serves 6

1 (7-ounce / 198-g) package baby spinach and arugula blend
3 tablespoons fresh lemon juice
5 tablespoons olive oil
⅛ teaspoon salt
Pinch (teaspoon) sugar

Freshly ground black pepper, to taste
½ red onion, thinly sliced
3 ripe nectarines, pitted and sliced into wedges
1 cucumber, peeled, seeded, and sliced
½ cup crumbled feta cheese

1. Place the spinach-arugula blend in a large bowl. 2. In a small bowl, whisk together the lemon juice, olive oil, salt, and sugar and season with pepper. Taste and adjust the seasonings. 3. Add the dressing to the greens and toss. Top with the onion, nectarines, cucumber, and feta. 4. Serve immediately.

Per Serving:

1 cup: calories: 178 | fat: 14g | protein: 4g | carbs: 11g | fiber: 2g | sodium: 193mg

Caprese Salad with Fresh Mozzarella

Prep time: 10 minutes | Cook time: 0 minutes | Serves 6 to 8

For the Pesto:
2 cups (packed) fresh basil leaves, plus more for garnish
⅓ cup pine nuts
3 garlic cloves, minced
½ cup (about 2 ounces / 57 g) freshly grated Parmesan cheese
½ cup extra-virgin olive oil
Salt

Freshly ground black pepper
For the Salad:
4 to 6 large, ripe tomatoes, cut into thick slices
1 pound (454 g) fresh mozzarella, cut into thick slices
3 tablespoons balsamic vinegar
Salt
Freshly ground black pepper

1. To make the pesto, in a food processor combine the basil, pine nuts, and garlic and pulse several times to chop. Add the Parmesan cheese and pulse again until well combined. With the food processor running, add the olive oil in a slow, steady stream. Transfer to a small bowl, taste, and add salt and pepper as needed. Slice, quarter, or halve the tomatoes, based on your preferred salad presentation. 2. To make the salad, on a large serving platter arrange the tomato slices and cheese slices, stacking them like fallen dominoes. 3. Dollop the pesto decoratively on top of the tomato and cheese slices. (You will likely have extra pesto. Refrigerate the extra in a tightly sealed container and use within 3 days, or freeze it for up to 3 months.) 4. Drizzle the balsamic vinegar over the top, garnish with basil leaves, sprinkle with salt and pepper to taste, and serve immediately.

Per Serving:

calories: 398 | fat: 32g | protein: 23g | carbs: 8g | fiber: 1g | sodium: 474mg

Chapter 13 Pizzas, Wraps, and Sandwiches

Barbecue Chicken Pita Pizza

Prep time: 5 minutes | Cook time: 5 to 7 minutes per batch | Makes 4 pizzas

1 cup barbecue sauce, divided
4 pita breads
2 cups shredded cooked chicken
2 cups shredded Mozzarella
cheese
½ small red onion, thinly sliced
2 tablespoons finely chopped fresh cilantro

1. Measure ½ cup of the barbecue sauce in a small measuring cup. Spread 2 tablespoons of the barbecue sauce on each pita. 2. In a medium bowl, mix together the remaining ½ cup of barbecue sauce and chicken. Place ½ cup of the chicken on each pita. Top each pizza with ½ cup of the Mozzarella cheese. Sprinkle the tops of the pizzas with the red onion. 3. Place one pizza in the air fryer. Air fry at 400ºF (204ºC) for 5 to 7 minutes. Repeat this process with the remaining pizzas. 4. Top the pizzas with the cilantro.

Per Serving:
calories: 530 | fat: 19g | protein: 40g | carbs: 47g | fiber: 2g | sodium: 672mg

Turkey and Provolone Panini with Roasted Peppers and Onions

Prep time: 15 minutes | Cook time: 1 hour 5 minutes | Serves 4

For the peppers and onions
2 red bell pepper, seeded and quartered
2 red onions, peeled and quartered
2 tablespoons olive oil
½ teaspoon salt
½ teaspoon freshly ground
black pepper
For the panini
2 tablespoons olive oil
8 slices whole-wheat bread
8 ounces (227 g) thinly sliced provolone cheese
8 ounces (227 g) sliced roasted turkey or chicken breast

1. Preheat the oven to 375°F(190ºC). 2. To roast the peppers and onions, toss them together with the olive oil, salt, and pepper on a large, rimmed baking sheet. Spread them out in a single layer and then bake in the preheated oven for 45 to 60 minutes, turning occasionally, until they are tender and beginning to brown. Remove the peppers and onions from the oven and let them cool for a few minutes until they are cool enough to handle. Skin the peppers and thinly slice them. Thinly slice the onions. 3. Preheat a skillet or grill pan over medium-high heat. 4. To make the panini, brush one side of each of the 8 slices of bread with olive oil. Place 4 of the bread slices, oiled side down, on your work surface. Top each with ¼ of the cheese and ¼ of the turkey, and top with some of the roasted peppers and onions. Place the remaining 4 bread slices on top of the sandwiches, oiled side up. 5. Place the sandwiches in the skillet or grill pan (you may have to cook them in two batches), cover the pan, and cook until the bottoms have golden brown grill marks and the cheese is beginning to melt, about 2 minutes. Turn the sandwiches over and cook, covered, until the second side is golden brown and the cheese is melted, another 2 minutes or so. Cut each sandwich in half and serve immediately.

Per Serving:
calories: 603 | fat: 32g | protein: 41g | carbs: 37g | fiber: 6g | sodium: 792mg

Bocadillo with Herbed Tuna and Piquillo Peppers

Prep time: 5 minutes | Cook time: 20 minutes | Serves 4

2 tablespoons olive oil, plus more for brushing
1 medium onion, finely chopped
2 leeks, white and tender green parts only, finely chopped
1 teaspoon chopped thyme
½ teaspoon dried marjoram
½ teaspoon salt
¼ teaspoon freshly ground black pepper
3 tablespoons sherry vinegar
1 carrot, finely diced
2 (8-ounce / 227-g) jars Spanish tuna in olive oil
4 crusty whole-wheat sandwich rolls, split
1 ripe tomato, grated on the large holes of a box grater
4 piquillo peppers, cut into thin strips

1. Heat 2 tablespoons olive oil in a medium skillet over medium heat. Add the onion, leeks, thyme, marjoram, salt, and pepper. Stir frequently until the onions are softened, about 10 minutes. Stir in the vinegar and carrot and cook until the liquid has evaporated, 5 minutes. Transfer the mixture to a bowl and let cool to room temperature or refrigerate for 15 minutes or so. 2. In a medium bowl, combine the tuna, along with its oil, with the onion mixture, breaking the tuna chunks up with a fork. 3. Brush the rolls lightly with oil and toast under the broiler until lightly browned, about 2 minutes. Spoon the tomato pulp onto the bottom half of each roll, dividing equally and spreading it with the back of the spoon. Divide the tuna mixture among the rolls and top with the piquillo pepper slices. Serve immediately.

Per Serving:
calories: 416 | fat: 18g | protein: 35g | carbs: 30g | fiber: 5g | sodium: 520mg

Herbed Focaccia Panini with Anchovies and Burrata

Prep time: 5 minutes | Cook time: 8 minutes | Serves 4

8 ounces (227 g) burrata cheese, chilled and sliced
1 pound (454 g) whole-wheat herbed focaccia, cut crosswise into 4 rectangles and split horizontally
1 can anchovy fillets packed in oil, drained
8 slices tomato, sliced
2 cups arugula
1 tablespoon olive oil

1. Divide the cheese evenly among the bottom halves of the focaccia rectangles. Top each with 3 or 4 anchovy fillets, 2 slices of tomato, and ½ cup arugula. Place the top halves of the focaccia on top of the sandwiches. 2. To make the panini, heat a skillet or grill pan over high heat and brush with the olive oil. 3. Place the sandwiches in the hot pan and place another heavy pan, such as a cast-iron skillet, on top to weigh them down. Cook for about 3 to 4 minutes, until crisp and golden on the bottom, and then flip over and repeat on the second side, cooking for an additional 3 to 4 minutes until golden and crisp. Slice each sandwich in half and serve hot.

Per Serving:

calories: 596 | fat: 30g | protein: 27g | carbs: 58g | fiber: 5g | sodium: 626mg

Open-Faced Eggplant Parmesan Sandwich

Prep time: 10 minutes | Cook time: 10 minutes | Serves 2

1 small eggplant, sliced into ¼-inch rounds
Pinch sea salt
2 tablespoons olive oil
Sea salt and freshly ground pepper, to taste
2 slices whole-grain bread, thickly cut and toasted
1 cup marinara sauce (no added sugar)
¼ cup freshly grated, low-fat Parmesan cheese

1. Preheat broiler to high heat. 2. Salt both sides of the sliced eggplant, and let sit for 20 minutes to draw out the bitter juices. 3. Rinse the eggplant and pat dry with a paper towel. 4. Brush the eggplant with the olive oil, and season with sea salt and freshly ground pepper. 5. Lay the eggplant on a sheet pan, and broil until crisp, about 4 minutes. Flip over and crisp the other side. 6. Lay the toasted bread on a sheet pan. Spoon some marinara sauce on each slice of bread, and layer the eggplant on top. 7. Sprinkle half of the cheese on top of the eggplant and top with more marinara sauce. 8. Sprinkle with remaining cheese. 9. Put the sandwiches under the broiler until the cheese has melted, about 2 minutes. 10. Using a spatula, transfer the sandwiches to plates and serve.

Per Serving:

calories: 355 | fat: 19g | protein: 10g | carbs: 38g | fiber: 13g | sodium: 334mg

Chicken and Goat Cheese Pizza

Prep time: 10 minutes | Cook time: 10 minutes | Serves 4

All-purpose flour, for dusting
1 pound (454 g) premade pizza dough
2 tablespoons olive oil
1 cup shredded cooked chicken
3 ounces (85 g) goat cheese, crumbled
Sea salt
Freshly ground black pepper

1. Preheat the oven to 475°F (245ºC) . 2. On a floured surface, roll out the dough to a 12-inch round and place it on a lightly floured pizza pan or baking sheet. Drizzle the dough with the olive oil and spread it out evenly. Top the dough with the chicken and goat cheese. 3. Bake the pizza for 8 to 10 minutes, until the crust is cooked through and golden. 4. Season with salt and pepper and serve.

Per Serving:

calories: 555 | fat: 23g | protein: 24g | carbs: 60g | fiber: 2g | sodium: 660mg

Moroccan Lamb Flatbread with Pine Nuts, Mint, and Ras Al Hanout

Prep time: 10 minutes | Cook time: 20 minutes | Serves 4

1⅓ cups plain Greek yogurt
Juice of 1½ lemons, divided
1¼ teaspoons salt, divided
1 pound (454 g) ground lamb
1 medium red onion, diced
1 clove garlic, minced
1 tablespoon ras al hanout
¼ cup chopped fresh mint
leaves
Freshly ground black pepper
4 Middle Eastern-style flatbread rounds
2 tablespoons toasted pine nuts
16 cherry tomatoes, halved
2 tablespoons chopped cilantro

1. Preheat the oven to 450°F(235ºC). 2. In a small bowl, stir together the yogurt, the juice of ½ lemon, and ¼ teaspoon salt. 3. Heat a large skillet over medium-high heat. Add the lamb and cook, stirring frequently, until browned, about 5 minutes. Drain any excess rendered fat from the pan and then stir in the onion and garlic and cook, stirring, until softened, about 3 minutes more. Stir in the ras al hanout, mint, the remaining teaspoon of salt, and pepper. 4. Place the flatbread rounds on a baking sheet (or two if necessary) and top with the lamb mixture, pine nuts, and tomatoes, dividing equally. Bake in the preheated oven until the crust is golden brown and the tomatoes have softened, about 10 minutes. Scatter the cilantro over the flatbreads and squeeze the remaining lemon juice over them. Cut into wedges and serve dolloped with the yogurt sauce.

Per Serving:

calories: 463 | fat: 22g | protein: 34g | carbs: 34g | fiber: 3g | sodium: 859mg

Dill Salmon Salad Wraps

Prep time: 10 minutes |Cook time: 10 minutes|

Serves:6

1 pound (454 g) salmon filet, cooked and flaked, or 3 (5-ounce / 142-g) cans salmon
½ cup diced carrots (about 1 carrot)
½ cup diced celery (about 1 celery stalk)
3 tablespoons chopped fresh dill
3 tablespoons diced red onion (a little less than ⅛ onion)

2 tablespoons capers
1½ tablespoons extra-virgin olive oil
1 tablespoon aged balsamic vinegar
½ teaspoon freshly ground black pepper
¼ teaspoon kosher or sea salt
4 whole-wheat flatbread wraps or soft whole-wheat tortillas

1. In a large bowl, mix together the salmon, carrots, celery, dill, red onion, capers, oil, vinegar, pepper, and salt. 2. Divide the salmon salad among the flatbreads. Fold up the bottom of the flatbread, then roll up the wrap and serve.

Per Serving:

calories: 185 | fat: 8g | protein: 17g | carbs: 12g | fiber: 2g | sodium: 237mg

Grilled Eggplant and Chopped Greek Salad Wraps

Prep time: 10 minutes | Cook time: 20 minutes |

Serves 4

15 small tomatoes, such as cherry or grape tomatoes, halved
10 pitted Kalamata olives, chopped
1 medium red onion, halved and thinly sliced
¾ cup crumbled feta cheese (about 4 ounces / 113 g)
2 tablespoons balsamic vinegar
1 tablespoon chopped fresh parsley
1 clove garlic, minced

2 tablespoons olive oil, plus 2 teaspoons, divided
¾ teaspoon salt, divided
1 medium cucumber, peeled, halved lengthwise, seeded, and diced
1 large eggplant, sliced ½-inch thick
½ teaspoon freshly ground black pepper
4 whole-wheat sandwich wraps or whole-wheat flour tortillas

1. In a medium bowl, toss together the tomatoes, olives, onion, cheese, vinegar, parsley, garlic, 2 teaspoons olive oil, and ¼ teaspoon of salt. Let sit at room temperature for 20 minutes. Add the cucumber, toss to combine, and let sit another 10 minutes. 2. While the salad is resting, grill the eggplant. Heat a grill or grill pan to high heat. Brush the remaining 2 tablespoons olive oil onto both sides of the eggplant slices. Grill for about 8 to 10 minutes per side, until grill marks appear and the eggplant is tender and cooked through. Transfer to a plate and season with the remaining ½ teaspoon of salt and the pepper. 3. Heat the wraps in a large, dry skillet over medium heat just until warm and soft, about 1 minute on each side. Place 2 or 3 eggplant slices down the center of each wrap. Spoon some of the salad mixture on top of the eggplant, using a slotted spoon so that any excess liquid is drained off. Fold in the sides of the wrap and roll up like a burrito. Serve immediately.

Per Serving:

calories: 233 | fat: 10g | protein: 8g | carbs: 29g | fiber: 7g | sodium: 707mg

Greek Salad Pita

Prep time: 15 minutes | Cook time: 0 minutes |

Serves 4

1 cup chopped romaine lettuce
1 tomato, chopped and seeded
½ cup baby spinach leaves
½ small red onion, thinly sliced
½ small cucumber, chopped and deseeded
2 tablespoons olive oil

1 tablespoon crumbled feta cheese
½ tablespoon red wine vinegar
1 teaspoon Dijon mustard
Sea salt and freshly ground pepper, to taste
1 whole-wheat pita

1. Combine everything except the sea salt, freshly ground pepper, and pita bread in a medium bowl. 2. Toss until the salad is well combined. 3. Season with sea salt and freshly ground pepper to taste. Fill the pita with the salad mixture, serve, and enjoy!

Per Serving:

calories: 123 | fat: 8g | protein: 3g | carbs: 12g | fiber: 2g | sodium: 125mg

Classic Margherita Pizza

Prep time: 10 minutes | Cook time: 10 minutes |

Serves 4

All-purpose flour, for dusting
1 pound (454 g) premade pizza dough
1 (15-ounce / 425-g) can crushed San Marzano tomatoes, with their juices
2 garlic cloves

1 teaspoon Italian seasoning
Pinch sea salt, plus more as needed
1½ teaspoons olive oil, for drizzling
10 slices mozzarella cheese
12 to 15 fresh basil leaves

1. Preheat the oven to 475ºF (245ºC). 2. On a floured surface, roll out the dough to a 12-inch round and place it on a lightly floured pizza pan or baking sheet. 3. In a food processor, combine the tomatoes with their juices, garlic, Italian seasoning, and salt and process until smooth. Taste and adjust the seasoning. 4. Drizzle the olive oil over the pizza dough, then spoon the pizza sauce over the dough and spread it out evenly with the back of the spoon, leaving a 1-inch border. Evenly distribute the mozzarella over the pizza. 5. Bake until the crust is cooked through and golden, 8 to 10 minutes. Remove from the oven and let sit for 1 to 2 minutes. Top with the basil right before serving.

Per Serving:

calories: 570 | fat: 21g | protein: 28g | carbs: 66g | fiber: 4g | sodium: 570mg

Croatian Double-Crust Pizza with Greens and Garlic

4½ cups all-purpose flour
1¼ teaspoons salt, divided
1½ cups olive oil, plus 3 tablespoons, divided
1 cup warm water
1 pound (454 g) Swiss chard or kale, tough center ribs removed,

leaves julienned
¼ small head of green cabbage, thinly sliced
¼ teaspoon freshly ground black pepper
4 cloves garlic, minced

1. In a medium bowl, combine the flour and 1 teaspoon salt. Add 1½ cups olive oil and the warm water and stir with a fork until the mixture comes together and forms a ball. Wrap the ball in plastic wrap and refrigerate for at least 30 minutes. 2. While the dough is chilling, in a large bowl, toss together the greens, cabbage, 2 tablespoons olive oil, the remaining ¼ teaspoon salt, and the pepper. 3. Preheat the oven to 400°F(205°C). 4. Halve the dough and place the halves on two sheets of lightly floured parchment paper. Roll or pat the dough out into two ¼-inch-thick, 11-inch-diameter rounds. 5. Spread the greens mixture over one of the dough rounds, leaving about an inch clear around the edge. Place the second dough round over the greens and fold the edges together to seal the two rounds together. Bake in the preheated oven until the crust is golden brown, about 20 minutes. 6. While the pizza is in the oven, combine 1 tablespoon of olive oil with the garlic. When the pizza is done, remove it from the oven and immediately brush the garlic-oil mixture over the crust. Cut into wedges and serve hot.

Per Serving:

calories: 670 | fat: 45g | protein: 10g | carbs: 62g | fiber: 5g | sodium: 504mg

Margherita Open-Face Sandwiches

2 (6- to 7-inch) whole-wheat submarine or hoagie rolls, sliced open horizontally
1 tablespoon extra-virgin olive oil
1 garlic clove, halved
1 large ripe tomato, cut into 8 slices

¼ teaspoon dried oregano
1 cup fresh mozzarella (about 4 ounces / 113 g), patted dry and sliced
¼ cup lightly packed fresh basil leaves, torn into small pieces
¼ teaspoon freshly ground black pepper

1. Preheat the broiler to high with the rack 4 inches under the heating element. 2. Place the sliced bread on a large, rimmed baking sheet. Place under the broiler for 1 minute, until the bread is just lightly toasted. Remove from the oven. 3. Brush each piece of the toasted bread with the oil, and rub a garlic half over each piece. 4. Place the toasted bread back on the baking sheet. Evenly distribute the tomato slices on each piece, sprinkle with the oregano, and layer the cheese on top. 5. Place the baking sheet under the broiler.

Set the timer for 1½ minutes, but check after 1 minute. When the cheese is melted and the edges are just starting to get dark brown, remove the sandwiches from the oven (this can take anywhere from 1½ to 2 minutes). 6. Top each sandwich with the fresh basil and pepper.

Per Serving:

calories: 176 | fat: 9g | protein: 10g | carbs: 14g | fiber: 2g | sodium: 119mg

Pesto Chicken Mini Pizzas

2 cups shredded cooked chicken
¾ cup pesto
4 English muffins, split

2 cups shredded Mozzarella cheese

1. In a medium bowl, toss the chicken with the pesto. Place one-eighth of the chicken on each English muffin half. Top each English muffin with ¼ cup of the Mozzarella cheese. 2. Put four pizzas at a time in the air fryer and air fry at 350°F (177°C) for 5 minutes. Repeat this process with the other four pizzas.

Per Serving:

calories: 617 | fat: 36g | protein: 45g | carbs: 29g | fiber: 3g | sodium: 544mg

Beans and Greens Pizza

¾ cup whole-wheat pastry flour
½ teaspoon low-sodium baking powder
1 tablespoon olive oil, divided
1 cup chopped kale
2 cups chopped fresh baby spinach

1 cup canned no-salt-added cannellini beans, rinsed and drained
½ teaspoon dried thyme
1 piece low-sodium string cheese, torn into pieces

1. In a small bowl, mix the pastry flour and baking powder until well combined. 2. Add ¼ cup of water and 2 teaspoons of olive oil. Mix until a dough forms. 3. On a floured surface, press or roll the dough into a 7-inch round. Set aside while you cook the greens. 4. In a baking pan, mix the kale, spinach, and remaining teaspoon of the olive oil. Air fry at 350°F (177°C) for 3 to 5 minutes, until the greens are wilted. Drain well. 5. Put the pizza dough into the air fryer basket. Top with the greens, cannellini beans, thyme, and string cheese. Air fry for 11 to 14 minutes, or until the crust is golden brown and the cheese is melted. Cut into quarters to serve.

Per Serving:

calories: 181 | fat: 6g | protein: 8g | carbs: 27g | fiber: 6g | sodium: 103mg

Turkish Pizza

Prep time: 20 minutes | Cook time: 10 minutes | Serves 4

4 ounces (113 g) ground lamb or 85% lean ground beef
¼ cup finely chopped green bell pepper
¼ cup chopped fresh parsley
1 small plum tomato, seeded and finely chopped
2 tablespoons finely chopped yellow onion
1 garlic clove, minced
2 teaspoons tomato paste
¼ teaspoon sweet paprika
¼ teaspoon ground cumin
⅛ to ¼ teaspoon red pepper flakes
⅛ teaspoon ground allspice
⅛ teaspoon kosher salt
⅛ teaspoon black pepper
4 (6-inch) flour tortillas
For Serving:
Chopped fresh mint
Extra-virgin olive oil
Lemon wedges

1. In a medium bowl, gently mix the ground lamb, bell pepper, parsley, chopped tomato, onion, garlic, tomato paste, paprika, cumin, red pepper flakes, allspice, salt, and black pepper until well combined. 2. Divide the meat mixture evenly among the tortillas, spreading it all the way to the edge of each tortilla. 3. Place 1 tortilla in the air fryer basket. Set the air fryer to 400°F (204°C) for 10 minutes, or until the meat topping has browned and the edge of the tortilla is golden. Transfer to a plate and repeat to cook the remaining tortillas. 4. Serve the pizzas warm, topped with chopped fresh mint and a drizzle of extra-virgin olive oil and with lemon wedges alongside.

Per Serving:

calories: 172 | fat: 8g | protein: 8g | carbs: 18g | fiber: 2g | sodium: 318mg

Za'atar Pizza

Prep time: 10 minutes | Cook time: 15 minutes | Serves 4 to 6

1 sheet puff pastry
¼ cup extra-virgin olive oil
⅓ cup za'atar seasoning

1. Preheat the oven to 350°F (180°C). 2. Put the puff pastry on a parchment-lined baking sheet. Cut the pastry into desired slices. 3. Brush the pastry with olive oil. Sprinkle with the za'atar. 4. Put the pastry in the oven and bake for 10 to 12 minutes or until edges are lightly browned and puffed up. Serve warm or at room temperature.

Per Serving:

calories: 374 | fat: 30g | protein: 3g | carbs: 20g | fiber: 1g | sodium: 166mg

Cucumber Basil Sandwiches

Prep time: 10 minutes | Cook time: 0 minutes | Serves 2

4 slices whole-grain bread
¼ cup hummus
1 large cucumber, thinly sliced
4 whole basil leaves

1. Spread the hummus on 2 slices of bread, and layer the cucumbers onto it. Top with the basil leaves and close the sandwiches. 2. Press down lightly and serve immediately.

Per Serving:

calories: 209 | fat: 5g | protein: 9g | carbs: 32g | fiber: 6g | sodium: 275mg

Moroccan Lamb Wrap with Harissa

Prep time: 10 minutes | Cook time: 10 minutes | Serves 4

1 clove garlic, minced
2 teaspoons ground cumin
2 teaspoons chopped fresh thyme
¼ cup olive oil, divided
1 lamb leg steak, about 12 ounces (340 g)
4 (8-inch) pocketless pita rounds or naan, preferably whole-wheat
1 medium eggplant, sliced ½-inch thick
1 medium zucchini, sliced lengthwise into 4 slices
1 bell pepper (any color), roasted and skinned
6 to 8 Kalamata olives, sliced
Juice of 1 lemon
2 to 4 tablespoons harissa
2 cups arugula

1. In a large bowl, combine the garlic, cumin, thyme, and 1 tablespoon of the olive oil. Add the lamb, turn to coat, cover, refrigerate, and marinate for at least an hour. 2. Preheat the oven to 400°F (205°C). 3. Heat a grill or grill pan to high heat. Remove the lamb from the marinade and grill for about 4 minutes per side, until medium-rare. Transfer to a plate and let rest for about 10 minutes before slicing thinly across the grain. 4. While the meat is resting, wrap the bread rounds in aluminum foil and heat in the oven for about 10 minutes. 5. Meanwhile, brush the eggplant and zucchini slices with the remaining olive oil and grill until tender, about 3 minutes. Dice them and the bell pepper. Toss in a large bowl with the olives and lemon juice. 6. Spread some of the harissa onto each warm flatbread round and top each evenly with roasted vegetables, a few slices of lamb, and a handful of the arugula. 7. Roll up the wraps, cut each in half crosswise, and serve immediately.

Per Serving:

calories: 553 | fat: 24g | protein: 33g | carbs: 53g | fiber: 11g | sodium: 531mg

Roasted Vegetable Bocadillo with Romesco Sauce

Prep time: 10 minutes | Cook time: 20 minutes | Serves 4

2 small yellow squash, sliced lengthwise
2 small zucchini, sliced lengthwise
1 medium red onion, thinly sliced
4 large button mushrooms, sliced
2 tablespoons olive oil
1 teaspoon salt, divided
½ teaspoon freshly ground black pepper, divided
2 roasted red peppers from a jar, drained
2 tablespoons blanched almonds
1 tablespoon sherry vinegar
1 small clove garlic
4 crusty multigrain rolls
4 ounces (113 g) goat cheese, at room temperature
1 tablespoon chopped fresh basil

1. Preheat the oven to 400°F(205ºC). 2. In a medium bowl, toss the yellow squash, zucchini, onion, and mushrooms with the olive oil, ½ teaspoon salt, and ¼ teaspoon pepper. Spread on a large baking sheet. Roast the vegetables in the oven for about 20 minutes, until softened. 3. Meanwhile, in a food processor, combine the roasted peppers, almonds, vinegar, garlic, the remaining ½ teaspoon salt, and the remaining ¼ teaspoon pepper and process until smooth. 4. Split the rolls and spread ¼ of the goat cheese on the bottom of each. Place the roasted vegetables on top of the cheese, dividing equally. Top with chopped basil. Spread the top halves of the rolls with the roasted red pepper sauce and serve immediately.

Per Serving:

calories: 379 | fat: 21g | protein: 17g | carbs: 32g | fiber: 4g | sodium: 592mg

Chapter 14 Pasta

Toasted Couscous with Feta, Cucumber, and Tomato

Prep time: 15 minutes | Cook time: 10 minutes |
Serves 8

1 tablespoon plus ¼ cup light olive oil, divided
2 cups Israeli couscous
3 cups vegetable broth
2 large tomatoes, seeded and diced
1 large English cucumber, diced
1 medium red onion, peeled and

chopped
½ cup crumbled feta cheese
¼ cup red wine vinegar
½ teaspoon ground black pepper
¼ cup chopped flat-leaf parsley
¼ cup chopped fresh basil

1. Press the Sauté button on the Instant Pot® and heat 1 tablespoon oil. Add couscous and cook, stirring frequently, until couscous is light golden brown, about 7 minutes. Press the Cancel button. 2. Add broth and stir. Close lid, set steam release to Sealing, press the Manual button, and set time to 2 minutes. When the timer beeps, let pressure release naturally for 5 minutes, then quick-release the remaining pressure until the float valve drops and open lid. 3. Fluff couscous with a fork, then transfer to a medium bowl and set aside to cool to room temperature, about 30 minutes. Add remaining ¼ cup oil, tomatoes, cucumber, onion, feta, vinegar, pepper, parsley, and basil, and stir until combined. Serve at room temperature or refrigerate for at least 2 hours.

Per Serving:
calories: 286 | fat: 11g | protein: 9g | carbs: 38g | fiber: 3g | sodium: 438mg

Chilled Pearl Couscous Salad

Prep time: 15 minutes | Cook time: 10 minutes |
Serves 6

3 tablespoons olive oil, divided
1 cup pearl couscous
1 cup water
1 cup orange juice
1 small cucumber, seeded and diced
1 small yellow bell pepper, seeded and diced
2 small Roma tomatoes, seeded and diced

¼ cup slivered almonds
¼ cup chopped fresh mint leaves
2 tablespoons lemon juice
1 teaspoon grated lemon zest
¼ cup crumbled feta cheese
¼ teaspoon fine sea salt
1 teaspoon smoked paprika
1 teaspoon garlic powder

1. Press the Sauté button and heat 1 tablespoon oil. Add couscous and cook for 2–4 minutes until couscous is slightly browned. Add

water and orange juice. Press the Cancel button. 2. Close lid, set steam release to Sealing, press the Manual button, and set time to 5 minutes. When the timer beeps, let pressure release naturally for 5 minutes. Quick-release any remaining pressure until the float valve drops and open lid. Drain any liquid and set aside to cool for 20 minutes. 3. Combine remaining 2 tablespoons oil, cucumber, bell pepper, tomatoes, almonds, mint, lemon juice, lemon zest, cheese, salt, paprika, and garlic powder in a medium bowl. Add couscous and toss ingredients together. Cover and refrigerate overnight before serving.

Per Serving:
calories: 177 | fat: 11g | protein: 5g | carbs: 12g | fiber: 1g | sodium: 319mg

Roasted Asparagus Caprese Pasta

Prep time: 10 minutes |Cook time: 15 minutes|
Serves: 6

8 ounces (227 g) uncooked small pasta, like orecchiette (little ears) or farfalle (bow ties)
1½ pounds (680 g) fresh asparagus, ends trimmed and stalks chopped into 1-inch pieces (about 3 cups)
1 pint grape tomatoes, halved (about 1½ cups)
2 tablespoons extra-virgin olive

oil
¼ teaspoon freshly ground black pepper
¼ teaspoon kosher or sea salt
2 cups fresh mozzarella, drained and cut into bite-size pieces (about 8 ounces / 227 g)
⅓ cup torn fresh basil leaves
2 tablespoons balsamic vinegar

1. Preheat the oven to 400°F(205ºC). 2. In a large stockpot, cook the pasta according to the package directions. Drain, reserving about ¼ cup of the pasta water. 3. While the pasta is cooking, in a large bowl, toss the asparagus, tomatoes, oil, pepper, and salt together. Spread the mixture onto a large, rimmed baking sheet and bake for 15 minutes, stirring twice as it cooks. 4. Remove the vegetables from the oven, and add the cooked pasta to the baking sheet. Mix with a few tablespoons of pasta water to help the sauce become smoother and the saucy vegetables stick to the pasta. 5. Gently mix in the mozzarella and basil. Drizzle with the balsamic vinegar. Serve from the baking sheet or pour the pasta into a large bowl. 6. If you want to make this dish ahead of time or to serve it cold, follow the recipe up to step 4, then refrigerate the pasta and vegetables. When you are ready to serve, follow step 5 either with the cold pasta or with warm pasta that's been gently reheated in a pot on the stove.

Per Serving:
calories: 317 | fat: 12g | protein: 16g | carbs: 38g | fiber: 7g | sodium: 110mg

Couscous with Crab and Lemon

Prep time: 10 minutes | Cook time: 7 minutes |

Serves 4

1 cup couscous	1 tablespoon minced fresh dill
1 clove garlic, peeled and minced	8 ounces (227 g) jumbo lump crabmeat
2 cups water	3 tablespoons lemon juice
3 tablespoons extra-virgin olive oil, divided	½ teaspoon ground black pepper
¼ cup minced fresh flat-leaf parsley	¼ cup grated Parmesan cheese

1. Place couscous, garlic, water, and 1 tablespoon oil in the Instant Pot® and stir well. Close lid, set steam release to Sealing, press the Manual button, and set time to 7 minutes. When the timer beeps, let pressure release naturally for 10 minutes, then quick-release the remaining pressure and open lid. 2. Fluff couscous with a fork. Add parsley, dill, crabmeat, lemon juice, pepper, and remaining 2 tablespoons oil, and stir until combined. Top with cheese and serve immediately.

Per Serving:

calories: 360 | fat: 15g | protein: 22g | carbs: 34g | fiber: 2g | sodium: 388mg

Puglia-Style Pasta with Broccoli Sauce

Prep time: 15 minutes | Cook time: 25 minutes |

Serves 3

1 pound (454 g) fresh broccoli, washed and cut into small florets	4 canned packed-in-oil anchovies
7 ounces (198 g) uncooked rigatoni pasta	½ teaspoon kosher salt
2 tablespoons extra virgin olive oil, plus 1½ tablespoons for serving	3 teaspoons fresh lemon juice
3 garlic cloves, thinly sliced	3 ounces (85 g) grated or shaved Parmesan cheese, divided
2 tablespoons pine nuts	½ teaspoon freshly ground black pepper

1. Place the broccoli in a large pot filled with enough water to cover the broccoli. Bring the pot to a boil and cook for 12 minutes or until the stems can be easily pierced with a fork. Use a slotted spoon to transfer the broccoli to a plate, but do not discard the cooking water. Set the broccoli aside. 2. Add the pasta to the pot with the broccoli water and cook according to package instructions. 3. About 3 minutes before the pasta is ready, place a large, deep pan over medium heat and add 2 tablespoons of the olive oil. When the olive oil is shimmering, add the garlic and sauté for 1 minute, stirring continuously, until the garlic is golden, then add the pine nuts and continue sautéing for 1 more minute. 4. Stir in the anchovies, using a wooden spoon to break them into smaller pieces, then add the broccoli. Continue cooking for 1 additional minute, stirring continuously and using the spoon to break the broccoli into smaller pieces. 5. When the pasta is ready, remove the pot from the heat and drain, reserving ¼ cup of the cooking water. 6. Add the pasta and 2 tablespoons of the cooking water to the pan, stirring until all the ingredients are well combined. Cook for 1 minute, then remove the pan from the heat. 7. Promptly divide the pasta among three plates. Top each serving with a pinch of kosher salt, 1 teaspoon of the lemon juice, 1 ounce (28 g) of the Parmesan, 1½ teaspoons of the remaining olive oil, and a pinch of fresh ground pepper. Store covered in the refrigerator for up to 3 days.

Per Serving:

calories: 610 | fat: 31g | protein: 24g | carbs: 66g | fiber: 12g | sodium: 654mg

Pine Nut and Currant Couscous with Butternut Squash

Prep time: 10 minutes | Cook time: 50 minutes |

Serves 4

3 tablespoons olive oil	1 (16-ounce / 454-g) can chickpeas, drained and rinsed
1 medium onion, chopped	4½ cups vegetable broth, divided
3 cloves garlic, minced	1-inch strip lemon zest
6 canned plum tomatoes, crushed	½ cup currants
1 cinnamon stick	4 cups (about 5 ounces / 142 g) chopped spinach
1 teaspoon ground coriander	Juice of ½ lemon
1 teaspoon ground cumin	¼ teaspoon pepper
1 teaspoon salt, divided	1 cup whole-wheat couscous
¼ teaspoon red pepper flakes	¼ cup toasted pine nuts
1½ pounds (680 g) diced butternut squash	

1. Heat the olive oil in a medium saucepan set over medium heat. Add the onion and cook, stirring frequently, until softened and lightly browned, about 10 minutes. Stir in the garlic, tomatoes, cinnamon stick, coriander, cumin, ½ teaspoon of the salt, and the red pepper flakes and cook for about 3 minutes more, until the tomatoes begin to break down. Stir in the butternut squash, chickpeas, 3 cups broth, lemon zest, and currants and bring to a simmer. 2. Partially cover the pan and cook for about 25 minutes, until the squash is tender. Add the spinach and cook, stirring, for 2 or 3 more minutes, until the spinach is wilted. Stir in the lemon juice. 3. While the vegetables are cooking, prepare the couscous. Combine the remaining 1½ cups broth, the remaining ½ teaspoon of salt, and the pepper in a small saucepan and bring to a boil. Remove the pan from the heat and stir in the couscous. Cover immediately and let sit for about 5 minutes, until the liquid has been fully absorbed. Fluff with a fork. 4. Spoon the couscous into serving bowls, top with the vegetable and chickpea mixture, and sprinkle some of the pine nuts over the top of each bowl. Serve immediately.

Per Serving:

calories: 549 | fat: 19g | protein: 16g | carbs: 84g | fiber: 14g | sodium: 774mg

Tahini Soup

Prep time: 5 minutes | Cook time: 4 minutes | Serves 6

2 cups orzo
8 cups water
1 tablespoon olive oil
1 teaspoon salt

½ teaspoon ground black pepper
½ cup tahini
¼ cup lemon juice

1. Add pasta, water, oil, salt, and pepper to the Instant Pot®. Close lid, set steam release to Sealing, press the Manual button, and set time to 4 minutes. When the timer beeps, quick-release the pressure until the float valve drops, and open lid. Set aside. 2. Add tahini to a small mixing bowl and slowly add lemon juice while whisking constantly. Once lemon juice has been incorporated, take about ½ cup hot broth from the pot and slowly add to tahini mixture while whisking, until creamy smooth. 3. Pour mixture into the soup and mix well. Serve immediately.

Per Serving:

calories: 338 | fat: 13g | protein: 12g | carbs: 49g | fiber: 5g | sodium: 389mg

Baked Ziti

Prep time: 10 minutes | Cook time: 55 minutes |
Serves 8

For the Marinara Sauce:
2 tablespoons olive oil
¼ medium onion, diced (about 3 tablespoons)
3 cloves garlic, chopped
1 (28-ounce / 794-g) can whole, peeled tomatoes, roughly chopped
Sprig of fresh thyme
½ bunch fresh basil
Sea salt and freshly ground

pepper, to taste
For the Ziti:
1 pound (454 g) whole-wheat ziti
3½ cups marinara sauce
1 cup low-fat cottage cheese
1 cup grated, low-fat mozzarella cheese, divided
¾ cup freshly grated, low-fat Parmesan cheese, divided

Make the marinara sauce: 1. Heat the olive oil in a medium saucepan over medium-high heat. 2. Sauté the onion and garlic, stirring until lightly browned, about 3 minutes. 3. Add the tomatoes and the herb sprigs, and bring to a boil. Lower the heat and simmer, covered, for 10 minutes. Remove and discard the herb sprigs. 4. Stir in sea salt and season with freshly ground pepper to taste. Make the ziti: 1. Preheat the oven to 375ºF (190ºC). 2. Prepare the pasta according to package directions. Drain pasta. Combine the pasta in a bowl with 2 cups marinara sauce, the cottage cheese, and half the mozzarella and Parmesan cheeses. 3. Spread the mixture in a baking dish, and top with the remaining marinara sauce and cheese. 4. Bake for 30–40 minutes, or until bubbly and golden brown.

Per Serving:

calories: 389 | fat: 12g | protein: 18g | carbs: 56g | fiber: 9g | sodium: 369mg

Mediterranean Pasta Salad

Prep time: 20 minutes | Cook time: 15 minutes |
Serves 4

4 cups dried farfalle (bow-tie) pasta
1 cup canned chickpeas, drained and rinsed
⅔ cup water-packed artichoke hearts, drained and diced
½ red onion, thinly sliced
1 cup packed baby spinach
½ red bell pepper, diced

1 Roma (plum) tomato, diced
½ English cucumber, quartered lengthwise and cut into ½-inch pieces
⅓ cup extra-virgin olive oil
Juice of ½ lemon
Sea salt
Freshly ground black pepper
½ cup crumbled feta cheese

1. Fill a large saucepan three-quarters full with water and bring to a boil over high heat. Add the pasta and cook according to the package directions until al dente, about 15 minutes. Drain the pasta and run it under cold water to stop the cooking process and cool. 2. While the pasta is cooking, in a large bowl, mix the chickpeas, artichoke hearts, onion, spinach, bell pepper, tomato, and cucumber. 3. Add the pasta to the bowl with the vegetables. Add the olive oil and lemon juice and season with salt and black pepper. Mix well. 4. Top the salad with the feta and serve.

Per Serving:

calories: 702 | fat: 25g | protein: 22g | carbs: 99g | fiber: 10g | sodium: 207mg

Meaty Baked Penne

Prep time: 10 minutes | Cook time: 40 minutes |
Serves 8

1 pound (454 g) penne pasta
1 pound (454 g) ground beef
1 teaspoon salt
1 (25-ounce / 709-g) jar marinara sauce

1 (1-pound / 454-g) bag baby spinach, washed
3 cups shredded mozzarella cheese, divided

1. Bring a large pot of salted water to a boil, add the penne, and cook for 7 minutes. Reserve 2 cups of the pasta water and drain the pasta. 2. Preheat the oven to 350ºF(180ºC). 3. In a large saucepan over medium heat, cook the ground beef and salt. Brown the ground beef for about 5 minutes. 4. Stir in marinara sauce, and 2 cups of pasta water. Let simmer for 5 minutes. 5. Add a handful of spinach at a time into the sauce, and cook for another 3 minutes. 6. To assemble, in a 9-by-13-inch baking dish, add the pasta and pour the pasta sauce over it. Stir in 1½ cups of the mozzarella cheese. Cover the dish with foil and bake for 20 minutes. 7. After 20 minutes, remove the foil, top with the rest of the mozzarella, and bake for another 10 minutes. Serve warm.

Per Serving:

calories: 454 | fat: 13g | protein: 31g | carbs: 55g | fiber: 9g | sodium: 408mg

Rotini with Spinach, Cherry Tomatoes, and Feta

Prep time: 5 minutes | Cook time: 30 minutes | Serves 2

6 ounces (170 g) uncooked rotini pasta (penne pasta will also work)
1 garlic clove, minced
3 tablespoons extra virgin olive oil, divided
1½ cups cherry tomatoes, halved and divided

9 ounces (255 g) baby leaf spinach, washed and chopped
1½ ounces (43 g) crumbled feta, divided
Kosher salt, to taste
Freshly ground black pepper, to taste

1. Cook the pasta according to the package instructions, reserving ½ cup of the cooking water. Drain and set aside. 2. While the pasta is cooking, combine the garlic with 2 tablespoons of the olive oil in a small bowl. Set aside. 3. Add the remaining tablespoon of olive oil to a medium pan placed over medium heat and then add 1 cup of the tomatoes. Cook for 2–3 minutes, then use a fork to mash lightly. 4. Add the spinach to the pan and continue cooking, stirring occasionally, until the spinach is wilted and the liquid is absorbed, about 4–5 minutes. 5. Transfer the cooked pasta to the pan with the spinach and tomatoes. Add 3 tablespoons of the pasta water, the garlic and olive oil mixture, and 1 ounce (28 g) of the crumbled feta. Increase the heat to high and cook for 1 minute. 6. Top with the remaining cherry tomatoes and feta, and season to taste with kosher salt and black pepper. Store covered in the refrigerator for up to 2 days.

Per Serving:

calories: 602 | fat: 27g | protein: 19g | carbs: 74g | fiber: 7g | sodium: 307mg

Whole-Wheat Spaghetti à la Puttanesca

Prep time: 5 minutes | Cook time: 20 minutes | Serves 6

1 pound (454 g) dried whole-wheat spaghetti
⅓ cup olive oil
5 garlic cloves, minced or pressed
4 anchovy fillets, chopped
½ teaspoon red pepper flakes
1 teaspoon salt
½ teaspoon freshly ground

black pepper
1 (28-ounce / 794-g) can tomato purée
1 pint cherry tomatoes, halved
½ cup pitted green olives, halved
2 tablespoons drained capers
¾ cup coarsely chopped basil

1. Cook the pasta according to the package instructions. 2. Meanwhile, heat the oil in a large skillet over medium-high heat. Add the garlic, anchovies, red pepper flakes, salt, and pepper. Cook, stirring frequently, until the garlic just begins to turn golden brown, 2 to 3 minutes. Add the tomato purée, olives, cherry tomatoes, and capers and let the mixture simmer, reducing the heat if necessary, and stirring occasionally, until the pasta is done, about 10 minutes. 3. Drain the pasta in a colander and then add it to the sauce, tossing

with tongs until the pasta is well coated. Serve hot, garnished with the basil.

Per Serving:

calories: 464 | fat: 17g | protein: 12g | carbs: 70g | fiber: 12g | sodium: 707mg

Bowtie Pesto Pasta Salad

Prep time: 5 minutes | Cook time: 4 minutes | Serves 8

1 pound (454 g) whole-wheat bowtie pasta
4 cups water
1 tablespoon extra-virgin olive oil
2 cups halved cherry tomatoes

2 cups baby spinach
½ cup chopped fresh basil
½ cup prepared pesto
½ teaspoon ground black pepper
½ cup grated Parmesan cheese

1. Add pasta, water, and olive oil to the Instant Pot®. Close lid, set steam release to Sealing, press the Manual button, and set time to 4 minutes. 2. When the timer beeps, quick-release the pressure until the float valve drops and open lid. Drain off any excess liquid. Allow pasta to cool to room temperature, about 30 minutes. Stir in tomatoes, spinach, basil, pesto, pepper, and cheese. Refrigerate for 2 hours. Stir well before serving.

Per Serving:

calories: 360 | fat: 13g | protein: 16g | carbs: 44g | fiber: 7g | sodium: 372mg

Rotini with Red Wine Marinara

Prep time: 10 minutes | Cook time: 25 minutes | Serves 6

1 pound (454 g) rotini
4 cups water
1 tablespoon olive oil
½ medium yellow onion, peeled and diced
3 cloves garlic, peeled and minced
1 (15-ounce / 425-g) can

crushed tomatoes
½ cup red wine
1 teaspoon sugar
2 tablespoons chopped fresh basil
½ teaspoon salt
¼ teaspoon ground black pepper

1. Add pasta and water to the Instant Pot®. Close lid, set steam release to Sealing, press the Manual button, and set time to 4 minutes. When the timer beeps, quick-release the pressure until the float valve drops and open the lid. Press the Cancel button. Drain pasta and set aside. 2. Clean pot and return to machine. Press the Sauté button and heat oil. Add onion and cook until it begins to caramelize, about 10 minutes. Add garlic and cook 30 seconds. Add tomatoes, red wine, and sugar, and simmer for 10 minutes. Add basil, salt, pepper, and pasta. Serve immediately.

Per Serving:

calories: 320 | fat: 4g | protein: 10g | carbs: 59g | fiber: 4g | sodium: 215mg

Rigatoni with Lamb Meatballs

Prep time: 15 minutes | Cook time: 3 to 5 hours | Serves 4

8 ounces (227 g) dried rigatoni pasta
2 (28-ounce / 794-g) cans no-salt-added crushed tomatoes or no-salt-added diced tomatoes
1 small onion, diced
1 bell pepper, any color, seeded and diced
3 garlic cloves, minced, divided

1 pound (454 g) raw ground lamb
1 large egg
2 tablespoons bread crumbs
1 tablespoon dried parsley
1 teaspoon dried oregano
1 teaspoon sea salt
½ teaspoon freshly ground black pepper

1. In a slow cooker, combine the pasta, tomatoes, onion, bell pepper, and 1 clove of garlic. Stir to mix well. 2. In a large bowl, mix together the ground lamb, egg, bread crumbs, the remaining 2 garlic cloves, parsley, oregano, salt, and black pepper until all of the ingredients are evenly blended. Shape the meat mixture into 6 to 9 large meatballs. Nestle the meatballs into the pasta and tomato sauce. 3. Cover the cooker and cook for 3 to 5 hours on Low heat, or until the pasta is tender.

Per Serving:

calories: 653 | fat: 29g | protein: 32g | carbs: 69g | fiber: 10g | sodium: 847mg

Quick Shrimp Fettuccine

Prep time: 10 minutes | Cook time: 10 minutes | Serves 4 to 6

8 ounces (227 g) fettuccine pasta
¼ cup extra-virgin olive oil
3 tablespoons garlic, minced
1 pound (454 g) large shrimp (21-25), peeled and deveined

⅓ cup lemon juice
1 tablespoon lemon zest
½ teaspoon salt
½ teaspoon freshly ground black pepper

1. Bring a large pot of salted water to a boil. Add the fettuccine and cook for 8 minutes. 2. In a large saucepan over medium heat, cook the olive oil and garlic for 1 minute. 3. Add the shrimp to the saucepan and cook for 3 minutes on each side. Remove the shrimp from the pan and set aside. 4. Add the lemon juice and lemon zest to the saucepan, along with the salt and pepper. 5. Reserve ½ cup of the pasta water and drain the pasta. 6. Add the pasta water to the saucepan with the lemon juice and zest and stir everything together. Add the pasta and toss together to evenly coat the pasta. Transfer the pasta to a serving dish and top with the cooked shrimp. Serve warm.

Per Serving:

calories: 615 | fat: 17g | protein: 33g | carbs: 89g | fiber: 4g | sodium: 407mg

Penne with Tuna and Green Olives

Prep time: 5 minutes | Cook time: 5 minutes | Serves 4

2 tablespoons olive oil
3 garlic cloves, minced
½ cup green olives
½ teaspoon salt
¼ teaspoon freshly ground black pepper
2 (6-ounce / 170-g) cans tuna in

olive oil (don't drain off the oil)
½ teaspoon wine vinegar
12 ounces (340 g) penne pasta, cooked according to package directions
2 tablespoons chopped flat-leaf parsley

1. Heat the olive oil in a medium skillet over medium heat. Add the garlic and cook, stirring, 2 to 3 minutes, just until the garlic begins to brown. Add the olives, salt, pepper, and the tuna along with its oil. Cook, stirring, for a minute or two to heat the ingredients through. Remove from the heat and stir in the vinegar. 2. Add the cooked pasta to the skillet and toss to combine the pasta with the sauce. Serve immediately, garnished with the parsley.

Per Serving:

calories: 511 | fat: 22g | protein: 31g | carbs: 52g | fiber: 1g | sodium: 826mg

Fresh Tomato Pasta Bowl

Prep time: 10 minutes | Cook time: 15 minutes | Serves 4

8 ounces (227 g) whole-grain linguine
1 tablespoon extra-virgin olive oil
2 garlic cloves, minced
¼ cup chopped yellow onion
1 teaspoon chopped fresh oregano
½ teaspoon salt

¼ teaspoon freshly ground black pepper
1 teaspoon tomato paste
8 ounces (227 g) cherry tomatoes, halved
½ cup grated Parmesan cheese
1 tablespoon chopped fresh parsley

1. Bring a large saucepan of water to a boil over high heat and cook the linguine according to the package instructions until al dente (still slightly firm). Drain, reserving ½ cup of the pasta water. Do not rinse the pasta. 2. In a large, heavy skillet, heat the olive oil over medium-high heat. Sauté the garlic, onion, and oregano until the onion is just translucent, about 5 minutes. 3. Add the salt, pepper, tomato paste, and ¼ cup of the reserved pasta water. Stir well and allow it to cook for 1 minute. 4. Stir in the tomatoes and cooked pasta, tossing everything well to coat. Add more pasta water if needed. 5. To serve, mound the pasta in shallow bowls and top with Parmesan cheese and parsley.

Per Serving:

calories: 310 | fat: 9g | protein: 10g | carbs: 49g | fiber: 7g | sodium: 305mg

Spicy Broccoli Pasta Salad

Prep time: 10 minutes | Cook time: 10 minutes | Serves 2

8 ounces (227 g) whole-wheat pasta
2 cups broccoli florets
1 cup carrots, peeled and shredded
¼ cup plain Greek yogurt

Juice of 1 lemon
1 teaspoon red pepper flakes
Sea salt and freshly ground pepper, to taste

1. Cook the pasta according to the package directions for al dente and drain well. 2. When the pasta is cool, combine it with the veggies, yogurt, lemon juice, and red pepper flakes in a large bowl, and stir thoroughly to combine. 3. Taste for seasoning, and add sea salt and freshly ground pepper as needed. 4. This dish can be served at room temperature or chilled.

Per Serving:

calories: 473 | fat: 2g | protein: 22g | carbs: 101g | fiber: 13g | sodium: 101mg

Greek Chicken Pasta Casserole

Prep time: 15 minutes | Cook time: 4 to 6 hours | Serves 4

2 pounds (907 g) boneless, skinless chicken thighs or breasts, cut into 1-inch pieces
8 ounces (227 g) dried rotini pasta
7 cups low-sodium chicken broth
½ red onion, diced
3 garlic cloves, minced
¼ cup whole Kalamata olives, pitted

3 Roma tomatoes, diced
2 tablespoons red wine vinegar
1 teaspoon extra-virgin olive oil
2 teaspoons dried oregano
1 teaspoon sea salt
½ teaspoon freshly ground black pepper
¼ cup crumbled feta cheese

1. In a slow cooker, combine the chicken, pasta, chicken broth, onion, garlic, olives, tomatoes, vinegar, olive oil, oregano, salt, and pepper. Stir to mix well. 2. Cover the cooker and cook for 4 to 6 hours on Low heat. 3. Garnish with the feta cheese for serving.

Per Serving:

calories: 608 | fat: 17g | protein: 59g | carbs: 55g | fiber: 8g | sodium: 775mg

Chapter 15 Staples, Sauces, Dips, and Dressings

Chermoula

Prep time: 10 minutes | Cook time: 0 minutes |
Makes about 1½ cups

2¼ cups fresh cilantro leaves
8 garlic cloves, minced
1½ teaspoons ground cumin
1½ teaspoons paprika
½ teaspoon cayenne pepper
½ teaspoon table salt
6 tablespoons lemon juice (2 lemons)
¾ cup extra-virgin olive oil

1. Pulse cilantro, garlic, cumin, paprika, cayenne, and salt in food processor until cilantro is coarsely chopped, about 10 pulses. Add lemon juice and pulse briefly to combine. Transfer mixture to medium bowl and slowly whisk in oil until incorporated and mixture is emulsified. Cover and let sit at room temperature for at least 30 minutes to allow flavors to meld. (Sauce can be refrigerated for up to 2 days; bring to room temperature before serving.)

Per Serving:
¼ cup: calories: 253 | fat: 27g | protein: 1g | carbs: 3g | fiber: 1g | sodium: 199mg

Creamy Grapefruit-Tarragon Dressing

Prep time: 5 minutes | Cook time: 0 minutes | Serves
4to 6

½ cup avocado oil mayonnaise
2 tablespoons Dijon mustard
1 teaspoon dried tarragon or
1 tablespoon chopped fresh tarragon
Zest and juice of ½ grapefruit
(about 2 tablespoons juice)
½ teaspoon salt
¼ teaspoon freshly ground black pepper
1 to 2 tablespoons water (optional)

1. In a large mason jar or glass measuring cup, combine the mayonnaise, Dijon, tarragon, grapefruit zest and juice, salt, and pepper and whisk well with a fork until smooth and creamy. If a thinner dressing is preferred, thin out with water.

Per Serving:
calories: 49 | fat: 4g | protein: 0g | carbs: 4g | fiber: 0g | sodium: 272mg

Cucumber Yogurt Dip

Prep time: 5 minutes | Cook time: 0 minutes | Serves
2 to 3

1 cup plain, unsweetened, full-fat Greek yogurt
½ cup cucumber, peeled, seeded, and diced
1 tablespoon freshly squeezed lemon juice
1 tablespoon chopped fresh mint
1 small garlic clove, minced
Salt and freshly ground black pepper, to taste

1. In a food processor, combine the yogurt, cucumber, lemon juice, mint, and garlic. Pulse several times to combine, leaving noticeable cucumber chunks. 2. Taste and season with salt and pepper.

Per Serving:
calories: 55 | fat: 3g | protein: 3g | carbs: 5g | fiber: 0g | sodium: 38mg

Piri Piri Sauce

Prep time: 5 minutes | Cook time: 0 minutes | Makes
about 1 cup

4 to 8 fresh hot, red chiles, stemmed and coarsely chopped
2 cloves garlic, minced
Juice of 1 lemon
Pinch of salt
½ to 1 cup olive oil

1. In a food processor, combine the chiles (with their seeds), garlic, lemon juice, salt, and ½ cup of olive oil. Process to a smooth purée. Add additional oil as needed to reach the desired consistency. 2. Pour the mixture into a glass jar or non-reactive bowl, cover, and refrigerate for at least 3 days before using. Store in the refrigerator for up to a month.

Per Serving:
calories:84 | fat: 10g | protein: 0g | carbs: 0g | fiber: 0g | sodium: 13mg

Marinated Artichokes

Prep time: 10 minutes | Cook time: 0 minutes |

Makes 2 cups

2 (13¾-ounce / 390-g) cans
artichoke hearts, drained and
quartered
¾ cup extra-virgin olive oil
4 small garlic cloves, crushed
with the back of a knife
1 tablespoon fresh rosemary

leaves
2 teaspoons chopped fresh
oregano or 1 teaspoon dried
oregano
1 teaspoon red pepper flakes
(optional)
1 teaspoon salt

1. In a medium bowl, combine the artichoke hearts, olive oil, garlic, rosemary, oregano, red pepper flakes (if using), and salt. Toss to combine well. 2. Store in an airtight glass container in the refrigerator and marinate for at least 24 hours before using. Store in the refrigerator for up to 2 weeks.

Per Serving:

¼ cup: calories: 228 | fat: 20g | protein: 3g | carbs: 11g | fiber: 5g | sodium: 381mg

Whole-Wheat Pizza Dough

Prep time: 10 minutes | Cook time: 10 to 12 minutes

| Makes 1 pound (454 g)

¾ cup hot tap water
½ teaspoon honey
1 envelope quick-rising yeast,
(2¼ teaspoons)
1 tablespoon olive oil, plus

more for oiling the bowl
1 cup whole-wheat flour
1 cup all-purpose flour
1 teaspoon salt

1. Preheat the oven to 500ºF (260ºC). 2. In a non-reactive bowl, stir together the hot water and honey. Sprinkle the yeast over the top, stir to mix, and let sit for about 10 minutes, until foamy. Add 1 tablespoon of olive oil. 3. In a food processor or the bowl of a stand mixer fitted with a dough hook, combine the whole-wheat and all-purpose flours, and the salt. With the food processor or mixer running, slowly add the yeast and water mixture until the dough comes together in a ball. The dough should be quite soft and tacky, but not overly sticky. If it is too dry, you can add warm water 1 tablespoon at a time, mixing after each addition, until the right consistency is achieved. Likewise, if it seems too wet, you can add all-purpose flour, 1 tablespoon at a time, until the desired consistency is achieved. Process for about 1 more minute to knead the dough. 4. Oil a large bowl lightly with olive oil. Put the dough in the bowl and turn to coat with oil. Cover the bowl with a clean dish towel and set it in a warm place (like on your stovetop or in a sunny spot on the kitchen counter) and let rise for 1 hour, during which time it should double in size. 5. Using your hands or a rolling pin, shape the dough into whatever shape you like. Top as desired and bake in a preheated oven for 10 to 12 minutes, until crisp and lightly browned.

Per Serving:

2 ounces / 57 g: calories: 135 | fat: 2g | protein: 5g | carbs: 24g | fiber: 3g | sodium: 294mg

Citrus Vinaigrette

Prep time: 2 minutes | Cook time: 0 minutes | Serves 4

Zest of 1 lemon
3 tablespoons fresh lemon juice
Pinch kosher salt

Pinch freshly ground black
pepper
2 tablespoons olive oil

1. In a small bowl, whisk together the lemon zest, lemon juice, 3 tablespoons water, the salt, and the pepper. While whisking, gradually stream in the olive oil and whisk until emulsified. Store in an airtight container in the refrigerator for up to 3 days.

Per Serving:

calories: 65 | fat: 7g | protein: 0g | carbs: 2g | fiber: 0g | sodium: 146mg

Pepper Sauce

Prep time: 10 minutes | Cook time: 20 minutes |

Makes 4 cups

2 red hot fresh chiles, seeded
2 dried chiles
½ small yellow onion, roughly
chopped

2 garlic cloves, peeled
2 cups water
2 cups white vinegar

1. In a medium saucepan, combine the fresh and dried chiles, onion, garlic, and water. Bring to a simmer and cook for 20 minutes, or until tender. Transfer to a food processor or blender. 2. Add the vinegar and blend until smooth.

Per Serving:

1 cup: calories: 41 | fat: 0g | protein: 1g | carbs: 5g | fiber: 1g | sodium: 11mg

Italian Dressing

Prep time: 5 minutes | Cook time: 0 minutes | Serves

12

¼ cup red wine vinegar
½ cup extra-virgin olive oil
¼ teaspoon salt
¼ teaspoon freshly ground
black pepper

1 teaspoon dried Italian
seasoning
1 teaspoon Dijon mustard
1 garlic clove, minced

1. In a small jar, combine the vinegar, olive oil, salt, pepper, Italian seasoning, mustard, and garlic. Close with a tight-fitting lid and shake vigorously for 1 minute. 2. Refrigerate for up to 1 week.

Per Serving:

calories: 82 | fat: 9g | protein: 0g | carbs: 0g | fiber: 0g | sodium: 71mg

Lemon Tahini Dressing

Prep time: 5 minutes | Cook time: 0 minutes | Makes ½ cup

¼ cup tahini
3 tablespoons lemon juice
3 tablespoons warm water
¼ teaspoon kosher salt

¼ teaspoon pure maple syrup
¼ teaspoon ground cumin
⅛ teaspoon cayenne pepper

1. In a medium bowl, whisk together the tahini, lemon juice, water, salt, maple syrup, cumin, and cayenne pepper until smooth. Place in the refrigerator until ready to serve. Store any leftovers in the refrigerator in an airtight container up to 5 days.

Per Serving:

2 tablespoons: calories: 90 | fat: 7g | protein: 3g | carbs: 5g | fiber: 1g | sodium: 80mg

Parsley-Mint Sauce

Prep time: 5 minutes | Cook time: 0 minutes | Serves 6

½ cup fresh flat-leaf parsley
1 cup fresh mint leaves
2 garlic cloves, minced
2 scallions (green onions), chopped

2 tablespoons pomegranate molasses
¼ cup olive oil
1 tablespoon fresh lemon juice

1. Combine all the ingredients in a blender and blend until smooth. Transfer to an airtight container and refrigerate until ready to use. Can be refrigerated for 1 day.

Per Serving:

calories: 90 | fat: 9g | protein: 1g | carbs: 2g | fiber: 0g | sodium: 5mg

Lemon-Dill Vinaigrette

Prep time: 2 minutes | Cook time: 0 minutes | Serves 6 to 8

4 large cloves of garlic
½ cup fresh dill
½ cup parsley
1 tablespoon sherry vinegar or

red wine vinegar
1 tablespoon lemon juice
½ teaspoon salt
½ cup extra-virgin olive oil

1. Put the garlic, dill, parsley, lemon juice, vinegar, and salt into a blender. Add olive oil and process until smooth. Refrigerate covered up to a day. (I put it into a Ball jar with a tight-fitting top so I can shake it to use later but it stays emulsified.)

Per Serving:

calories: 165 | fat: 18g | protein: 0g | carbs: 1g | fiber: 0g | sodium: 198mg

Olive Tapenade

Prep time: 10 minutes | Cook time: 0 minutes | Makes about 1 cup

¾ cup pitted brine-cured green or black olives, chopped fine
1 small shallot, minced
2 tablespoons extra-virgin olive oil

1 tablespoon capers, rinsed and minced
1½ teaspoons red wine vinegar
1 teaspoon minced fresh oregano

1. Combine all ingredients in bowl. (Tapenade can be refrigerated for up to 1 week.)

Per Serving:

¼ cup: calories: 92 | fat: 9g | protein: 0g | carbs: 2g | fiber: 1g | sodium: 236mg

Mint Pesto

Prep time: 5 minutes | Cook time: 0 minutes | Makes about 1 cup

1 tablespoon toasted walnuts
2 cups packed fresh mint leaves
1 clove garlic
1 tablespoon lemon juice

½ teaspoon lemon zest
¼ teaspoon salt
⅔ cup olive oil
½ cup grated Pecorino cheese

1. Place the walnuts, mint, and garlic in a food processor and pulse to mince finely. Add the lemon juice, lemon zest, and salt and pulse to grind to a paste. 2. With the processor running, add the olive oil in a thin stream. Process until the mixture is well combined. 3. Add the cheese and pulse to combine.

Per Serving:

calories: 113 | fat: 12g | protein: 3g | carbs: 1g | fiber: 0g | sodium: 234mg

Miso-Ginger Dressing

Prep time: 10 minutes | Cook time: 0 minutes | Serves 4

1 tablespoon unseasoned rice vinegar
1 tablespoon red or white miso
1 teaspoon grated fresh ginger

1 garlic clove, minced
3 tablespoons extra-virgin olive oil

1. In a small bowl, combine the vinegar and miso into a paste. Add the ginger and garlic, and mix well. While whisking, drizzle in the olive oil. 2. Store in the refrigerator in an airtight container for up to 1 week.

Per Serving:

calories: 100 | fat: 10g | protein: 1g | carbs: 2g | fiber: 0g | sodium: 159mg

Berry and Honey Compote

Prep time: 5 minutes | Cook time: 15 minutes |
Serves 2 to 3

½ cup honey
¼ cup fresh berries

2 tablespoons grated orange
zest

1. In a small saucepan, heat the honey, berries, and orange zest over medium-low heat for 2 to 5 minutes, until the sauce thickens, or heat for 15 seconds in the microwave. Serve the compote drizzled over pancakes, muffins, or French toast.

Per Serving:

calories: 272 | fat: 0g | protein: 1g | carbs: 74g | fiber: 1g | sodium: 4mg

White Bean Hummus

Prep time: 10 minutes | Cook time: 30 minutes |
Serves 12

⅔ cup dried white beans, rinsed and drained
3 cloves garlic, peeled and crushed

¼ cup olive oil
1 tablespoon lemon juice
½ teaspoon salt

1. Place beans and garlic in the Instant Pot® and stir well. Add enough cold water to cover ingredients. Close lid, set steam release to Sealing, press the Manual button, and set time to 30 minutes. 2. When the timer beeps, let pressure release naturally, about 20 minutes. Press the Cancel button and open lid. Use a fork to check that beans are tender. Drain off excess water and transfer beans to a food processor. 3. Add oil, lemon juice, and salt to the processor and pulse until mixture is smooth with some small chunks. Transfer to a storage container and refrigerate for at least 4 hours. Serve cold or at room temperature. Store in the refrigerator for up to one week.

Per Serving:

calories: 57 | fat: 5g | protein: 1g | carbs: 3g | fiber: 1g | sodium: 99mg

Tabil (Tunisian Five-Spice Blend)

Prep time: 2 minutes | Cook time: 0 minutes | Makes
2 tablespoons

1 tablespoon ground coriander
1 teaspoon caraway seeds
¼ teaspoon garlic powder

¼ teaspoon cayenne pepper
¼ teaspoon ground cumin

1. Combine all the ingredients in a small bowl. 2. It may be stored in an airtight container for up to 2 weeks.

Per Serving:

calories: 13 | fat: 1g | protein: 1g | carbs: 2g | fiber: 1g | sodium: 2mg

Bagna Cauda

Prep time: 5 minutes | Cook time: 20 minutes |
Serves 8 to 10

½ cup extra-virgin olive oil
4 tablespoons (½ stick) butter
8 anchovy fillets, very finely chopped
4 large garlic cloves, finely

minced
½ teaspoon salt
½ teaspoon freshly ground black pepper

1. In a small saucepan, heat the olive oil and butter over medium-low heat until the butter is melted. 2. Add the anchovies and garlic and stir to combine. Add the salt and pepper and reduce the heat to low. Cook, stirring occasionally, until the anchovies are very soft and the mixture is very fragrant, about 20 minutes. 3. Serve warm, drizzled over steamed vegetables, as a dipping sauce for raw veggies or cooked artichokes, or use as a salad dressing. Store leftovers in an airtight container in the refrigerator for up to 2 weeks.

Per Serving:

calories: 145 | fat: 16g | protein: 1g | carbs: 0g | fiber: 0g | sodium: 235mg

Tahini Dressing

Prep time: 5 minutes | Cook time: 0 minutes | Serves
8 to 10

½ cup tahini
¼ cup freshly squeezed lemon juice (about 2 to 3 lemons)
¼ cup extra-virgin olive oil

1 garlic clove, finely minced or
½ teaspoon garlic powder
2 teaspoons salt

1. In a glass mason jar with a lid, combine the tahini, lemon juice, olive oil, garlic, and salt. Cover and shake well until combined and creamy. Store in the refrigerator for up to 2 weeks.

Per Serving:

calories: 121 | fat: 12g | protein: 2g | carbs: 3g | fiber: 1g | sodium: 479mg

Appendix 1: Measurement Conversion Chart

MEASUREMENT CONVERSION CHART

VOLUME EQUIVALENTS(DRY)

US STANDARD	METRIC (APPROXIMATE)
1/8 teaspoon	0.5 mL
1/4 teaspoon	1 mL
1/2 teaspoon	2 mL
3/4 teaspoon	4 mL
1 teaspoon	5 mL
1 tablespoon	15 mL
1/4 cup	59 mL
1/2 cup	118 mL
3/4 cup	177 mL
1 cup	235 mL
2 cups	475 mL
3 cups	700 mL
4 cups	1 L

VOLUME EQUIVALENTS(LIQUID)

US STANDARD	US STANDARD (OUNCES)	METRIC (APPROXIMATE)
2 tablespoons	1 fl.oz.	30 mL
1/4 cup	2 fl.oz.	60 mL
1/2 cup	4 fl.oz.	120 mL
1 cup	8 fl.oz.	240 mL
1 1/2 cup	12 fl.oz.	355 mL
2 cups or 1 pint	16 fl.oz.	475 mL
4 cups or 1 quart	32 fl.oz.	1 L
1 gallon	128 fl.oz.	4 L

TEMPERATURES EQUIVALENTS

FAHRENHEIT(F)	CELSIUS(C) (APPROXIMATE)
225 °F	107 °C
250 °F	120 °C
275 °F	135 °C
300 °F	150 °C
325 °F	160 °C
350 °F	180 °C
375 °F	190 °C
400 °F	205 °C
425 °F	220 °C
450 °F	235 °C
475 °F	245 °C
500 °F	260 °C

WEIGHT EQUIVALENTS

US STANDARD	METRIC (APPROXIMATE)
1 ounce	28 g
2 ounces	57 g
5 ounces	142 g
10 ounces	284 g
15 ounces	425 g
16 ounces (1 pound)	455 g
1.5 pounds	680 g
2 pounds	907 g

Appendix 2: The Dirty Dozen and Clean Fifteen

The Dirty Dozen and Clean Fifteen

The Environmental Working Group (EWG) is a nonprofit, nonpartisan organization dedicated to protecting human health and the environment Its mission is to empower people to live healthier lives in a healthier environment. This organization publishes an annual list of the twelve kinds of produce, in sequence, that have the highest amount of pesticide residue-the Dirty Dozen-as well as a list of the fifteen kinds ofproduce that have the least amount of pesticide residue-the Clean Fifteen.

THE DIRTY DOZEN	THE CLEAN FIFTEEN
• The 2016 Dirty Dozen includes the following produce. These are considered among the year's most important produce to buy organic:	• The least critical to buy organically are the Clean Fifteen list. The following are on the 2016 list:

THE DIRTY DOZEN

Strawberries	Spinach
Apples	Tomatoes
Nectarines	Bell peppers
Peaches	Cherry tomatoes
Celery	Cucumbers
Grapes	Kale/collard greens
Cherries	Hot peppers

• *The Dirty Dozen list contains two additional itemskale/collard greens and hot peppers-because they tend to contain trace levels of highly hazardous pesticides.*

THE CLEAN FIFTEEN

Avocados	Papayas
Corn	Kiw
Pineapples	Eggplant
Cabbage	Honeydew
Sweet peas	Grapefruit
Onions	Cantaloupe
Asparagus	Cauliflower
Mangos	

• *Some of the sweet corn sold in the United States are made from genetically engineered (GE) seedstock. Buy organic varieties of these crops to avoid GE produce.*

Made in the USA
Coppell, TX
03 July 2023

18726584R00077